The City on the Hill
from Below

The City on the Hill from Below

THE CRISIS OF PROPHETIC BLACK POLITICS

Stephen H. Marshall

TEMPLE UNIVERSITY PRESS PHILADELPHIA

TEMPLE UNIVERSITY PRESS
Philadelphia, Pennsylvania 19122
www.temple.edu/tempress

Copyright © 2011 by Temple University
All rights reserved
Published 2011
Paperback edition published 2012

Library of Congress Cataloging-in-Publication Data

Marshall, Stephen H.
   The city on the hill from below : the crisis of prophetic Black politics /
Stephen H. Marshall.
      p. cm.
   Includes bibliographical references and index.
   ISBN 978-1-4399-0655-2 (cloth : alk. paper) — ISBN 978-1-4399-0657-6 (e-book)
   1. African Americans—Politics and government. 2. African Americans—Politics and
government—Philosophy. 3. African Americans—Social conditions. 4. United States—
Politics and government. I . Title.
   E185.615.M296 2011
   323.1196'073—dc22

                                                                        2010046507

ISBN 978-1-4399-0656-9 (paperback : alk. paper)

Printed in the United States of America

091312P

For Shirley and Solomon

Contents

Acknowledgments

This book could not have been written were it not for the extraordinary support I have received over the years. Three persons in particular have played herculean roles. I am permanently indebted to Mary Hawkesworth, my teacher and friend, whose encouragement inspired the genesis of the book and whose careful reading of the entire manuscript saw the book through to completion. I am similarly beholden to Shirley Thompson, without whose editorial skill and less-than-gentle prodding at the midnight hour, I would still be writing. Finally, I am deeply indebted to Cornel West, my teacher and friend, whose writings awakened me to the importance of the prophetic tradition and whose guidance trained me to read black political thought as political and social theory.

I have also received generous assistance from friends and colleagues who read partial drafts and/or provided me with invaluable suggestions that were later incorporated into the book. Among the members of this group, Juliet Hooker—who has been and remains an invaluable interlocutor and who read early versions of the manuscript—deserves special mention. I also thank Jafari Allen, Matt Richardson, Christen Smith, David Kim, Jeff Tulis, John Lewis, Keith Wright, Mike Wilcox, Eddie Glaude, Jim Fuerst, Mark Jefferson, Tom Pangle, Lorraine Pangle, and Ted Gordon.

I am grateful as well for the nurturing and stimulating intellectual community provided by the John L. Warfield Center for African and African American Studies at the University of Texas at Austin. As a departmental home, the Warfield Center has offered me financial and administrative support. As a community of scholars, activists, and students, the Warfield Center has provided me with much-appreciated compatriots. The same can be said of the support I have received from my colleagues in the Department of American Studies. A wonderful community of interdisciplinary scholars and fabulous graduate students, the Department of American Studies at the University of Texas at Austin has given me a context for rediscovering my groove.

When my soul looks back in wonder, I have answered and will continue to answer with a prayer of gratitude for my family. The love and faith of my parents, Lois Christine Houston Marshall and Isaiah Willis Marshall, continue to sustain me. The friendship and unconditional love of my sisters, Carol, Andrea, and Shelly, continue to hold me up, while my brilliant nephew, Bjorn, constantly engenders my hope. My father-in-law and mother-in-law, Dr. Joseph Thompson and Dr. Shirley W. Thompson, have provided me with love and much-appreciated acceptance.

Shirley and Solomon Marshall are my condition of possibility. Were it not for my beautiful wife and beloved son, I'd be a tossed and driven vessel on an open and angry sea. I dedicate this book to them.

The City on the Hill from Below

Introduction

The City on the Hill from Below

The Crisis of Prophetic Black Politics

Prophetic political critique of the "City on the Hill" is an old and esteemed political philosophy within black America, yet today this project is in crisis. Born within the fugitive public space of black churches and constructed from the multivalent language of biblical scripture, African American quests for freedom, security, and communal autonomy began as insurgent resistance to slavery, terror, and dishonoring dislocation. What began as resistance, however, flowered into a vital and sustained mode of political reflection and politics, as inspired political intellectuals conceived sophisticated social and political analyses that situated the predicament of African Americans within larger and more urgent pathologies of the American polity. They also disseminated ennobling visions of personal and societal transformation that spoke to the hopes of an oppressed people and the conscience and anxieties of white Americans. Prophetic political critique, then, is both a genre of political theory and a mode of political action.

The political imaginary associated with the City on the Hill reflects an older and more durable set of social meanings and practices that conceive and reproduce American political life as the secular instantiation of the sacred. Born aboard a ship that bore colonial settlers from the profane and exhausted space of Old World Europe to lands they planned to consecrate as "New Jerusalem," this imagined community emerged as a religious quest to found and consolidate a new order of human existence.[1] What began as a religious quest, however, flowered into a nation-state of unprecedented power, as Puritan settlers bequeathed to their heirs a public memory of their origins as a covenant, articulated their project as a sacred errand, and established a narrative of divine providence as popular historiography. The figure of the City on the Hill captures both the biblical metaphor mobilized by the community of Puritan settlers and their heirs to describe their fateful political project and a symbol of national identity taken up by successive generations of Americans. The multiple discursive practices that come together under this theologico-political symbol connect the meanings of settlement, conquest, revolution, state formation, and national consolidation into an archetypal conception of intergenerational political community and transhistorical national purpose. The City on the Hill is perhaps best understood as a political imaginary that founds and sustains a unique and enduring solidarity within the American polity, an architectonic cultural formation that unites political desire with religious hope. At stake in the crisis of African American prophetic political critique, then, is neither simply the fate of a venerable but declining tradition of black politics nor the dissipation of a once vital mode of theoretical reflection. At stake is the demise of an indigenous New World tradition of rigorous American self-criticism. To be sure, the fundamental theological presuppositions of the political culture of the United States tend to inoculate it from assessing the excesses it systematically produces. However, these presuppositions contain the possibility to destabilize and to help dissolve the forces that produce such excesses.[2]

This book explicates the character, historical role, and current status of African American prophetic political critique as a capacious and once vital tradition of American political theorizing and political engagement. With a few notable exceptions, this tradition of political theorizing has been largely neglected within the discipline of American political science and the field of political theory, an omission that is puzzling, given the centrality of this tradition to the history of American political thought, African American studies, American political development, and assessments of the current status of post–civil rights black politics and American democracy. There are excellent cultural and intellectual histories of this tradition of politics and a rich and growing literature of incisive theoretical analyses of African American cultural production during all phases of American historical development.[3] There is also a smaller but growing and rich literature on African American political theory. Yet only a handful of works substantively address prophetic political critique as a form of political theorizing.[4] To redress this omission, I explore this vibrant tradition, describe the historical context and intellectual milieu in which it emerged, and situate its central preoccupations in relation to the concerns of canonical and contemporary political theory. By treating their texts as works of political theory, I demonstrate that some of the principal thinkers of the African American prophetic tradition—David Walker, Frederick Douglass, W.E.B. Du Bois, and James Baldwin—provide critical insights into the most intractable questions of American political life.

Any appreciative retrieval of an underappreciated and imperiled tradition risks nostalgic veneration, especially amid the current atmosphere of rapid social change.[5] One might be tempted to invoke the past in order to manage or to avoid grappling with the contingency of the present or to construe the present as the detritus of some former golden age. On the other hand, one might be tempted to use the embarrassments of the past primarily to disrupt the sanctioned ignorance of the present. In this case, exposing the ignoble roots of current commitments and practices could make a scapegoat of the past that absolves the present of the responsibility to change. Succumbing to either interpretive temptation can blind thought to the power of history and the value of historical achievement, concealing the continuing presence of the past in contemporary life and obscuring past achievements that might constructively educate the present.[6] Guarding against the twin pitfalls of nostalgia and irony, I lay the groundwork for a substantive retrieval of a mode of African American political reflection that addresses the unresolved problems of race in America and provides resources for thinking constructively about these problems.

The City on the Hill as Political Education

References to the City on the Hill surface frequently in American political discourse. Republicans and Democrats, candidates and elected officials alike, adopt this biblical reference to suggest that the American polity has a unique destiny caught up with liberty and the right of self-determination. In recent memory, Ronald Reagan is perhaps most closely associated with this political rhetoric, having invoked the "shining City on the Hill" in his bid for the Presidency and, once elected, deploying this image to legitimate his foreign policy: "We cannot escape our destiny, nor should we try to do so. The leadership of the free world was thrust upon us two centuries ago in that little hall in Philadelphia." Democrats too have used this symbol as a touchstone to vindicate their preferred public policies and to criticize their political opponents for failing to realize American ideals. In his keynote address to the 1984 Democratic National Nominating Convention, Governor Mario Cuomo condemned Reagan administration policies that excluded the poor, the working class, and racial minorities from American prosperity. Using terms borrowed from Charles Dickens, Cuomo characterized the increasing inequality in the United States as a fundamental betrayal of America's sacred mission: "Mr. President, you ought to know that this nation is more a 'Tale of Two Cities' than it is a 'Shining City on a Hill.'"

Both speakers invoked the idea of the City on the Hill because they knew that this idea captures a distinctively American political self-understanding, one that unites a conception of community, a mode of belonging, and a sense of historical destiny. Combining a vision of political possibility, a goal for national aspiration, and a set of standards by which to measure progress, the symbol of the City on the Hill invokes an imaginary of American political community. Hence, the speeches of both men call American citizens to imagine an experience of politics that is beyond partisanship, interest group affiliation, and the particular policy debates of the day. Each reveals to American citizens that the true and proper experience of the political lies in associating with a particular form of political solidarity that accrues from recognizing America's exemplary service to humanity. The controlling vision that inspires these calls involves certain civic competences that citizens can acquire only through the practice of certain excellences identified by John Winthrop. Although seldom explicitly discussed in political science classrooms, these excellences are lodged deep within American political culture, resonating in the lives of those privileged by the American political system as well as in the lives of those marginalized and disenfranchised by it.

Despite the constitutional guarantee of the separation of church and state and the First Amendment prohibition on establishing any official religion, the founding documents of the American republic ground a "civic faith" in the imagery of the City on the Hill. The earliest articulation of this faith was crafted by John Winthrop, who envisioned a compact between the English settlers in this "New World" and their God. Invoking biblical notions of a "chosen people," Winthrop suggested that if these new "Americans" lived in accordance with a strenuous moral ideal, then God would dwell among them and bless them, enabling them to resist all enemies.

At the heart of Winthrop's "A Modell of Christian Charitee" lies an ideal of community that traces its ancestry to the New Testament. The very first formulation of the City on the Hill is found in the Sermon on the Mount, recorded in the Gospel according to Matthew (5:14). In this passage, Jesus explains to his followers that if they would truly follow him, they must become "like a city set upon a hill." As formulated by Jesus, the City on the Hill is a metaphor for a religious ethic of care. The deeper roots of this metaphor, however, are tied to an implicit invocation of the ancient conception of the "city" as a political community. Anchored in the experiences of the Greek city-states and the Roman republic, the city was far more than a geographical space. It was the precondition for the good life, providing the physical, moral, and intellectual conditions for human flourishing. Embodying the values cherished by a particular community of people, the city was a form of human association that preserved traditions, institutions, and mores. As Aristotle noted in *The Politics*, the identity of the city was provided by its distinctive constitution, which codified a determinate mode of life.[7] Thus, as the ancient cities of Athens and Rome demonstrate, the idea of the city encapsulates freedom, the freedom of a self-sufficient community to govern its own affairs, according its members the final authority to determine all matters pertaining to their common life.

John Winthrop's vision of the City on the Hill, like that of its New Testament precursor, linked the institutional conditions for collective self-determination to the fulfillment of a divine mandate. The political independence of the people was tied to the strenuous demands required by the new faith. Living in accordance with the model of Christian charity required a certain selflessness, a willingness to assume responsibility for the well-being of one's neighbors. Knit together in the shared project of freedom, citizens were to expand the horizons of their personal concerns to encompass the needs of others. The duty to provide community members with "the necessities" of existence was to be complemented by a particular demeanor, a "brotherly affection," which enabled all to "delight in each other" as they undertook the arduous challenges of communal self-sufficiency and self-determination. The demands of this virtuous political community would not be easy to fulfill, nor was their achievement a certainty. With what he expected to be the whole world watching this noble experiment, Winthrop emphasized that the settlers had it in their power to succeed or to fail. They could fulfill their destiny as a chosen nation, creating a unique political community set apart from other nations of the world by their performance of exemplary service to humanity, or they could be seduced by "pleasures and profits" and fail in their sacred mission, incurring God's curse and perishing in the process.

The uncertainty of outcomes noted in John Winthrop's challenge to the new settlers was echoed by Alexander Hamilton as he crafted his first editorial designed to persuade his fellow countrymen to ratify the proposed U.S. Constitution:

> It seems to have been reserved to the people of this country, by their conduct and example, to decide the important question, whether societies of men are really capable or not of establishing good government from reflection and choice, or whether they are forever destined to depend for their political constitutions on accident and

force. If there be any truth in the remark, the crisis at which we are arrived may with propriety be regarded as the era in which that decision is to be made; and a wrong election on the part we shall act may, in this view, deserve to be considered as the general misfortune of mankind.[8]

For Hamilton, as for Winthrop, Americans possessed the unprecedented opportunity to institutionalize a modern republic through deliberate choice. The 1787 Constitution designed a durable and energetic federal government capable of uniting the diverse citizens populating the large geographic expanse of the thirteen original states. It claimed to be able to preserve both the rights of member states and the liberties of individual citizens. By offering the people within the states the opportunity to freely adopt the Constitution, the draft document enshrined the principle of popular sovereignty. Yet because the people might not choose to ratify the document, it also posed a serious challenge to the continuance of the American experiment in self-government. Thus, the ratification campaign represented a decisive historical test of whether republican government was a genuine possibility for modern politics. The process of ratification also raised questions about effective governance: Could a sovereign coercive power sufficient to repel external enemies and regulate citizens be established by the assent of citizens who held a dual status as both rulers and subjects, as equal participants in constitution making and as those equally bound to the laws established by the constitution? For Hamilton, America had been assigned, by whatever forces governing human history, the awesome task of answering the question for all time. America could prove that a good government, contrived by conscious human design, could be legitimated through popular assent.

Hamilton's formulation of the City on the Hill secularized Winthrop's vision. Where Winthrop had insisted that diligent observation and rigorous practice of Christian religious precepts would afford living testimony of God's plan, Hamilton suggested that enlightened self-interest generated by the extreme exigencies of post-revolutionary history would enable Americans to momentarily rise above their narrow selfish interests and bind themselves to a new constitutional order. James Madison, Hamilton's co-author of the *Federalist Papers*, reintroduced the language of divine providence in Federalist 37. To explain the unlikely emergence of consensus at the Constitutional Convention among delegates with wildly divergent interests, Madison wrote, "The real wonder is that so many difficulties should have been surmounted, and surmounted with a unanimity almost as unprecedented as it must have been unexpected. It is impossible for any man of candor to reflect on this circumstance without partaking of astonishment. It is impossible for the man of pious reflection not to perceive in it a finger of *that almighty hand* that has been so frequently and signally extended to our relief in the critical stages of the revolution."[9] Whether credited to overarching historical forces or to the hand of God, the founders agreed that the United States had a unique and distinctive mission that accorded the nation particular responsibilities on the world stage.

If the founders appealed to the City on the Hill with a sense of profound possibility, more recent politicians have debated whether the United States has fulfilled or betrayed its historic mission. In his 1974 speech "The Shining City on the Hill" aspiring presidential candidate Ronald Reagan resurrected this old political vision to vindicate the American project and reinvigorate U.S. foreign policy initiatives in the aftermath of a decade of dissent. Following more than a decade of intensive social unrest characterized by massive public demonstrations for civil rights and against the Vietnam War, political assassinations of national leaders (John F. Kennedy, Medgar Evers, Malcolm X, Martin Luther King, Robert Kennedy), and riots in major American cities, Reagan insisted that America had *fulfilled* the covenant first articulated by Winthrop. Taking issue with wrenching critiques of domestic and foreign policies, Reagan argued that such debilitating self-examination was unwarranted. Indeed, attacking those who dared criticize the United States, Reagan suggested that it was the critics themselves who had lost their way. War protestors had foolishly mistaken America's defense of freedom abroad for imperial predation. Critics of American capitalism had failed to acknowledge unprecedented productivity, economic growth, and improved standards of living. Critical discourse about America's "race problem" simply ignored the prodigious accomplishments in race relations over the course of the twentieth century, culminating in the extension of constitutional rights to African Americans. With his characteristic simplicity, Reagan responded to Winthrop's challenge, "We have not dealt falsely with our God, even if he is temporarily suspended from the classroom."[10] Casting cold war politics in terms of good and evil, Reagan suggested that Americans had divine right on their side as they engaged a historic mission to destroy the "evil" communist empire. Echoing themes from Winthrop, Hamilton, and Madison, he insisted, "You can call it mysticism if you want to, but I have always believed there was some divine plan that placed this continent between two oceans to be sought out by those who were possessed of an abiding love of freedom and a special kind of courage." In response to Hamilton's probing question concerning the destiny of the nation, Reagan confidently asserted, "We are today, the last best hope of man on earth."

Reagan's rhetorical brilliance consisted, in part, of setting Winthrop's founding prophecy against increasingly trenchant cultural and political critique of the seventies and early eighties, especially critiques leveled by black power advocates, New Left and Third World Marxists such as the Black Panther Party, and leaders of the women's movement. The brilliance of Reagan's rhetoric, however, also goes beyond mere recuperation of the language of the City on the Hill. He effectively wrested this central symbol of the American public imaginary from the long series of critical interrogations undertaken by successive generations of African American prophetic critics. The Reverend Martin Luther King has come to define this tradition within American public memory, in part because he was a transcendent orator with extraordinary compassion and courage and in part because his later writings and speeches criticizing American militarism and empire are rarely discussed in public.[11] Yet while King may be the greatest practitioner of prophetic critique—insofar as his extraordinary integrity enabled him to lead by example and his rhetorical virtuosity enabled him to fix the attention of the entire nation and the world—he is but a representative of a larger and more capacious tradition. I trace this tradition in the work of David Walker, Frederick Douglass, W.E.B. Du Bois, and James Baldwin. In different ways, each thinker I consider developed comprehensive analyses of the American polity in terms of the normative commitments prescribed by the political imaginary of the City on the Hill. Each articulated unsettling truths about the failings of the American polity, and each devised rhetorical and programmatic strategies for political redress and transformation. The brilliance of Reagan's rhetorical achievement consists, then, of having convinced the American polity that he—rather than African American prophetic critics—spoke the truth about America. Indeed, Reagan convinced Americans that the prophetic political critics were no more than false prophets. To help adjudicate the contest between Reagan and these prophetic political critics concerning the true heir to the rhetoric of the City on the Hill, I turn to John Winthrop himself and examine his works in the context of a longer tradition of political theorizing that Winthrop both engaged and helped to create.

The City on the Hill: A Model of Political Desire

"The eies of all people are uppon us," John Winthrop preached to fellow émigrés aboard the Arbella. As he explained to this first generation of Puritans, their great migration was an "errand into the North American wilderness," a sacred mission grounded in a covenant with God, undertaken to provide reformation Christianity with a model of ecclesiastical and civil government.[12]

As the seventeenth-century vessel sailed across the Atlantic, Winthrop delivered the sermon that would establish him as the most venerable ancestor of the future republic's pre-constitutional past. In this remarkable sermon, "A Modell of Christian Charitee," Winthrop bequeathed to succeeding generations "The City on the Hill," a richly evocative theologico-political symbol of national purpose, a model of political desire tailor-made for soulcraft as statecraft under conditions of New World modernity. Importantly, Winthrop's sermon embeds a model of political desire within the imagined community he conjures with his invocation of the City on the Hill. Winthrop advances a metaphor of care for the powerless at the heart of a community in which God's residence instantiates the sacred, supplies the arms that secure the community's perpetual military advantage, and grounds the claim of exemplariness. He envisions a polity entitled to claim leadership over the world. "Wee shall finde that the God of Israell is among us, when tenn of us shall be able to resist a thousand of our enemies, when hee shall make us a prayse and glory, that men shall say of succeeding plantacions: the lord make it like that of New England: for wee must Consider that wee shall be as a Citty upon a Hill, the eies of all people are upon us."[13]

"A Modell of Christian Charitee" can best be understood as a model of political desire. Winthrop's sermon deliberately explicates and prescribes an order of love, an order of erotic desire, which must obtain if the Puritan errand is to succeed. Winthrop anticipates and rejects the appeal to sovereign rationality as the architectonic human faculty much celebrated by later liberal political theorists. In his view, rationality is a derivative power whose primary function is to help clarify and defend love, the source of human action. There was ample philosophical precedent for Winthrop's approach. St. Augustine, the Christian philosopher of late antiquity, argued that a polity is none other than "an assembled multitude of rational creatures united in agreement about the objects of their loves."[14] Reason, in this political context, may facilitate agreement among citizens by mediating and bringing their loves into accord, but the fruit of this intercourse of reason and desire (*logos and eros*), according to Augustine, is a higher and more generalized order of love, an order that can best be described as an authoritative and comprehensive regime of desire (*nomos of eros*). Because he believed human sinfulness yoked the most virtuous loves to pride and vanity, however, Augustine concluded that the sovereignty of love in politics doomed the very best polities to corruption.[15] Winthrop appropriated Augustine's account of the formative power of desire, but he believed he had discovered the means to circumvent Augustine's pessimism concerning the fate of political undertakings.

According to Winthrop, justice affords the correct principles for regulating desire, principles that would be furnished by nature. By the law of nature, "man is commanded to love his neighbor as himself," to "help another in want or distress," and to "perform this out of the same affection which makes him care for his own good."[16] Because nature gave these principles to humans in "the state of innocence," adherence to them is almost impossible for selves who have suffered the permanent disfigurement of human sinfulness. Although Winthrop seems to accede to Augustine's prevailing pessimism, he shifts the terms of debate to enable an alternative outcome.[17] For Winthrop, the real problem is not that sin precludes the observance of natural law, but rather that natural law is grossly inadequate to the project he and his fellows are undertaking.[18] The Puritan settlers believed themselves to be establishing something altogether unprecedented, an order of community whose freedom from the corruptions of the *saeculum* was vouchsafed by a new covenanted dispensation: "Thus stands the cause between God and us, wee are entered into a Covenant with him for this worke, wee have taken out a Commission, the Lord hath given us leave to drawe our own Articles."[19] The ends of this covenant were uniquely tied to religious purposes: "[Our] end is to improve our lives to do more service to the Lord, the comfort and increase of the body of Christ that ourselves and posterity may be better preserved from the common corruption of this evil world to serve the Lord and work out our salvation under the power and purity of his holy ordinances."[20] For this extraordinary venture, the "law of grace" rather than the "law of nature" was to be their guide. Thus, natural law's inadequacy in the face of original sin no longer posed an insuperable obstacle to their success. As a covenanted community—an association of persons "commissioned" directly by God—the Puritans could escape from "the common corruption of the evil world." Envisioning escape as safe passage cleared by new law rather than fugitive passage sanctioned by old, Winthrop argued that a new form of solidarity was required in the City on the Hill, a solidarity predicated on principles of self-sacrifice rather than virtue. As he explained to his fellow travelers: "Wee must be knitt together in this worke as one man, wee must entertaine each other in brotherly Affeccion, wee must be willing to abridge our selves of our superfluities, for the supply of others' necessities, wee must uphold a familiar Commerce together in all meekness, gentleness, patience and liberallity, wee must delight in eache other, make others' Condicions our owne rejoice together, labor, and suffer together, alwayes haveing before our eyes our Commission and Community in the worke."[21]

Novelists and political theorists have popularized a depiction of Puritans as rigid, self-righteous, and morally exacting.[22] However, Winthrop's Puritans did not fit this stereotype. The form of association elaborated by Winthrop forged bonds among persons who were not necessarily virtuous but who were capable of self-denial under appropriate circumstances. Community of this kind is different from a community of moral exemplars, although its requirements may be no less taxing. The community of sacrifice, according to Winthrop, presupposed an altogether different order of desire given to the elect "in the state of regeneracy," that is, the altered condition of the self who has been regenerated by Puritan Christianity.[23] In particular, "the law of grace" revealed to the regenerated a new set of principles concerning the duties of mercy. Mercy prescribed a "measure" for practices of "giving," "lending," and "forgiving," a measure appropriate to "a difference of seasons and occasions." In other words, Winthrop suggested that the requirements of mercy were different in extraordinary circumstances than they were in ordinary conditions.[24] Under normal circumstances, mercy prescribes what individuals must be prepared to give to others in need, how they should value their property, and how they should treat persons who owe them debts. The principles of mercy under these normal circumstances are not terribly different from the principles of justice established by natural law, which require individuals to do good to all and give out of abundance. However, under extraordinary circumstances, such as those permanently built into "an errand into the wilderness," the requirements of mercy are quite distinctive. Winthrop suggests that the errand mandates a permanent state of exception: "Here we cannot be content with ordinary means or with means we deploy in England."[25] Under circumstances governed by the Lord's commission, the principles of mercy are exacting. Individuals must be prepared to devote all their energies and efforts to the community, even if the community requires the entirety of their personal force. They must give beyond the exhaustion of abundance to others who have squandered their portions if the errand is at stake. They must be able to release others from promises made, if for whatever reason, they lack the means to fulfill them. In short, community members must sacrifice. The security of the covenant requires each person to give precedence to the needs of fellow travelers over the demands of their own integrity and their own needs.[26]

The "law of grace," then, is both an unprecedented emancipation from ordinary morality and an extravagant burden. It frees members of the covenanted community to supplement principles of justice with principles of mercy, but it requires them to enshrine sacrifice as the necessary civic competence for all who wish to inhabit the City on the Hill. To enter and reside in this city, then, everyone must be prepared to sacrifice everything. Winthrop was keenly aware of the arduous demands required by this ethic of sacrifice.

The strategy he devised to address these demands demonstrates his acuity as a political founder and his talents as a poet. Winthrop insisted that where grace or "regeneracy" was genuine, God's "delight to dwell among us" would not require transcendence of sin; it would require only sinners' deference to the new set of demands required by their unprecedented experiment in self-government. In a polity where the "law of grace" functioned as a rule of law, sacrifice and covenant fused to institutionalize an exceptional form of mercy as public practice.

Winthrop noted that his task was to "lay open the grounds" of mercy, knowing full well that "draw[ing] men to works of mercy is not [accomplished by] force of argument from goodness or necessity of the work."[27] Appeals to reason would be largely ineffective in habituating people to the duty of sacrifice. "For this might persuade some rational mind to some present act of mercy (as is frequent in experience) but it cannot worke such a habit in a soul as shall make it prompt upon all occasions to produce the same effect but by framing the affections of love in the hearte."[28] Invoking the authority of St. Paul, architect and venerated martyr of Christianity, Winthrop insisted that love must be framed in the heart, "for it is this love which makes mercy easy." To frame love in the heart, Winthrop advocated three interrelated strategies and, in so doing, underscored the constitutive role of rhetoric in covenant politics. First, he described what love is and explained what it is for, revealing love's existential basis and the rewards that flow from its exercise. Second, he extolled what love has done to create the conditions of possibility for this particular covenanted community. Third, he promised God's blessings for successful completion of the errand in the wilderness and God's curses for deviating from it. Winthrop used his considerable oratorical power to articulate the shape and color of "love in the heart," this all-important desire, and to inflame it through poetic invocation of ancestral heroes whose sacrificial love founded the community. He then appealed to a strict and jealous God as an invisible, yet ever-present special prosecutor poised to ensure community compliance with its covenanted mission.

Arguing that "love is the bond of perfection," Winthrop accords a particular role to certain aspects of community in "unfolding" the "inward exercise" of love. "Wee must take in our way that maxime of philosophy Simile simili gaudet or like will to like."[29] For Winthrop's conception of love, just as for Aristotle's conception of justice, the principle of resemblance shapes the parameters for the exercise of virtue in community. In Winthrop's words, "For as it is things which are carved with disafeccion to each other, the ground of it is from dissimilitude or ariseing from the contrary or different nature of the things themselves, soe the ground of love is an apprehension of some resemblance in the things loved to which affects it."[30] The capacity to recognize similarity and difference is essential to the communal practice of love. In relationships with others, an individual can restrain self-interestedness and fulfill the demands of sacrifice as long as the individual apprehends that another is not "the other." Indeed, Winthrop suggests that the rewards for love for others within a homogeneous community are intense pleasure and secure contentment and that these rewards constitute the true key to the kingdom.[31] "Soe is it in all the labour of love, among christians, the partie loving, reapes love againe as was shewed before, which soule covetts more than all the wealthe in the world. nothing yeilds more pleasure and content to the soule then when it findes that which it may love fervently for to love and live beloved is the soules paradise, both heare and in heaven."[32] Within Winthrop's frame, love is a form of identification that enables difficult acts of mercy, and the reward for this identification is a form of pleasure that can be had in no other way.[33] Appealing to those who have encountered the pleasures of such identification as his authorities, Winthrop insists, "Let those with experience say if there is sweetness comparable to mutual love."

By explicating love as an "unfolding" of philosophical principles regarding matters that are impervious to rational demonstration, Winthrop subordinates philosophy to politics and conflates politics with religion. Philosophical authority is enlisted to support a political imperative that fosters competence in distinguishing beloved compatriots from others, or as Plato had suggested many centuries earlier, friends from enemies. Although philosophy shores up the capacity to distinguish relevant similarities and differences in defining the boundaries of community, it pales in comparison to the decisive support provided by religion. Within Winthrop's conception of covenanted communal membership, political solidarity is forged by sacrifice. Winthrop construes the meaning of sacrifice as the expression of an exceptional love predicated on resemblance. Uniquely suited to the extraordinary circumstances of settlers in a New World, solidarity in sacrifice for those like oneself promises unprecedented pleasure in the future. In addition to such unparalleled satisfaction, Winthrop consolidates his vision with the threat of divine punishment for communal failure and divine elevation for communal success. Winthrop weaves together the fearsome prospect of God's abandonment or destruction and the promise that God's chosen people will enjoy an exalted status among other polities. "If wee shall neglect the observation of these articles which are the ends wee have propounded, and, dissembling with our

God, shall fall to embrace this present world and prosecute our carnall intentions, seeking great things for ourselves and our posterity, the Lord will surely breake out in wrathe against us; be revenged of such a [sinful] people and make us knowe the price of the breache of such a covenant."[34] To avoid this catastrophe and court glory, however, Winthrop enjoins his listeners to the counsel of the prophet Micah: "To doe justly, to love mercy, [and] to walk humbly with our God."

The City on the Hill envisioned by Winthrop had markedly different consequences for those within the homogeneous community and those identified as sufficiently different to be cast outside its borders. Justice supplemented by mercy and mercy as a political practice of sacrifice legitimated the colonization of the New World and the displacement of indigenous peoples. It also legitimated the importation and exploitation of enslaved Africans. The "souls' paradise" consolidated by love of those like oneself was simultaneously a living hell for those defined as different. African American prophetic critics documented atrocities within this bifurcated world in ways that European-American political theorists consistently failed to do. However, they took over Winthrop's politics of sacrifice, convinced of its necessity for their purposes, yet insufficiently attentive to its consequences. Before we turn our attention to the terms of their critique, it is worth surveying the problems presented by colonialism.

New World Modernity and the Parameters of the Political Imaginary

Hannah Arendt described the colonial settlement of the New World as one of the outstanding achievements of Europe. Lacking "a culture and a history of their own," Arendt explained, the Americas provided empty space for "the founding of new settlements which adopted the legal and political institutions of the mother country."[35] In addition to expelling victims of genocidal violence from history, Arendt's story failed to engage the politics implicit in the creation of New World modernity.[36] Had she engaged the catastrophic upheavals of New World early modernity with the care that animated her engagement with the disintegration of European late modernity, she might have been more circumspect in her claims concerning such "achievements."[37] Colonial settlement of the New World justified its violence against and exploitation of native populations by appeal to a long-standing rationale: Settlement required expropriation, and expropriation required conquest.[38] Estranged from "European civilization," colonial settlers and their heirs wrestled with deep fears of cultural decline and assimilation into "barbarism," which contributed to the exercise of violence against various excluded others.[39] Settlement of the New World proceeded according to predatory political logic established by the realities of competitive acquisition among imperial states. Expropriation of native populations through violence cleared political space, but it created borders that separated settlers from native inhabitants with prudential warrants for violent aggression. Settlers also had to grapple with the continued arrival of agents of Old World empires, who sought to protect their own acquisitions and extend them into space "cleared" by prior expropriators. As Niccolò Machiavelli had suggested at the genesis of European imperial expansion into the New World, the best way to consolidate power in space claimed by violence is to expand outward. Following Machiavelli's thinking, New World colonialism encouraged the continuous immigration of "assimilable aliens," while building durable and powerful governing structures to secure and manage acquired space. As the frontiers of this vast continent receded with the expansion of white settlement across the West, white settlers wrestled with interior frontiers. Territorial expansion and political consolidation ambivalently and imperfectly incorporated increasing numbers of "internal aliens," peoples whose "difference" precluded assimilation as settler-citizens.

As Winthrop anticipated, a society of restive individuals actively involved in nation-building and dispersed across vast tracts of appropriated space required authority—power that is inspired as well as effective. Inspired power was required to manage fluid and multiple forms of commerce among such individuals and to authorize (in various ways) extreme inequalities and moral excesses resulting from the conquest, subjugation, and displacement of indigenous populations. Inspired power was also needed to mask other exigent economies of violence and violation associated with the expansion and consolidation of a settler society. "Theologico-politics" is one name for such an inspired authority. Conjuring a powerful image of selfhood and community that unites the theological and the political into a single norm of worldly activity, the City on the Hill has functioned as an ingenious form of modern soulcraft and statecraft. Over the past four centuries, this theologico-political discourse has produced citizen-subjects with rich resources and unique abilities to meet the exigencies of New World political modernity. Appropriated for multiple purposes, the City on the Hill has manifested resilience and power that surpass, yet are peculiarly bound up with, the world historic purposes pursued by the small and rather unlikely settlement at Massachusetts Bay.[40]

Contemporary scholarly debates on the question of American theologico-politics have focused on questions of empirical evidence and theoretical adequacy. Is there a civil religion in America? If so, what are its doctrines, and how might we account for its hegemony in a doctrinally diverse polity?[41] Some scholars who suspect the presence of theologico-politics but doubt that there is sufficient empirical support to prove the existence of an American civil religion posit ideology or civil mythology as an alternative rubric for understanding the dynamics of the bifurcated politics of the City on the Hill. For some writers, "ideology" offers a conceptual category that can account for the hegemony of theologico-politics by locating the reproduction of citizens' religious understanding of American politics in secular rhetorical practices that appeal to and reinscribe religious ideas and practices.[42] The notion of ideology captures the continuity between the past and the present and highlights the conservative political role of these practices. Yet it often reduces these complex theologico-political practices to false consciousness and thus masks the multiple dimensions of self-interest that inform them. The notion of ideology also obscures the spiritual resonance of these practices in a polity constituted by varying political interests and diverse forms of religious belief.[43]

As an alternative to ideology, some scholars have turned to the conception of the "political imaginary."[44] As contemporary philosopher Charles Taylor explains, a political imaginary refers to "the ways people imagine their social existence, how they fit together with others, how things go on between them and their fellows, their expectations that are normally met, and the deeper normative notions and images that underlie these expectations."[45] An imaginary may be informed by older theories, ideology, civil religion, or various other civic myths, but it is a much looser set of beliefs that is not reducible to these constitutive elements. Held by ordinary persons rather than political or intellectual elites, Taylor suggests that a social imaginary remains causally efficacious within social life, even though it is not tightly structured, elite-driven, or theoretically coherent. More suspicious of the partisan character of "political imaginary" than Taylor, political theorist Sheldon Wolin describes the concept as a potent "fantasy" that serves the immediate political objectives of particular actors or groups of actors. Within Wolin's frame, a political imaginary is an "organization of resources, ideal as well as material, in which a potential [within a particular conceptualization of resources] becomes a challenge to realize it. What is conceived by the imagination is not mere improvement but a quantum leap that nonetheless preserves elements of the familiar."[46] Wolin provides an account of how a political imaginary works and why imperially inclined, corporate-elite-dominated politics favor the proliferation of political imagination. Even so, he does not address those conditions in which political imagination is inoperative or, if operative, is unable to flourish. Nor does he consider the complex ways in which the "political imagination," as an individual faculty and as a collective mode of political perception, can become a source of political knowledge.

Legal scholar Paul Kahn has argued that the political imaginary is in fact the true basis of the modern nation-state. In his view, "the basic structures of our self understanding—family, religion, and state—share an overlapping narrative form."[47] This overlapping narrative captures accounts of sacrificial violence suffered by the self's imagined ancestral precursors. What appear to be autonomous discourses about state formation, family history, and religious community—construed by liberalism as separate spheres of association—are seen as parallel inventions of political imagination that situate the conditions of possibility for the modern self in heroic ancestral battles against violence, suffering, and death. As Kahn argues, these narratives incite the modern self to deep and concerted forms of reverent identification with imagined communities of predecessors engaged in grand historical struggles. This reverence fosters the modern self's willing compliance with determinate ideas of human flourishing—ideas that flow from imagined communities of sacrifice rather than actual ones. Embodied in modern selves, these imagined pasts result in the internalization and the voluntary performance of the very real sovereignty of the modern nation-state.

Kahn's account of the identifications fostered by these parallel imaginaries of predecessors, saints, and heroes shares marked similarities with the views advanced by Winthrop. Kahn argues that these identifications produce a potent form of political desire, indeed, a form of love. "Love binds us to particular political communities just as it binds us to particular families. We locate ourselves—really, we find ourselves—in communities that have a particular history and territory. That history is not universal history but rather the narrative of the successful overcoming of challenges by a particular community."[48] Whether the City on the Hill is conceived as a love-inducing communal identification, a narrative structure that grounds and shapes fundamental conceptions of American selfhood, a loose but causally efficacious set of background conditions, or a thoroughly contingent political construct deployed discretely by specific groups of political actors to secure particular objectives, it has operated powerfully for four centuries to establish the parameters of the American political imaginary. These parameters are thoroughly inflected by race, and the African American prophetic tradition has long examined the effects of such sustained racialization.

Prophetic Political Critique and the Problem
of Political Evil

Prophets are a distinguished group of inspired social critics who remind the community of their constitutive covenanted obligations to God and interpret prevailing social contradictions in light of these originary covenanted obligations.[49] Bearing God's assessment of the justice of their communal practices, prophets warn of impending calamity that will result from the community's continued failure to honor their covenant and place before the community the moment of decision, the moment when the community must choose whether they will honor their commitments or suffer the consequences for their failure to do so.[50] Prophets illuminate the ways in which communal observances of divine ordinances have ossified into empty ritual and how communal deference to established forms of social order have devolved into institutional practices of self-congratulatory idolatry.[51] Prophets often bear witness to the experiences of the poor, marginalized, and unprotected. They often insist that the proliferation of practices that generate and justify these kinds of vulnerabilities bear directly on compliance with covenanted obligations to God.[52] When prophets raise the question of the status of the covenant, what is at stake is not simply the quality, form, and distribution of religious piety, but rather the security and integrity of the community established by the covenant. Addressing the national community about its collective fate, prophecy is a profoundly political discourse.[53]

African American prophetic critics appropriated and revised this ancient tradition of Hebrew prophecy to interpret and transform their New World political predicament. Old Testament narratives of captivity, exile, persecution, and deliverance expressed and validated black people's experiences of isolation, physical vulnerability, and dishonor. They powerfully articulated the experiences of blacks who were hoping, waiting, and preparing for deliverance from slavery and other forms of social denigration. Biblical narratives provided African Americans a larger historical frame within which to situate their own experiences of captivity, exile, and persecution in America.[54] When read alongside the Christian Gospel, these biblical stories afforded a political theology of individual dignity that opposed white supremacist discourses of black inferiority. They also provided a theory of human depravity that helped to render intelligible the motives and methods of American mastery.[55] Prophetic language also facilitated a convergence of the ultimate concerns of African Americans and white Americans. Enacting the dreaded proposition that African Americans read from the same texts as white Americans, prophetic political critics asked the national community about the content and status of America's constitutive obligations. They asked whether American citizens' deference to the celebrated forms and glorious practices of the republic were practices of idolatry. They asked whether, in a Christian community, slavery, segregation, and exploitation could be indicators of anything other than the ways in which the community attends to the poor and powerless it systematically creates and tolerates. Prophetic political critics conceived the problems of slavery, segregation, and other forms of white supremacy as critical national questions that demanded a decision whose continued deferral or wrong-headed outcomes would result in disaster for the polity.[56]

Writing in the prophetic tradition, David Walker, Frederick Douglass, W.E.B. Du Bois, and James Baldwin provided African Americans (and their allies) inspiring yet credible visions of societal transformation, grounded in white repentance for the evils perpetrated against blacks. Yet black prophetic political intellectuals also attempted to help African Americans to flourish in a political and cultural context where practices of mercy between whites rendered black pain not only invisible but also integral to settled practices of American "public happiness." Thus, prophetic political critics were forced to grapple seriously and productively with the problem of political evil.[57] I understand the problem of political evil to be distinct from the problem of moral evil, which has engaged theologians and moral philosophers over the centuries, and different, as well, from the modern theoretical effort, described by Susan Neiman in *Evil Modern Thought*, to reconceive political life in response to the problem of moral evil. In my understanding, the problem of political evil is a subaltern theoretical problematic pursued seriously by only a few political theorists—Augustine, Machiavelli, and Alexis de Tocqueville, among canonical political philosophers, and George Kateb, William Connolly, and Judith Shklar, among contemporary political theorists.[58] Notwithstanding the insightful interventions of these contemporary scholars, however, the problem of political evil, for the most part, has been studiously avoided by American intellectuals, statesmen, and citizens, past and present.[59] Against the grain, then, black prophetic political critique developed an incisive, profound, and instructive program of theory and action that was uniquely attuned to American political problems, yet fully engaged with urgent, if subaltern, questions of Western political philosophy.[60] To appreciate the theoretical profundity of this tradition, then, we need to consider this problem of evil—chief, I would argue, among subaltern questions—in its complex and awesome specificity.

The problem of political evil refers to a range of phenomena associated with a polity's systematic production and concealment of the unwarranted

pain and unjustifiable harm of human beings as the product of its normal operations. The problem of political evil includes an assessment of the
institutional operations that produce and sustain harm as well as the consequences of remedial, insurgent, or transformative strategies devised by survivors of political evil to contain, redress, and transcend these harms. George
Kateb has conceived of political evil as the unjustifiable harm of undeserving persons caused, endorsed, or knowingly tolerated by states, lower-level
political associations, or private citizens who act under the protection of
states.[61] Within this frame, "political evil" refers to communal and institutional practices and comprises individual actions (or failures of action) that
cannot be reduced to individual deeds. As Kateb notes, political evil is problematic not simply because culprits are collective entities, such as states, associations, and movements, whose sovereignty (or legitimacy with a sovereign
state) shelters them from accountability. Rather, the problem is the "susceptibility for political evil" that is built into politics itself. These exigencies of
politics foster modes of abstract thinking among political elites that conceal the human costs of the policies that they pursue and promote group
identities that secrete images of enemies who can be violated without scru-
ple.[62] Judith Shklar also wrestled with this question of "susceptibilities" and
located them in ordinary vices, the perennial flaws of human character that,
however troublesome, detestable, or shunned in social life, map onto the
particular needs of different kinds of regimes. Of these vices, cruelty is the
worst, in her view, because its direct product is fear, the passion that provides
the generative conditions for the proliferation of most of the other vices.[63]
Shklar concluded, as Kateb would later, that liberalism, the theory of politics
that upholds the sanctity of individual rights and the enshrinement of these
rights by governments as the principle of their political legitimacy, was not
simply the *best* but rather the *only* modern regime sufficiently cognizant of
the problem of political evil.[64]

William E. Connolly's sensitivity to this problem of susceptibility is just
as acute, but his intervention takes a very different form. For Connolly, the
problem of political evil inheres in various cultural practices, but one of its
most acute forms resides within faith, a crypto-Augustinian religious imperative that inhabits insecure ethico-politico commitments of all kinds—
whether those of overtly religious groups or those with overtly secular aims
who simply conceal from themselves their abiding faith in secularism.[65]
According to Connolly, "to be human is to be inhabited by existential faith,
hence the tendency to evil in faith is this. The instance in which the faith of
others incites you to anathematize it as inferior or evil can usher into being
the demand for revenge against them for the internal disturbance they sow,

even if they have not otherwise limited your ability to express your faith."[66] Connolly suggests that this imperative is akin to madness because it seeks to extirpate anything that it perceives as a threat to itself.

These provocations occasion a return to St. Augustine, one of the most penetrating theorists of political evil. In contrast to these recent conceptualizations of political evil as a "susceptibility" of the political—a susceptibility that is rooted in ordinary vice and is at once fostered and concealed by faith—Augustine advanced an account of political evil particularly useful for an understanding of the institutionalization of Winthrop-inspired public practices of mercy in the New World. For Augustine, self-sacrifice on the basis of resemblance constituted a criminal solidarity.[67] Indeed, he suggested that the choice of criminal solidarity was the constitutive act of human community. Grounding his analysis in an interpretation of the biblical story of Adam and Eve, Augustine argued that individuals not only would countenance the crime of others if sufficiently invested in or erotically attached to them; they would also sacrifice their highest good as long as they could sustain their connection to their beloved. Augustine suggests that inordinate desire for recognition by those we desire is so basic to human life that obvious and greater goods will be continually sacrificed in order to maintain this solidarity. In recognizing how criminal solidarity can bind those within a community constituted by resemblance, Augustine demonstrates how Christian religiosity is at once a peculiarly effective form of modern political solidarity and a peculiarly ferocious incarnation of the problem of political evil. Individuals providentially sanctioned as a covenanted community and educated in habits of sacrifice will be especially prone to acts of political evil, even and especially when such acts violate their respective consciences and perhaps even threaten the safety of the covenanted community itself. Augustine illuminates the problem of political evil in a manner that is more comprehensive than the accounts provided by Kateb, Shklar, or Connolly. His account helps to illuminate how the problem of political evil has become embedded into the theological politics of America.

Augustine provides additional conceptual resources for thinking about the problem of political evil. The wily Bishop of Hippo also quietly counseled that the remembrance of communal crime was the best way to manage discord. To remember communal crime is to remind ourselves of sin, our propensities for self-seeking, shortsighted, and inordinately desirous pursuits. "For there is nothing so social by nature as [the human] race no matter how discordant it has become through this fault; and human nature can call upon nothing more appropriate, either to prevent discord from coming into existence, or heal it where it already exists, than remembrance of that first parent of us all."[68] To remember Adam is to remember sacrifice and to remember that the human condition is inaugurated by Adam's act of preference for corrupt solidarity with Eve over divine communion according to higher principles of justice. Reflection on this biblical crime that fixed the fate of all humanity demonstrates that deep-seated human needs for recognition permanently threaten the human capacity to act on what individuals know to be right and true.

Augustine offers a plausible account of the criminal solidarity that is foundational to Christian communities, an account that provides firm canonical warrant for reading Winthrop's explication of the exceptional demands of mercy in the New World context as a theologico-political vindication of the problem of political evil. I do not mean to suggest that Winthrop advanced a program of "evil as policy."[69] Nonetheless, the consequences of his exceptionalist account of Christian solidarity produced and legitimated political evil. The program of sacrifice inaugurated by his explication of covenant politics facilitated imperatives of compromise, habits of forgiveness, and exigencies of differentiation based on resemblance. These practices enabled a community at odds over issues that they regarded as fundamental questions of good and evil to sustain deep, satisfying, and all-too-often untroubled bonds of solidarity, with devastating consequences for indigenous and enslaved people. An examination of Christian solidarity as a foundational mode of racial solidarity in the New World is the starting point for African American prophetic political reflection on and critique of the City on the Hill.

In the following pages, I tell the story of prophetic critique as a tradition of political theorizing and practice that is especially attuned to the problem of political evil that resides within the theologico-politics of America. In Chapter 1, I analyze the explosive but virtually unexplicated political theory of David Walker, the mysterious political intellectual whose publication of *An Appeal to the Colored Citizens of the World* established him as one of the most notorious men of his day. Walker's provocative text is the first systematic political account of the institution of American slavery and the first explicit attempt to found a new political imaginary to organize and animate black politics. Walker unmasks the Winthropian mercy lurking behind Thomas Jefferson's apology for slavery and defense of white supremacy. Launching an alternative constitutional project, he issues a call to blacks throughout the Atlantic diaspora to consider the necessity and glory of black sacrifice in attempting, within a "city of enmity," to build a different kind of City on the Hill.

Chapter 2 analyzes the writings and speeches of Frederick Douglass. As a theorist who was a former slave and bore on his body the manifold scars of slavery, Douglass possessed a keen grasp of the problem of political evil. Yet as an exceptionally graceful and charismatic figure who managed to ascend to a position of leadership within the abolition movement, Douglass focused his extraordinary acumen on envisioning the possibilities within America for multiracial liberal democracy. Douglass appropriated Walker's critique and developed a more sophisticated theory of political evil. I suggest that Douglass launched a campaign against political evil on two fronts at once. On the first front, Douglass sought to reclaim the dignity of Winthropian aspirations incarnated in the American Revolution and founding, exposing the vulnerability of this inheritance to the corruptions unleashed by the political evil of slavery. On the second front, Douglass waged a battle to neutralize the political imaginary conceived and disseminated by Walker. Toward that end, ensconced within a "city of mastery," Douglass devised a narrative of the problem of political evil, which, for reasons of public credibility and personal sanity, led him to publicize the evils of mastery but privatize the experience of slavery. This chapter suggests that the genius of Douglass's prophetic critique may consist of having rendered masters intelligible as enemies of the republic at the cost of banishing the lived atrocity of slavery from history into the relative obscurity of African American memory.

A brilliant and accomplished scholar, W.E.B. Du Bois wrestled with the complex consequences of lived atrocity in his great work *The Souls of Black Folk*. He also examined the advantages and disadvantages of the public imaginary of the City on the Hill as a means to mobilize white citizens around black political needs. Du Bois envisioned critique as a scholarly pursuit taken up by the polity's best minds and accorded a special and protected sphere within society. Chapter 3 analyzes how Du Bois deployed his intimate knowledge of the spiritual aspirations of American cultural and political elites. Acutely aware of their mounting worries about the social leveling associated with mass democratization, Du Bois was able to breach the walls of the "gilded city" and develop a patrician narrative of Winthropian sacrifice that could promote black interests in the twentieth century.

Chapter 4 examines the writings of James Baldwin, the author of six novels, two plays, a screenplay, and a book of poetry, and best remembered for his searing and beautifully written essays. Confronting his sense of exile in the "dishonorable city," Baldwin resuscitated the praxis of prophetic critique, despite his grave reservations about theologico-politics of any kind. Articulating a self-critical prophetic political critique of radical social and political transformation, Baldwin revised Winthropian politics in a skeptical and self-conscious effort to quell deep and abiding suspicions that Walker's initial project might be justified. Investigating the contours and moral complexity of a black political imaginary, Baldwin illuminated the vulnerability and insufficiency of the American self buoyed by Winthropian mercy. In its place, Baldwin offered a political practice of love as provocation to be undertaken by lovers struggling with and on behalf of a beloved society. Baldwin attempted to create a new New World identity that could sustain more humane and more human politics.

Taken together, Walker, Douglass, Du Bois, and Baldwin delineate a tradition of prophetic critique that offers powerful challenges to the American political imaginary, even as it attempts to preserve some of its more hopeful insights. Nonetheless, examination of the political thought of these four thinkers reveals telling omissions in this mode of political analysis, not the least of which concerns the status of black women's testimony for its purposes. Concerned with reconstituting themselves as founders of a new polity, these thinkers (with the exception, perhaps, of Baldwin) more often than not reproduced the heteronormative, patriarchal norms of society at large. They constructed masculinist models of sacrifice and honor that affirmed for them the duties of citizenship. In the process, they sought to (literally and figuratively) domesticate the violations and vulnerabilities suffered by enslaved women, even rendering those experiences invisible when they did not suit the authors' overarching political purposes. This tendency is one of this tradition's enduring problems.

The Conclusion addresses the contemporary crisis of prophetic critique. I examine the literary critique of the prophetic political tradition advanced by Toni Morrison. Morrison exposes the limitations of gendered constructions of personal vulnerability and citizenship and, in so doing, synthesizes and extends a tradition of black feminist skepticism regarding prophetic political critique. As an avowed legatee of Baldwin, author of nine novels and countless essays, and an African American woman who labored at the crux of the civil rights movement and the women's movement, Morrison exposes the glaring blindness and insuperable limits of this tradition as a contemporary mode of political inquiry, tradition of political action, and form of American self-criticism. I also provide a genealogy of the shifting vocations of black politics associated with the praxis of prophetic critique and assess past articulations in the context of contemporary issues and future prospects. In light of recent declarations of a "post-racial" era in American political life, I analyze the rise to prominence of Barack Obama to explore how this once vital tradition may dissipate into an instrument of black political entrepreneurialism.

In telling the story of African American critical engagement with an American political imaginary forged by the City on the Hill, I also reclaim the work of exemplary American political thinkers. In so doing, I hope to add to the canon of American political theory the critical works of David Walker, a freeborn son of a slave who sought to be a founder; Frederick Douglass, a former slave who became a statesman but longed to be a citizen; W.E.B. Du Bois, a scholar whose quest to become a statesman in an era dominated by aristocrats and demagogues led him to become an exile and a revolutionary; and James Baldwin, an artist turned founder whose failure makes him a candidate for sainthood.

1

Black Liberty in the City of Enmity

The Political Theory of David Walker

I therefore, in the name and fear of the Lord God of Heaven and of earth, divested of prejudice either on the side of my color or that of the whites, advance my suspicion of them, whether they are as good by nature as we are or not.[1]

The world will have the opportunity to see whether it is unfortunate for us, that our creator *has made* us darker than the whites.[2]

Here and there in the early part of the century came other exceptional men. . . . [T]here was that Voice crying in the Wilderness, David Walker.[3]

When David Walker wrote his infamous *Appeal to the Colored Citizens of the World, but in Particular, and Very Expressly, to Those of the United States of America*, Winthrop's "shining city on a hill" had become for aspiring "colored citizens," a "city of enmity," a place where American happiness was contingent on racial slavery, social ostracism, and terroristic violence. Indeed, the pursuit of happiness, with property rights as its precondition and slavery as its corollary, had begun, systematically, to make an enemy of the very notion of "black liberty." David Walker was neither the first African American political intellectual nor the first thinker to employ prophetic Christian language as a political vocabulary. However, Walker can lay claim to having inaugurated the transformation of prophetic exhortation from a theologico-political rhetoric of insurgency into a literary genre of systematic reflection and critique. Suspicious that Winthrop's political imaginary fused with white supremacy and the lust for mastery in the writings of the American republic's leading spokespersons, Walker's insurgent political writings sought to answer several interrelated theoretical questions. How should blacks understand the U.S. social and political order, given the polity's official commitment to the fundamental dignity of all men, its profession of faith in its covenanted origins and obligations, and its equally resolute commitment to disregard, if not destroy, the dignity of blacks? Should American slavery and white supremacy be understood as deficiencies in an otherwise decent society, or are they constitutive practices within a system of political evil? Which of the harms suffered by blacks have most undermined black dignity and freedom, and what must blacks do to reconstitute themselves as subjects in full possession of human dignity within and outside of slavery?

Walker drew from the ancient Roman historian Sallust to facilitate his effort to reconceive and reconstruct prevailing conceptions of black agency and solidarity. In doing so, he recast Christian ethics in light of what he learned from Roman antiquity of political virtue. Approaching the predicament of African Americans through the lens of these questions and with these intellectual investments enabled Walker to pierce the horizon of exclusively religious and moral criticism of slavery prevailing in the Anglo-American world and to reconfigure what amounted to a cultural criticism into a sophisticated political-theoretical analysis and normative critique.[4] For these reasons, among others that I explore in this chapter, Walker can be described as an important founder of the African American tradition of prophetic political critique.[5]

Walker's *Appeal to the Colored Citizens of the World*

Two curiosities in particular should strike even the most casual reader of David Walker's *Appeal to the Colored Citizens of the World, but in Particular, and Very Expressly, to Those of the United States of America*: the provocative title of the work itself and the particular literary form Walker cobbles together from disparate sources and deploys on behalf of a vision of black liberty. As the full title of the work suggests, Walker delineated an audience comprising blacks residing in the United States and blacks who lived beyond the boundaries of that specific American nation-state. The pamphlet heralds a transnational public of "colored citizens" that did not yet exist, but that, if carefully constituted, would be interested and invested in the claims and grievances the text advanced.[6] Walker's reference to citizenship here is complicated and utopian: He writes to, for, and about black persons who are neither citizens in the formal sense of persons who enjoy protections and privileges provided by a recognized state nor in the informal sense of persons who identify with and participate within a purposive solidarity oriented toward a common good.[7] His mode of salutation for each section of the *Appeal* indicates the fractured nature of his "citizenry" and seeks to forge a relationship among "citizens." He addresses the preamble of his *Appeal* to "my dearly beloved Brethren and Fellow Citizens," a salutation that associates the intimate religious and familial affiliation of brethren—which blacks had actualized to varying degrees of success in a range of contexts—with the formal, political designation of "citizen," a status, Walker argued, blacks had achieved only in the Republic of Haiti. Aside from its Catholicism, Haiti was, for Walker, "the glory of the blacks and terror of tyrants," a polity composed of "men who would be cut off to a man before they would yield to the combined forces of the whole world."[8] After invoking this sweeping utopian political vision in the title and preamble, Walker addresses each remaining article to "my brethren," a more humble salutation meant to address the particular, if limited, affiliations blacks had managed to sustain against the onslaught of a quickening white supremacy. The series of rhetorical moves indicated by his salutations provides an important clue to an underappreciated aspect of the theoretical ambitions of Walker's *Appeal*. By appealing to a utopian transnational public of colored citizens, Walker fortifies a basis for imagining how the seeds of familial intimacy implied by the term "brethren" might, through careful nurturing (and sustained philosophical reflection), mature into genuine political solidarity. In yoking together these two entities—brethren and fellow citizens—Walker begins to prepare the provocative intellectual ground he ultimately stakes to fuse and extend the various experiences of the constituencies that make up the title's utopian vision: a "colored [citizenry] of the world, but in particular and very expressly . . . [that] of the United States of America."

Walker also constitutes this citizenry by invoking and combining a range of sacred and secular forms and, in so doing, performs the multifaceted role of prophet, herald, tribune, and statesman. As scholars have noted, the forms issuing from religious faith are vital to Walker's project. Wilson Moses situates Walker within a "black messianic tradition," a tradition of black theological interpretation that appropriates apocalyptic literatures and exegetical practices from Hebrew traditions and deploys them as the critical lens through which to assess American covenantal theology. According to Moses, black messianism holds that blacks are God's chosen people and that God will send a deliverer to redeem their suffering. On Moses's reading, the *Appeal* "mingles the conciliatory and strident tones" of this tradition and reflects a perspective of religious certainty, a certainty grounded in the "people's" access to revelation, powers of divinization, and skills of scriptural exegesis.[9] Eddie Glaude further excavates the religious sources of Walker's forms by emphasizing the *Appeal*'s function as a jeremiad, a reading that is ultimately more subtle and complex than that advanced by Moses. Walker's jeremiad, Glaude explains, is "a rhetorical form [that] ought to be understood as a paradigm of the structure of ambivalence that constitutes African Americans' relation to American culture."[10]

I do not wish to dispute the significance of religious faith as a constitutive element of the theoretical view that informs Walker's *Appeal*. However, I would like to focus my own analysis of the *Appeal* around the concerns that arise from its political-theoretical sources. At times, this will entail reading the religious sources as political sources, as I believe Walker intended.[11] Indeed, it is widely noted that Walker arranged the structure of the *Appeal* to mirror the form of one of the most emblematic documents of state formation: the U.S. Constitution. Similarly to the Constitution, the text of the *Appeal* commences with a preamble, in which Walker introduces his subject, followed by four (rather than seven) articles in which he develops four separate arguments that seek to illuminate particular aspects of the problems confronting a "colored citizenry." He also grounds his authority by surveying the geographical, social, racial, moral, and philosophical boundaries of the polity in a way that parallels Thomas Jefferson's work, for example, in his *Notes on the State of Virginia*. In this respect, both founders—Walker and Jefferson—deploy a literary device political theorist Sheldon Wolin reminds us was a standard convention for political philosophers in the ancient world.[12] As Wolin explains, these figures sought to acquire and disseminate political knowledge and often presented their insights in the form of a record of their travels to distant and foreign lands. In the hands of someone such as Jefferson, this record could then be deployed in the imperial interest as known and therefore conquerable territory.[13] This is the spirit in which Jefferson sent Lewis and Clark to chart and domesticate the territory of the Louisiana Purchase in 1804. In contrast, Walker aims to constitute a geographically based political community that might counter and resist the effects of that imperialist thrust. As the free son of an enslaved father and a free mother, Walker spent his early years in Wilmington, North Carolina, before traveling south and west and finally settling among the venerable free black community of Boston, Massachusetts. As the local distributor of *Freedom's Journal*, a newspaper edited by the New York–based free blacks John Russworn and Samuel Cornish, and as a salesman of secondhand clothing serving merchant seamen as his clients, Walker situated himself within well-trod circuits of knowledge and information.[14] "Having travelled over a considerable portion of the United States, and having, in the course of my travels, taken the most accurate observations of things as they exist," Walker begins his testimony. "The result of my observations has warranted the full and unshaken conviction, that we (coloured people of these United States) are the most degraded, wretched, and abject set of beings that ever lived since the world began."[15] Walker closes the *Appeal* with the same point, stated more emphatically: "I have travelled and observed nearly the whole of those things myself, and what little I did not get by my own observation, I received from those among the whites and blacks, in whom the greatest confidence may be placed."[16] The extent, accuracy, and trustworthiness of Walker's information, then, helps to legitimate his construction of a possible black political community.

In framing his "constitution" and establishing his authority as someone who knows the actual and theoretical terrain it encompasses, Walker aligns his aims with the aims of founders of political community more generally. Aristotle, the first theorist of constitutions in the Western tradition, explained that constitutions do many things. They create, institutionalize, and authorize particular offices of government for a polity. They delineate the powers held by particular offices within a structure of governance and elaborate the relations among governmental offices and between the government and the people. Equally importantly, they specify the ends that are to be pursued by the political community. These ends reflect the highest and most publicly shared commitments of a political community. Through the designation of these ends, the constitution not only organizes power and authority and distributes honors and offices but also brings a people into being as a collective political entity.[17] Reading Walker's *Appeal* within the framework of constitutional analysis, as I do in the following pages, raises new questions. What kind of regime does Walker envision? Who are to be the citizens of this new polity? What principles will guide this constitutional order? What kinds of laws will govern this new people? Reading the *Appeal* (particularly and very expressly) in the context of U.S. constitutional analysis, as Walker clearly invites us to do, encourages us to consider how black political theorizing might help to evaluate and recast American political thought.

Awakening Spirits and Wrestling with Paradox:
The Political Work of Walker's Preamble

In the preamble to the *Appeal*, Walker identifies the aim that animates the work as a whole: "To awaken in the breasts of my afflicted, degraded, and slumbering brethren a spirit of inquiry and investigation respecting our miseries and wretchedness in this Republican land of Liberty."[18] With this formulation, Walker emphasizes two distinct but interrelated political problems, which, if not more fundamental than enslavement and marginalization of blacks, are nonetheless conceptually and programmatically before white oppression.[19] The first problem, as Walker characterizes it, is the absence among blacks of a genuine spirit of inquiry. By referring to his "slumbering brethren," Walker suggests that blacks have been sleeping, lulled into a complacency and latency that ultimately prevented them from apprehending the conditions of black suffering. The second problem, which Walker suggests by way of his ironic invocation of "the Republican land of liberty," encapsulates the predicament that historian Edmund Morgan identified as the central "American paradox"—that the status of the United States as a slave society was the economically and politically necessary precondition for its constitution as a "free" nation.[20] Walker writes so that he and other black theorists might shine a light on the blind eye that "Christian Americans" turn to the moral and political paradox in their midst.

To that end (and in contrast to many Anglo-American abolitionists who both preceded and followed him), Walker was not content merely to dramatize the horrendous cruelties of slavery for white consumption. Walker realized that political order is constituted, at least in part, by the settled pragmatic adjustments of individuals to circumstances not of their choosing and that political transformation often required persons to controvert these very adjustments. For these reasons, Walker surmised that inculcating a passion for philosophical investigation among blacks was far more constructive than cultivating resentment or proliferating outrage. After addressing the political problem of the absence of the spirit of inquiry among blacks and awakening his slumbering brethren, the preamble to Walker's *Appeal* calls not primarily for bloody revolt but for the development of an adequate theorization of the fatuous happiness of the white American republic.

In Walker's view, one of the major challenges for "coloured citizens" was not simply a deficiency of knowledge but a lack of desire and motivation to know. Walker opens space for other more fundamental questions. What precisely prevents blacks from mobilizing enough desire to pursue the source of their misery and wretchedness? What factors contribute to this slumbering complacency and smoldering latency? It is clear from the preamble that Walker is speaking to a multiply situated, variously interested population of colored "brethren," stunning in its diversity of status, class, national affiliation, and political orientation. The diorama of the New World presented black subjects with a seeming contradiction: an upward trajectory of emancipatory energies as well as an exacting retrenchment of slavery. In 1829, a decades-long policy of gradual emancipation had finally achieved a qualified black freedom in New York and other mid-Atlantic states. In 1833, the British Empire undertook its own gradual emancipation, which was officially completed in 1838. Through the decades since their revolution, French republican proponents of emancipation, having secured black freedom for almost a decade during the revolutionary era, sustained strong arguments on its behalf until 1848, when France emancipated its enslaved colonial subjects once and for all. The Haitian Republic was an ambivalent beacon of hope for the cause of black liberty, fraternity, and equality. Black abolitionists and their radical white counterparts drew sustenance from Haitian history, but expressed dismay at the difficult time Haiti had establishing economic prosperity and the terms of freedom for its poorest citizens. In the United States, as Walker penned his *Appeal*, President Andrew Jackson's support of Indian removal and national expansion helped to spur the internal slave trade, which, according to many abolitionists, occasioned the worst examples of slavery's injustice and brutality. Against this confusing backdrop, Walker urged blacks to think comparatively across national and historical contexts, to maintain a critical edge, and to mine these contradictory forces in the service of black liberation.[21]

Thus, in part, the purpose of his preamble is to expose black complicity and solidify a radical, rather than accommodationist, grounds for solidarity. Aiming a vivid critique at blacks themselves is a hallmark of Walker's *Appeal* and is explored in greater detail later. "I am fully aware in making this appeal to my much afflicted and suffering brethren, that I shall not only be assailed by those . . . who are of the firm conviction that Heaven has designed us and our children to be slaves and beast of burden to them and their children," Walker acknowledges in his preamble. "But I am persuaded, that many of my brethren, particularly those who are ignorantly in league with slave-holders or tyrants . . . and not a few of those too, who are too ignorant to see an inch beyond their noses, will rise up and call me cursed."[22] According to Walker, those blacks who have been able to glimpse opportunity in their limited emancipation—"the jealous among us" Walker calls them—"will perhaps use more abject subtlety, by affirming that this work is not worth perusing, that we are well situated, and there is no use in trying to better our condition, for we cannot." For Walker, black "citizens'" sense of urgency is slumbering for multiple reasons, abjection, ignorance, complacency, and complicity among them. The central aims of the *Appeal*, then, are to disrupt this predicament by awakening a passion for critical inquiry among blacks, to illuminate the forces that produced their collective slumber in the first place, and to devise and circulate a therapy of personal and collective transformation through applied historiographical, moral, and political analysis.

Toward these ends, Walker advances a critique that exposes the peculiar happiness of the U.S. political community. In addition to the grave problem of black slavery and the open question of whether blacks lack the power and material resources to transform their circumstances, Walker suggests that American happiness itself is a philosophical as well as a political problem that black Americans must address. Indeed, during the Jacksonian period, an atmosphere of economic and cultural anxiety and a general sense among elites of declension from the heroic age of the founding spurred a culture of willed happiness. In the wake of the fiftieth anniversary of the nation's independence, Americans embraced a persistent monumental culture premised on an adoration of the founders and a disavowal of the paradox of slavery and freedom. A speech delivered by Abraham Lincoln in 1838, "The Perpetuation of Our Institutions," is indicative of such a cultural turn. Lincoln intoned the civil religionist view that liberty was the unprecedented and sacred inheritance bequeathed to Americans by founding patriarchs, an inheritance unsullied by the existence of slavery. In Lincoln's words:

> We find ourselves under the government of a system of political institutions, conducing more essentially to the ends of civil and religious liberty, than any of which the history of former times tells us. We, when mounting the stage of existence, found ourselves the legal inheritors of these fundamental blessings. We toiled not in the acquirement or establishment of them—they are a legacy bequeathed us, by a once hardy, brave, and patriotic, but now lamented and departed race of ancestors. Theirs was the task (and nobly they performed it) to possess themselves, and through themselves, us, of this goodly land; and to uprear upon its hills and its valleys, a political edifice of liberty and equal rights; 'tis ours only, to transmit these.[23]

This, for Walker, was the crux of American hypocrisy and (he seems to imply) lunacy. "Some may ask," Walker writes, "what is the matter with this united and happy people?"[24] The capacity of this peculiar people—to whom Walker refers throughout as "white Christian Americans" or simply "Christian Americans"—to remain inordinately pleased with themselves required a thorough consideration. It required that he refine a moral language that could be deployed as political rhetoric aimed at counteracting a political evil. For him, this language would not merely seek to alleviate spiritual malaise and cultivate moral sentiment in putatively Christian hearts and minds, the attenuated aim of much of British abolitionism and what was soon to emerge in the Garrisonian strain of American abolitionism with the 1831 publication of *The Liberator*.[25] It would assert the necessity and primacy of the exegetical and political-theoretical labors of slaves and other "coloured citizens."

The fundamental contradiction at the heart of American happiness revealed itself in the true moral character of the institution of slavery, and Walker's preamble took direct aim at this moral conundrum. Using recognizably religious language, Walker argued that slavery was a "curse to nations" wherever it was practiced.[26] By "curse," Walker implies a polluting and corrupting force, a force whose essential power is the ability to degrade and disfigure whatever it touches, turning good to bad, and perhaps bad to worse.[27] For Walker, in the American context, slavery not only contravened principles of Christian equity but also, more significantly, placed Christianity, republicanism, and every other valid moral and political precept in the service of political evil. Moreover, slavery concealed the human costs of this political evil—including the spiritual value of their own souls—from those who continued to perpetrate and benefit from it. The inhabitants of Christian America, Walker explains, are "so happy to keep in ignorance and degradation, and to receive the homage and the labor of the slaves, they forget that God rules in the armies of heaven and among the inhabitants of the earth, having his ears continually open to the cries, tears, and groans of his oppressed people."[28]

Far from being an individual spiritual problem, Walker argues, slavery quickly contaminates the American body politic, particularly in the way it becomes entrenched in the U.S. political economy. According to Walker, slavery was desirable because it provided cheap labor to masters. Cheap labor forcibly extracted from slaves awakens and energizes the vice of avarice not only among masters but also among those who aspire to become masters. The existence of slavery, therefore, fuels the desire of some to exploit the labor of others. When the vice of avarice is awakened and energized, people become habituated to modes of desire and courses of action that corrode their moral fitness. "The fact is, the labor of slaves comes so cheap to the avaricious usurpers, and is (as they think) *of such great utility to the country where it exists*, they overlook the evils, which will as sure as the Lord lives, follow after the good."[29] In particular, Walker argues that some persons become habituated to expect and demand more luxury, comfort, and deference than are compatible with individual moral well-being. In purely moral terms, such persons are made greedy. However, greed of this caliber constituted a distinct political danger. Once avarice has been awakened and legitimated among citizens, Walker argues, citizens lose the capacity to see the evil they do. Once citizens' desires and expectations have been distorted and disfigured by avarice, they become blind to the evils they commit in pursuit of inordinate desires. Walker notes with bitter irony that if Americans were not so inured in their greed, they would see the obvious contradiction that slavery poses to their own most deeply held Christian beliefs. Indeed, if Christians understood themselves to worship a jealous God, who alone "is the *sole proprietor* or *master* of the WHOLE human family," how could they not— with their adored founder Thomas Jefferson—"tremble that God is just." If God were willing to overlook their greed and acts of oppression, Walker asks, "Could he be the God Americans claim that he is?"[30] Could the God who dispensed the blessings of liberty on a nation be so capricious in determining the nation's beneficiaries within the nation? By invoking the language of "cursedness," Walker claims that the American political community is constituted by an evil that corrupts it from within, a corruption that disfigures its quest for liberty to such an extent that the very terms of liberty become a shelter for license.

It is interesting to note that by the time of the Civil War, more than thirty years after the initial composition of Walker's *Appeal* and after a popular republication of it by black abolitionist Henry Highland Garnet in 1848, Walker's moral critique of the American polity had gained traction in an unlikely arena. By 1864, the year of his second inaugural, Abraham Lincoln had come to share Walker's understanding of the moral effects of slavery, and he, like Walker, pressed his sense of religious justice in the service of a political theoretical claim. In his Second Inaugural Address, President Lincoln asked, "If we shall suppose that American slavery is one of those offenses which, in the providence of God, must needs come, but which having continued through his appointed time, he now wills to remove, and that he gives to both the North and South this terrible war as the woe due to those by whom the offenses came, shall we discern therein any departure from those divine attributes which the believers in a living God always ascribe to him?"[31] Unlike his 1838 speech, where he spoke of the transmission of unblemished values from sacred founders to their worthy descendants, Lincoln adopted the language of offenses against God, and, perhaps more importantly, deployed such rhetoric as holder of the highest political office of the land. As Walker had done, Lincoln suggests that American slavery is more than a mere deficiency that could be subtracted from the sum total of American achievements. Instead, slavery is to be understood as an institution that actively corrupts and undermines the entire political system's claim to moral goodness. In the midst of the most destructive war in American history, Lincoln seemed to endorse Walker's view that full atonement for slavery might have required the destruction of America itself.

In writing his preamble, Walker was in keeping with the tradition of constitution making. However, in important respects, Walker might be said to have had a larger, subtler theoretical end in mind than those who drafted the preamble to the U.S. Constitution, which introduced the American political community to itself and to the world at large. In addition to defining the broad ends for which the government is being constituted, the preamble also identified the subjects in whose name political power would be organized and deployed. The writing of the preamble was a highly self-conscious legitimating moment in the making of the American political community. By articulating the purposes and naming the subjects of the American political community, and claiming authority to serve both, the preamble constituted the sovereign power of the American state as a consensual creation of an actual public, the making of "we, the people." Walker, by contrast, advances an argument about the making of a great political evil whose effect is the *unmaking* of a people. Does Walker attempt a comparable legitimating moment through his account of the unmaking of a people? Does he aim to remake this unmade people? Does he seek to unmake the peculiar happiness of the people who made and continue to remake the curse? If he seeks to found a new political community, what, precisely, is to be its form? Alternatively, if he seeks to undermine the white republic, does he argue for its total destruction, its reconstitution, or something altogether different?

Constituting the Slave as a New Political Subject

In Article I, Walker deploys a comparative method to analyze what he regards as the distinctiveness of American slavery, identifying the peculiar features that distinguish it from the other great slave regimes of Western history. "My beloved brethren," he begins, the peculiar thing about American slavery, the unique feature that distinguishes it from the other slave regimes of Western history, is that it denies the very humanity of its slaves: "All the inhabitants of the earth, (except, however, the sons of Africa) are

called men, and of course are, and ought to be free. But we, (colored people) and our children are brutes!! And of course are, and ought to be slaves
to the American people and their children forever."[32] Other slave regimes
debased the social identity of slaves through some form of dishonor, but the
peculiar cruelty of American slavery is the justification offered—that blacks
are rightly enslaved because they are inferior as human beings. They are not
seen as mere human instruments, whether made so because of defeat in battle or because, although human, they lacked sufficient rationality to order
their lives—the classic justifications advanced by Aristotle to explain the enslavement of conquered barbarians and women. Rather than recognizing the
humanity of the enslaved, American slavery, Walker notes, rests on the fundamental conviction that blacks are somehow less than fully human.

To appreciate the radical character of this view, Walker says that we
must consider the predicament of the Jews in Egypt, perhaps the most famous of all enslaved peoples. Walker explains that the Jews were subjected
to indefensible treatment by the "heathen" Egyptians, yet the suffering produced by this treatment does not compare with the sufferings of blacks at
the hands of white Americans. Joseph was able to rise to a position of honor
within Pharaoh's house, an indication, according to Walker, of the possibility for upward mobility for Jews in Egypt and an illustration of the relative humaneness of the Egyptian system. Joseph was able to demonstrate
his superior talents precisely because he was not quarantined from the rest
of humanity by a stigma that ascribed an inhuman identity to Jews. Once
having demonstrated his superior talents, he was able to scale the heights of
Egyptian society. As another token of the Egyptian recognition of his humanity, Walker notes that Joseph was allowed to take wives in Egypt. By
contrast, American blacks, free or enslaved, were forbidden to marry whites.
Although Walker insists, in an aside, that he could never desire to inter-
marry with whites, and holds nothing but scorn for those blacks who harbor such desires, the possibility for intermarriage within Egyptian society
illustrates, for him, the rigidity of the white commitment to the absolute alterity of blacks. As grievous as the absence of social mobility and the rigidity of white investment in black alterity are, they represent only some of the
many barriers to blacks' admittance to the community of humanity. Where
Joseph was able to acquire property in Egypt, blacks in America could not
do so in most cases, and where they could, they were routinely and systematically cheated, robbed, and terrorized out of what property they had managed to acquire. Moreover, Jews were not told by the Egyptians that they
were inhuman: They were enslaved and degraded, but they were not divested
of their claim to human status. Similarly, the Helots of Sparta were degraded

as an entire ethnic group, but unlike the American slave system, the Spartans left Helot families intact. Rome's slave regime recognized the humanity of its slaves by permitting them to learn, but under American slavery, forced illiteracy was the universally recognized norm of effective mastery. When measured against analogous systems throughout human history, American slavery failed.

It might seem, at first glance, that Walker goes to inordinate lengths to illustrate what, for many contemporary readers, is an obvious point: American slavery was horrendously unjust. However, to limit interpretation of Walker's work to this truism is to miss his larger point. For Walker, American slavery is not merely unjust: It is the *most* unjust system of slavery the world has ever known. American slavery is exceptional in its injustice, he insists, because its peculiar theoretical construction effectively seeks (if not always successfully) to eviscerate natural familial relations; to withhold rights of property to blacks, irrespective of status; to attenuate social mobility by effacing distinctions of merit among slaves; and to prevent individual whites from recognizing the desirability of individual blacks by prohibiting intermarriage. In combination, these multiple factors set a new standard for the age-old political evil of slavery.

Although Walker does not explicitly formulate a theory of race, the arguments he makes point to an unarticulated conception that locates the novelty of American mastery in America's wholesale adoption of a metaphysics of white supremacy and racial difference. Popular representations of blacks contrived to support the legitimacy of the exclusive enslavement of blacks, engendered uniquely demeaning and thoroughly demoralizing ascription of them, and helped to produce avaricious and tyrannical inclinations in whites. In their quest for moral legitimacy, defenders of American slavery propagated dehumanizing generalizations about black character, biology, and intellect, generalizations that, in turn, facilitated the inhumane treatment of slaves. Yet for Walker, constituting black subjects would require more than simply redressing demeaning depictions of blacks that proliferated in the American imagination. For him, this particular dimension of the evil of American slavery only partially explained how and why the subjectivity of blacks remained politically impotent. To supplement this picture, Walker offers a deeply troubling account of the extent to which American slavery has succeeded in debilitating the character of blacks by inculcating ignorance. Walker's political vision is unique in its account of the nature of ignorance, the content of the wisdom that blacks lack, the relation of wisdom to the place in which most blacks found themselves in 1829, and the means required to acquire this wisdom. It is to this dimension of the political problem facing "colored citizens" that Walker turns in Article II, where he develops the core concepts of his political theory.

"Our Wretchedness in Consequence of Ignorance"

In Article II, Walker examines the problem of "ignorance," a problem he characterizes as "a mist, low down into the very dark and almost impenetrable abyss in which our fathers for many centuries have been plunged."[33] According to Walker, the problem of ignorance is the problem of the systematic disfiguration of the intellect of blacks. Affecting blacks as individuals and as a community, this disfiguration is the purposeful creation of and an indispensable support for the maintenance of American slavery. Although it is the effect of white action, this ignorance is nonetheless a pervasive and crippling problem that blacks themselves must address. In Walker's view, while it is absolutely critical for blacks to understand that intellectual and cultural underdevelopment are the effect rather than the cause of enslavement, it is more important for them to recognize the problem in its political rather than its historical sense. Politically, the problem boils down to this: Independent of its origins, ignorance is a crippling deficiency within the individual black character. Furthermore, because this deficiency is institutionalized in black communal life, it must be corrected by blacks themselves, if they are to be truly free. For Walker, black freedom requires that blacks squarely and immediately confront the problem of ignorance, and confront this problem independently of the unprecedented cruelties of American slavery or even of the limited prospects for slavery's immediate abolition.

Attacking the unashamed and uncritical white supremacy informing his contemporary G.W.F. Hegel's *Philosophy of History* and anticipating arguments that would resurface one hundred years later in the writings and rhetoric of twentieth-century black nationalism, Walker insists that, contrary to popular Western beliefs, higher learning originated in Africa, resurfaced in Athens (where Westerners insist it originated), and then moved on to Rome.

> When we take a retrospective view of the arts and sciences—the wise legislators—the Pyramids, and other magnificent buildings—the turning of the channel of the river Nile, by the sons of Africa or of Ham, among whom learning originated, and was carried thence to Greece, where it was improved upon and refined. Thence among the Romans, and all over the then enlightened parts of the world, and it has been enlightening the dark and benighted minds of men from then, down to this day.[34]

In Walker's view, this learning would have brought Rome to its knees were it not for Carthaginian political disorganization, the very obstacle he claims plagues blacks of his own day. "I give it as my candid opinion, that had Carthage been well united and given him good support, [Hannibal] would have carried that cruel and barbarous city by storm. But they were disunited as the colored people are now, in the United States of America, the reason our natural enemies are enabled to keep their feet on our throats."[35]

Because the true origins of higher learning resided in Africa rather than in Greece or Rome, Walker advances the claim that ignorance reflects a decline from great heights occurring over time as the direct consequence of slavery's deliberate extraction of knowledge, learning, and literacy from black communities. In no way is it to be understood as the natural aptitude of an inferior race, which is understood as given and unalterable. With this claim, Walker defends against a longtime staple of the repertoire of white supremacist defenses of slavery and more moderate positions about the unfitness of blacks for American citizenship. The belief in the innate intellectual inferiority of African-descended persons was taken for granted by most white Americans, whether they were unlettered or as highly literate as Thomas Jefferson, the Founding Father with whom Walker sustains an engagement over the course of the *Appeal*. Although Walker concedes the sorry state of intellectual affairs among blacks as an undeniable empirical reality that must be addressed, he denies that intellectual inequality has any natural foundation, insisting instead that black intellectual underdevelopment is the result of social and political processes that can be redressed.

Walker's account of ignorance stands in marked contrast to contemporary understandings advanced by liberal pluralists and humanists. Liberal pluralists often construe the problem of ignorance in terms of a paucity of communal resources that must be put to productive use if blacks are to thrive, either individually or collectively, in a political economy that privileges specialized skills. Humanists, on the other hand, perceive ignorance as a problem of individual or collective underdevelopment of those quintessentially human powers by which humans distinguish themselves from beasts. The crux of the problem of ignorance, as Walker understands it, however, is more fundamentally political. Ignorance entails modes of treachery and deceit that distort blacks' understanding of their own interests.

> Ignorance and treachery one against the other—a groveling servile and abject submission to the lash of tyrants, we see plainly my brethren, are not the natural elements of the blacks, as the Americans try to make us believe; but these are misfortunes which God has suffered

our fathers to be enveloped in for many ages, no doubt in consequence of disobedience to their Maker, and which does indeed, reign
at this time among us, almost to the destruction of all other principles: for I must truly say, that ignorance, the mother of treachery and
deceit, gnaws into our very vitals.[36]

In Walker's view, ignorance facilitates slavery by encouraging blacks to systematically misidentify their true interests. In other words, the condition of
ignorance—endemic to America—debilitates blacks by promoting a false
and crippling sense of what is valuable and possible for them politically.
"Ignorance, as it now exists among us, produces a state of things, Oh my
Lord! too horrible to present to the world."[37]

Whether one were enslaved or free, whether one believed slavery just or
hopelessly durable despite its injustice, every black person in America suffered the pervasive effects of ignorance. According to Walker, those blacks
who had been taught to perceive slavery as an impregnable and stable, if not
legitimate, institution were precisely those persons most likely to betray the
efforts of enlightened and courageous blacks to undertake the dangerous
but necessary risks required to gain black freedom. Thus, ignorance should
be understood not only as a problem facing individual blacks but also as
one of the most pressing political problems for blacks as a collective and for
blacks as a potentially free people. In his discussion of ignorance, the central issue for Walker is not white distortion of black intellect. Rather, Walker's main concern is the more delicate question of the political capacity of
blacks, enslaved and free, who may have been conditioned to make pragmatic adjustments to white supremacy. Walker seeks to understand the dispositions inculcated by ignorance, their effects on the character of enslaved
and free blacks, and the obstacles they raise to blacks constituting themselves
as a free people. For Walker, confronting the problem of ignorance is central
to identifying the conditions of possibility for blacks' constitution as a free
citizenry. Confronting ignorance, for Walker, is the crucial first step in the
constitution of a new people capable of acting on behalf of their distinctive
conception of the common good.

To illuminate the political dangers of ignorance, Walker provides a number of arresting examples of blacks misidentifying their interests. In one case,
he recounts the story of a male slave whipping his mother. In another case,
a slave beats his pregnant wife until she is so traumatized she gives birth to
a dead child. In both cases, the offending slaves have turned the implement
of violence characteristic of enslavement—the whip—against another slave,
who is, significantly, also an intimate relation. Walker's attempt to illustrate

the political problem of ignorance, however, is not restricted to stories about slaves. Even worse than these appalling scenes involving slaves are cases involving free blacks who aid and abet masters in their purchase or capture of slaves. Walker interprets the actions of some "free" blacks for his reader:

> When my curious observer comes to take notice of those who are said to be free (which assertion I deny) and who are making some frivolous pretentions to common sense, he will see that branch of ignorance among the slaves assuming a more cunning and deceitful course of procedure. He may see some of my brethren in league with tyrants, selling their own brethren into hell upon earth, not dissimilar to the exhibitions in Africa, but in more secret, servile, and abject manner.[38]

For Walker, this brand of ignorance, as an abuse of one's free status, is more "cunning" and more "deceitful" than even the shocking examples of slaves imitating the violence of masters on one another.

As bad as both sets of examples are, however, and despite their powerful support for Walker's thesis that ignorance functions as the critical support for the institution of slavery, they are nonetheless merely preparatory for the final, and, according to Walker, most instructive example, drawn from a case that is purported to have occurred on August 22, 1829, in Portsmouth, Kentucky. When several white slave drivers attempted to convey a cargo of slaves to the plantations of their new masters, a few of the slaves managed to free themselves from the chains that bound them together in the back of the transport wagon. After they attacked and successfully subdued the drivers, the escapees freed the rest of the slaves and seized the contents of the wagon. All of the drivers had been killed except one. The lone survivor, Walker reports, was aided to his feet by a slave woman, who, moved by Christian charity, could not countenance leaving him to die. After gaining his composure, this man mounted his horse and rode to the nearest town, where he was able to mobilize a search party, who subsequently located and recaptured the escaped slaves. As Walker describes it, "The neighborhood was immediately rallied, and a hot pursuit given—which we understand, has resulted in the capture of the whole gang and recovery of the greatest part of the money. Seven of the negro men and one woman, it is said, were engaged in the murders, and will be brought to trial at the next court in Greenupsburg."[39]

For Walker, this case illustrates the problem of ignorance in bold relief. He charges the woman who assisted the fallen slave driver with two counts of ignorance. First, this woman's understanding of Christian charity was grossly mistaken: "It is no more harm for you to kill a man, who is trying to kill you," according to Walker's judgment, "than it is for you to take a drink of water when thirsty."[40] Since God created all human beings to be free, Walker reasons, slavery and slaveholders must be at war with God. Not only would slaveholders be undeserving of Christian charity; they must be actively resisted and perhaps even peremptorily vanquished by true Christians. Hence, the slave woman's generosity was not simply misguided; it was positively sinful precisely because she aided persons who not only meant her harm but were also in rebellion against God. Her second failure is, in some ways, more important for Walker than the first and constitutes a political rather than a religious transgression. In the political-theoretical sense, the ignorant woman failed to make the most elementary and important distinction: She failed to distinguish her enemies from her friends, which, as Plato noted in the *Republic*, is the fundamental task of every political leader.[41] When she assisted the slave driver, she extended kindness to a person who sought to degrade and dehumanize her and her people, and by virtue of this act, she effectively harmed (indirectly and unintentionally, to be sure) the very persons who sought to promote her interests. For Walker, this slave woman is the very picture of ignorance. Although she believed she had acted piously and knowingly when, in the heat of battle, she extended kindness to her oppressors, she had actually acted treacherously. She had abandoned not only God but also her people. Enacting the effects of imposed ignorance, she is, in Walker's view, the exemplary slave. She is also the embodiment of the problem of political ignorance that, in Walker's view, afflicted too many of his "brethren." Before they could become "citizens," the political problem of ignorance had to be fully apprehended and addressed.

Christianity Corrupted

If the ability to distinguish between enemies and friends is one of the paramount political problems facing blacks, then this problem is compounded by the Christian commitments of Walker and his ideal black citizenry. Indeed, Walker wields the term "Christian" more like an epithet than a term of brotherly affection. In Article III, Walker takes up the issue of American Christianity, in particular, the question of the role of American Christianity in supporting slavery and white supremacy. In brief, Walker argues that American Christianity is, by and large, utterly and thoroughly corrupted, having, at a decisive moment in its history, countenanced and condoned the institution of slavery. "Having introduced slavery among them," Walker explains, Americans "have become almost seared, as with a hot iron, and

God has nearly given them up to believe a lie in preference to the truth."[42] In making this argument, however, Walker finds himself in a peculiar position. On the one hand, he wants to demonstrate to his readers that the reigning interpretations and practices of Western Christianity are morally and spiritually bankrupt. On the other hand, because he is himself a Christian, he ultimately stands on and appeals to Christianity for the moral and theological norms that ground his critique of American slavery. Even more delicately, he wants to highlight and privilege his own prophetic reading of Christianity as the true religion.[43] This presents a vexing problem because Walker knows that Christian support for the institution of slavery is quite old, much older than the practice of slavery in America. Hence, he cannot simply portray American institutions as the source of Christianity's corruption. Moreover, he realizes that African Americans only had access to Christianity as the result of the African encounter with Christian Europe, an encounter inextricably knotted with the enslavement of Africans. If he is to maintain his view that the Christianization of Africans was part of God's providential plan, then he is compelled either to accept that the enslavement of Africans was part of God's plan or to tell an entirely different story about the historical development of Western Christianity. Walker is tempted to treat the corruption of Christianity as a matter of white supremacist propaganda: "Indeed, the way in which religion was and is conducted by the Europeans and their descendents, one might believe it was a plan fabricated by themselves and the devils to oppress us."[44] Barring this wholesale repudiation of Christianity—which was unlikely, given his status as a committed believer—Walker was compelled to reconcile his religion with the pernicious practices executed in its name and to press his reconciliation into the service of authorizing and providing moral legitimacy for the political community he envisions.

Not one to rely on divine revelation or strict biblical exegesis to reveal a pristine Christianity untainted by its historical complicity with slavery, Walker turned to history and sought to discern the fateful moment when Western Christianity lost its footing. In taking up the challenge, then, to simultaneously vindicate Christianity and expose it as having a degenerate and corrupt doctrine of slavery and white supremacy, Walker expands and transforms the jeremiad tradition that Bercovitch and Glaude have identified as the central discourse of American national formation.[45] Walker highlighted not only the declension of "white Christians" from American covenantal faith but also the declension of "the brethren" from the ancestral glories of ancient Africa. Walker fleshes out his jeremiad by first insisting that true religion is always a rarity. "Religion, my brethren is a substance of deep consideration among all nations of the earth. . . . But pure and unde-filed religion, such as was practiced by Jesus Christ and his apostles is hard to be found in all the earth."[46] Most persons who outwardly express a commitment to religious principles do so as a pretext or façade to conceal self-interested aims and commitments. Christianity is no different from other religions in this regard, but according to Walker, Western Christianity is guilty of a more serious crime. This crime consists of not only perverting the true religion to oppress persons in the broad sense but also using faith to justify the oppression of other Christians. History, according to Walker, would instruct us in why and where this perversion of the faith occurs.

In the *Appeal*, Walker dates the origins of this perversion of the faith to the writings of Bartholomé de las Casas, the sixteenth-century Catholic priest, who, appalled by the cruel treatment suffered by Indians at the hands of the Spanish, proposed the enslavement of Africans as an acceptable alternative.[47] Walker is unimpressed with the irony that las Casas's infamous and quite influential proposal was informed by a sincere commitment to oppose the torture and enslavement of indigenous persons. For him, las Casas's endorsement of African slavery is decisive: "It is well known to the Christian world, that Bartholomew Las Casas, that very notorious avaricious Catholic priest or preacher, and adventurer with Columbus in his second voyage, proposed to his countrymen, the Spaniards in Hispaniola to import the Africans from the Portuguese settlement in Africa, to dig up gold and silver, and work their plantations for them."[48] For Walker, las Casas's complete disregard for the well-being of Africans reveals perfectly how slavery unleashes the vice of avarice among its defenders. Although las Casas is motivated by an admirable concern for the welfare of Indians, his overriding commitment to finding an alternative labor source for work he acknowledges to be dehumanizing reveals, in Walker's analysis, a more fundamental motivation to pursue commodities at the expense of their human cost. Minimally, these costs included the effacement of the humanity of Africans. However, because the effacement of the humanity of any of God's human creatures is such an obvious violation of Christian principles, Walker suggests that its motivation must be systematic, tied to a comprehensive and totalizing corruption. Echoing the writings of the Roman historian Sallust, Walker concludes that the vice of avarice underlies this systemic corruption, which, in turn, infects Christian ethical norms. Thus, Article III leads back to the discussion of the corrupting force of avarice that Walker described in the preamble.

In Walker's view, Christian evangelism built on this corrupted foundation had proved itself to be a hollow pretense that served only to mask the extent to which Western Christianity had become an active force of human evil. Furthermore, the horrendous example American Christians present to non-Christians exacerbates the hypocrisy of Christian doctrine among slaveholders. "American ministers send out missionaries to convert the heathen, while they keep us and our children sunk at their feet in the most abject ignorance and wretchedness that ever a people was afflicted with since the world began."[49] In sharp contrast to the exceptionalist self-understanding of American civil religion, such as that expressed, for example, in Lincoln's speech, "The Perpetuation of Our Institutions," Walker insists that American Christians had become inured in their own evil. "The wicked and ungodly, seeing their preachers treat us with so much cruelty, they say: Our preachers, who must be right, if anybody are, treat them like brutes, and why cannot we? They think it is no harm to keep them in slavery and put the whip to them and why cannot we do the same?"[50]

Were American Christians simply failing to project a good face for Christendom, failing, in other words, to be the City on the Hill, Walker might rebuke them, but he would perhaps see no difference between Americans and other backsliders from the faith. For Walker, however, the true cost and consequence of the American perversion of the faith is much worse. The practice of American Christianity has resulted in the corruption of non-Christians, persons, in his view, who are most in need of genuine representations of the true faith. In particular, Walker is concerned with how Western Christianity has resulted in the corruption of Africans. We have already seen how Walker regards ignorance as the chief vice of the African American character and the fundamental achievement of the practice of enslavement. In the discussion of Christianity in Article III, Walker insists that the impact of slavery extends well beyond the experiences of the enslaved to make an indelibly deleterious mark on those places the slaves were forced to leave. The rapacious greed of slave traders and capturers, Walker argues, sets in motion the cultural and moral decay that is ultimately institutionalized as an international slave market, implicating Africans in this great evil every bit as much as Americans and Europeans. Walker especially indicts European and American Christians: "Have you not, on the contrary, entered among us, and learnt us the art of throat cutting, by setting us to fight, one against another, to take each other as prisoners of war, and sell to you for small bits of calicoes, old swords, knives, &c. to make slaves for you and your children."[51] Walker overstates the case when he suggests that Europeans are responsible for introducing the arts of war and enslavement to Africans. He is certainly aware that war and slavery among the various peoples of Africa predate the arrival of Europeans on African soil. However, his blatant overstatement underscores his larger point, which is, quite simply, that Christianity has functioned as an intellectual, moral, and existential support for the practice of slavery and has become a force for human evil.

Walker focuses his critique of Western Christianity on its moral consequences for Africans caught up—either as slaves or captors—in the transatlantic slave trade because he wants to trace the historical corruption of American Christianity. However, his critique serves his current political purposes as well. As the title of the *Appeal* suggests, Walker wants to lay the basis—utopian though it is—for a colored citizenry that encompasses the world. However, he also wants to constitute blacks in the United States— "particularly and very expressly"—as citizens. These two goals resonated in the broader U.S. debate over the repatriation of U.S. free and freed blacks to Africa, a debate that raged at fever pitch as Walker wrote the *Appeal* in the late 1820s. He turns to this specific question in Section IV of the *Appeal*.

The Moral Defects of "Repatriation"

In Article IV, Walker attacks a plan that initially sought to "repatriate" free blacks to Africa. Over the course of the early nineteenth century, this plan grew into a proposal for colonization, the creation of a colony in Africa and the recolonization of all blacks, as the ultimate solution to the problem of the black presence in America. Eventually giving rise to the influential organization the American Colonization Society, this view was championed over the course of the century by persons no less illustrious than Thomas Jefferson, Henry Clay, and Abraham Lincoln. Repatriation was an unwieldy alternative, with limited reach, especially given that the vast majority of enslaved blacks had been born on American soil. However limited in actual practice, though, the debate over colonization engaged the American public, white and black, because it touched on a range of concerns and anxieties regarding black fitness for citizenship. Proponents presented this view, however, as the most humane answer to the race problem. Moreover, colonization was a proposal supported not by professed enemies of blacks, but rather by persons who claimed to be their sympathetic advocates. As Walker reports Henry Clay to have said, "There was a peculiar, a moral fitness, in restoring them [blacks] to the land of their fathers, and if instead of evils and sufferings which we had been the innocent cause of inflicting upon the inhabitants of Africa, we can transmit to her the blessings of our arts, our civilization, and our religion."[52] Here, Clay seemed to respond directly to Walker's critique of the impact of African colonization on people of African descent and offered a different account of the relationship between Christian (civilized) Americans and Africans. The moral transgression of slavery, in Clay's view, was best understood as an "innocent" mistake—one that could be remedied by the return of sufficiently Christianized U.S. blacks to Africa. Walker sees through what he considered to be the great statesman's ruse of concern for the welfare of blacks and provided an alternative explanation for his apparent charity: It was "a plan to get those colored people who are said to be free, away from among those of our brethren whom they unjustly hold in bondage, so that they may be enabled to keep them the more secure in ignorance and wretchedness, to support them and their children, and consequently they would have the more obedient slaves."[53]

Walker counseled free blacks to stay put. "This country is as much ours as it is the whites, whether they will admit it now or not, they will see it bye and bye,"[54] Walker affirmed, offering an opposition to colonization that was by no means innovative. As he freely admits, he shared the same position as the Reverend Richard Allen, the powerful founder and leader of the African Methodist Episcopal Church, as well as a number of other important opinion leaders in free black communities across the United States. Indeed, he quotes liberally from Allen's sermons on the subject.[55] What is novel about Walker's treatment of the issue, however, is his attentiveness to the political motives he discerned in the plan and his vocal opposition to the professions of sympathy for blacks. In his view, the humanitarian gloss presented by the plan's sponsors was merely a pretense of sympathy for blacks that cloaked a true desire to consolidate American slavery. Advocates of colonization, he argued, sought to expel free blacks from America because they feared the continued presence of free blacks presented a constant source of insurrectionary thought and activity that might find its way to slaves. " For if the free are allowed to stay among the slaves, they will have intercourse together, and, of course, the free will learn the slaves bad habits by teaching them that they are men, as well as other people, and certainly ought and must be free."[56] Removing this source of agitation, Walker explained, would prove to be an effective means of maintaining good order in a slave society. It would also cut enslaved blacks off from the emergent black citizenry that Walker sought to constitute in his *Appeal*. If free blacks were removed a good distance from slaves, Walker reasoned, slavery's simultaneous and systematic production of ignorance among slaves and avarice among masters would ensure the continued vitality of the institution.[57]

Walker's interpretation of the motives of colonization's advocates is not far-fetched. In an early defense of the colonization plan, Thomas Jefferson had argued unequivocally that repatriation was the only viable solution to the Negro problem, in part, because even freed blacks can only be supposed to harbor deep and unshakable resentments at the myriad indignities they have suffered at the hands of whites. As Jefferson explained, "Ten thousand recollections by blacks, of the injuries they have sustained; new provocations; the real distinctions which nature has made; and many other circumstances will divide us into parties, and produce convulsions which will probably never end but in the extermination of the one or the other race."[58] Roughly thirty years later, Alexis de Tocqueville expressed a similar view when he suggested the antipathy between blacks and whites was so deep and widespread that an apocalypse of racial violence resulting in the defeat of one race or the other was more likely than peaceful coexistence between the races. "Until now, everywhere that whites have been most powerful they have held Negroes in degradation or in slavery. Everywhere that Negroes have been strongest, they have destroyed the whites; this is the only account that has ever been opened up between the races."[59] As this parallel with Jefferson suggests, the only distinction Tocqueville claimed for his work on American democracy was that he had not necessarily seen more than earlier political philosophers—he had only seen further.

Walker did not have the benefit of Tocqueville's insights, but he was a careful reader of Thomas Jefferson. Analyzing Jefferson's writings, Walker pierced the founding father's putative antipathy toward slavery and illuminated his more resolute commitment to black moral, aesthetic, and intellectual inferiority—views Jefferson admitted quite candidly that he held without good intellectual grounds.[60] According to Walker's theorization of ignorance, Jefferson's irrational commitments to black moral and intellectual unfitness should be understood in the context of his refusal to free his own slaves. As Walker explained, it was "indeed surprising, that a man of such learning, combining such excellent natural parts, should speak so of a set of men in chains."[61] Disseminating erroneous and unfounded views about black abilities enabled Jefferson to manifest solidarity with southern planters and to help preserve their distinctive quality of life. It also mitigated the sting of moral contradiction Jefferson must have wrestled with as a slaveholder who penned the abstract moral demands of the Declaration of Independence. For Walker, cold self-interest rather than humanitarianism likely motivated Jefferson's support for colonization. Walker held equally cynical views of Henry Clay, asking ironically, "Do you believe that Mr. Henry Clay, late Secretary of State, and now in Kentucky, is a friend to the blacks, further than his personal interest extends?"[62]

Walker concludes by judging American slavery to be the worst slave regime in history because it seeks to legitimate itself by denying the human competence of its slaves. Predicated on a rogue perversion of Christianity, this new and monstrous form of slavery unleashed vices among its defenders and beneficiaries, transforming the vaunted "blessings of liberty" into vicious license. Slavery's great achievement, Walker argued in Article II, was to have set in motion through forced illiteracy a process of intellectual and cultural decline among blacks, the most immediate and crippling effect of which was the production of treachery and defeatism. This defeatism among blacks is reinforced by subjection to corrupted religious doctrines that justify their enslavement. Slaves' defeatism was refined and strengthened through continued efforts of leading Americans to consolidate slavery by expelling potentially dangerous blacks to remote corners of the globe. In sum, Walker argues that blacks are caught in an evil system, without genuine allies and with no place to go, and predicts that, as long as they remain mired in ignorance, they will be unable to muster the internal resources required to reverse their predicament.

Ignorance and Enmity

Had Walker left matters here, he would have provided little more than a courageous indictment of American slavery. However, as a founder of African American prophetic political critique, he took the further step to offer a solution designed to overturn slavery in the long run and to build a foundation on which blacks could exercise their capacity for citizenship broadly conceived. While he acknowledged that his solution might not produce immediate results, he argued that it would nonetheless knit blacks together in a communal political project that could prepare them for the day when slavery would finally be vanquished. He also suggested that his solution would afford blacks the necessary measure of dignity to sustain them until the great day of emancipation arrived. As we have seen, Walker argued that ignorance was a problem that had dramatic manifestations among blacks and whites. Ignorance fostered complacency and resignation among blacks and avariciousness and greed among whites. Ignorance led blacks and whites to conflate the interests of slaves with those of their masters. Ignorance also produced habits of character and reflexive modes of action that are inimical to black solidarity and to the true precepts of Christianity. What kind of moral and political instruction would educate his "citizenry" away from this pervasive ignorance?

In Article II, as we have seen, Walker compared American blacks to the Carthaginians, who failed to defeat Rome.[63] His aim was to show how black Americans shared the traits of disorganization and disunity with the Carthaginians, but he was also concerned with demonstrating that white Americans shared common traits with the Romans. At the end of Article

IV, Walker makes these shared traits explicit in a way that recalls his discussion of the quintessential servility of the exemplary slave woman who aided and abetted the white slave driver, when he asks rhetorically, "What set of men can you point to, in all the world, who are so abjectly employed by their oppressors as we are by our natural enemies?"[64] Just as the Romans were the natural enemies of the Carthaginians, Walker suggests that white Americans are the natural enemies of blacks.[65] It is one of the chief accomplishments of political ignorance that this fundamental relation of antagonism is masked. The careful cultivation of ignorance among blacks, coupled with the circulation of ignorant and erroneous depictions of black abilities, mystified, concealed, and distorted this fundamental relation between whites and blacks. For Walker, natural enmity names the predicament that enables whites to stand on the necks of blacks, and it names the predicament in which the supposed piety of the slave woman is revealed as treacherous folly. Ignorance keeps blacks from recognizing the fundamental political relationship of natural enemies. Contrary to the pretensions of enlightened statesmen, concerned or benevolent masters, or even putatively disinterested whites, the real situation, according to Walker, is that blacks and whites stand to one another in an objective relation of mutual antagonism. As Walker characterized this relation, "[Whites] have kept us in so much ignorance, that many of us know no better than to fight against ourselves, and by that means, strengthen the hands of our *natural enemies*, to rivet their infernal chains of slavery upon us and our children."[66] In the context of this political relation, individual preferences and hopes are epiphenomenal and ultimately unimportant.

Walker's analysis of ignorance emerges in the interstices of two major intellectual traditions, and his conception of natural enmity reflects and challenges those traditions. On the one hand, his views reflect the hugely popular but grotesquely unrealized doctrine of natural equality, which characterized the modern political philosophy of Hobbes and Locke and the revolutionary doctrines of Thomas Paine and the Declaration of Independence. Hobbes and Paine might have provided Walker with an account of natural enmity, although there is little in the *Appeal* that would indicate that he subscribed to either of their views. Moreover, there is no discussion of the state of nature, the social contract, or the right of revolution in Walker's work. Given his many references to civic republican literature, this suggests either a lack of familiarity with or a lack of interest in John Locke or Thomas Hobbes. In particular, Walker's conception of natural equality does not indicate his exposure to or belief in a Hobbesian corollary that equality leads naturally to violent conflict. On the contrary, there is no doubt that Walker carefully studied the writings of Thomas Jefferson, whose multiple texts he quotes often, as we have seen.[67] Approaching the question from the vantage point of the Declaration of Independence, Walker might have argued that our common origin in God's creation implied a natural civility that was corrupted by human choice rather than one that was given in nature.

The other major intellectual trend emerging during Walker's lifetime was a scientific discourse on racial difference, a discourse developed in large part to validate prescientific judgments about the inferiority of nonwhites.[68] Paradoxically, it was a discourse initiated by Thomas Jefferson, who suspected that black people, "whether originally a distinct race, or made distinct by time and circumstances, are *inferior* to the whites in the endowments both of body and mind." He encouraged fellow empiricists to prove his hypothesis by making "many observations, even where the subject may be submitted to the anatomical knife, to optical glasses, to analysis by fire, or by solvents."[69] Walker urges his would-be colored citizens to do the painstaking work of refuting Jefferson and other such proponents of the racial science that would soon be popularized as the American School of Ethnology. "I hope," he admonished them, "you will not let it pass unnoticed."[70] Walker's impassioned defense of the humanity of blacks and his argument that the ignorance of blacks results from history rather from nature confirm his belief in natural equality. However, Walker also provocatively argued that blacks and whites were natural enemies. What did he mean in asserting both a natural equality and a natural enmity among races?

In Article IV, Walker argues that blacks and whites are not enemies *by nature*. He concurs with the Declaration of Independence that all men are created equal. Central to this natural equality is a common psychology: Equal persons naturally desire freedom and naturally resent abrogation of that freedom. By "freedom," Walker refers to the human capacity for meaningful action, and he testifies that the freedom experienced by all U.S. blacks comes up short: "Look into our freedom and happiness, and see of what kind they are composed!! They are of the very lowest kind—they are the *dregs!*"[71] Walker's conception of freedom is markedly similar to the classic characterization of liberty that Isaiah Berlin associated with the canon of Western political philosophy.[72] Freedom entails negative liberty, the opportunity to act without illegitimate interference. In this respect, the situation of blacks is dire: "If any of you wish to know how FREE you are, let one of you start and go through the southern and western States of this country, and unless you travel as a slave to a white man . . . or have your free papers (which if you are not careful they will get *from* you) if they do not take you up and put you in jail, and if you cannot give good evidence of your freedom, sell you into eternal slavery, I am not a living man."[73] Freedom also entails positive liberty, or autonomy, the capacity to initiate and achieve goals of one's own choosing. Again, blacks, in Walker's experience, know nothing of this kind of freedom: "For if we are men, we ought to be thankful to the Lord for the past, and for the future. Be looking forward with thankful hearts to higher attainments than *wielding the razor* and *cleaning boots and shoes.*"[74] By arguing for a common human psychology consisting in the desire for freedom, Walker suggests that one's individual desire to act independently of arbitrary interference and to pursue worldly purposes according to one's own desires are given in nature and remain fundamental aspirations, diminished only through relentless and concerted violation. He also suggests that resentment of the abrogation of freedom is thoroughly natural. When human beings are prevented from meaningful action through coercive violence, including arbitrary restraint and externally imposed discipline, they will naturally regard such constraining forces as a violation. Walker insists that blacks and whites are identical in this regard.

Because American slavery institutionalized the abrogation of black freedom, it institutionalized the condition for the evocation of black resentment. Walker maintains that white persons know in their hearts that blacks are humans. Indeed, it is precisely this knowledge that triggers anxieties over predictable black resentment, anxieties that ironically fuel cruelty and contribute to heightened black resentment. As Walker noted:

> Man is a peculiar creature—he is the image of God, though he may be subjected to the most wretched condition upon earth, yet the spirit and feeling which constitute the creature man, can never be entirely erased from his breast, because God who made him after his own image, planted it in his heart. The whites, knowing this, they do not know what to do; they know that they have done us so much injury, they are afraid that we, being men and not brutes, will retaliate, and woe will be to them.[75]

Natural enmity then is a natural consequence of the purely conventional predicament of slavery.

Natural enmity is also a crucial part of the wisdom that blacks must acquire if they are to be truly free. Awakening blacks to this wisdom constitutes one of the principal practical objectives of the *Appeal.* Walker's vision of political possibility in wisdom was remarkably attuned to the unique predicament that circumscribed most black lives at the time of his writing. His account of wisdom as knowledge of the true relation of blacks and whites—the ability to distinguish between friends and enemies—is particularly suited to a world of enforced illiteracy. Within Walker's frame, literacy is less important than the candid consideration of personal experience, a radical and transformative view that placed genuine and useful wisdom within the grasp of black slaves. His program of action is prudent: He seeks to develop communal virtues that can exist within the context of the intransigence of slavery in 1830, even as such virtues lay the foundation for a different future.

Free Black Political Subjectivity and the Political Virtue of Glory

Fulfilling what is arguably its most fundamental purpose, Walker's *Appeal* provides a vision of a new mode of black subjectivity that might arise once blacks had awakened themselves from their incapacitating slumber. The love of wisdom requires not only a desire for knowledge of natural enmity but also a clear comprehension of the mandate it conveys. It would be essential for black citizens to develop the courage—or the willingness to "glory in death"[76]—to act on this mandate. Walker extols a variety of public spirited-ness rooted in the willingness to sacrifice oneself:

> When I reflect that God is just and that millions of my wretched brethren would meet death in glory—yea, more, would plunge into the very mouths of cannons and be torn into particles as minute as the atoms which compose the elements of the earth, in preference to a mean submission to the lash tyrants, I am with streaming eyes, compelled to shrink back into nothingness before my Maker, and exclaim again, thy will be done, O Lord God Almighty.[77]

Walker's overblown prose strains to capture the sense of glory and public honor the sacrifice of these virtuous citizens should inspire among their brethren—enough, Walker is hoping, to achieve the founding of a great and lasting political community. His portrait of sacrifice and its sentimental effects confirm that private good can be attained only by "working for the salvation of our whole body."[78] Walker advises his colored citizens that "your full glory and happiness, as well as all the other colored people under Heaven, shall never be fully consumable, but with the *entire emancipation of your enslaved brethren all over the world*."[79] Walker's conception of civic virtue drew inspiration from the Roman historian Sallust, a foundational source of classical civic republican thought. Sallust's *The War with Jurgurtha*, a text Walker cites on multiple occasions, opens, "If men had as great regard for honorable enterprises as they have ardour in pursuing what is foreign to their interests and bound to be unprofitable and often even dangerous, they would control fate rather than be controlled by it, and would attain to the height of greatness where from mortals their glory would make them immortal."[80] In seeking to delineate the relation between black interests and black political virtue, Walker articulates a distinctively black modern conception of "honorable enterprises."[81] By imagining and valorizing black quests for glory, Walker attempts to articulate the conditions of possibility for black immortality. Inspired by Sallust, Walker offers a public philosophy that identifies necessary character traits suited to a world that is both oppressive and uncertain. His conception of virtue is particularly appropriate for the task of uniting blacks in a public quest for freedom, a quest that will require courage, strength, and the willingness to sacrifice one's life to counter white violence and achieve emancipation. "If you can only get courage into the blacks, I do declare it, that one good black man can put to death six white men."[82]

As the founder of systematic African American political theory, Walker's role might be compared with that of Plato in that both theorists articulated a utopia, a vision of human possibility that is instructive, even if unrealizable.[83] Laudable though they may be, Walker's conception of human possibility and his requirements for political virtue raise some troubling questions about the gendered dimensions of his theoretical commitments, questions that can be glimpsed by returning to one of his most memorable examples. In maligning ignorance and inculcating glory, Walker uses the "foolish" slave woman who foiled the escape of her fellow slaves as his point of reference. Indeed, he creates of her a spectacle of ignorance, which is, in his view, the most egregious character defect. "For my own part, I cannot think it was anything but servile deceit, combined with the most gross ignorance: for we must remember that humanity, kindness and fear of the Lord does not consist in protecting devils."[84] Here, Walker, in effect, feminizes treachery, a move in keeping with contemporary discourse on the inferior nature and limited capacity of women. In falling victim to this convention, however, Walker masks certain features of the experience of enslavement. Within the institution of slavery, all slaves—men and women—were vulnerable to sexual violation. By using a gendered trope to embody the effects of enslavement, Walker hides this equal vulnerability. In so doing, Walker is able to mobilize men's martial energies and confrontational sensibilities without naming the source for them. Moreover, Walker's vision privileges masculine ideals as the aim of black politics and celebrates manly virtues as essential to the production of new black political subjects. Finally, in tying ignorance to the metaphor of "womanly servility," Walker pathologizes the vulnerability that was inescapable for black slaves and later for freed blacks as well. Within Walker's vision of free black subjectivity, the transcendence of womanly servility necessitates an embrace of manly virtues with strong martial overtones. His extensive reflections on the virtues of glory, courage, and sacrifice serve to underscore the gendered nature of citizenship. Indeed, one wonders if Walker's deployment of these gendered tropes and his inability to rehabilitate the particular experiences of enslaved black women render women, in his view, unfit for his brand of citizenship.

Walker's utopian vision of blacks throughout the world violently contending on behalf of freedom is the starting point for systematic philosophical reflection about the black experience within the City on the Hill. His concealment of critical aspects of the experience of enslavement and his linkage of black freedom to the quest for the rights and privileges of black men, unfortunately, however, constitute some of his most durable contributions. As I present successive thinkers in this tradition of African American prophetic political thought—Douglass, Du Bois, and Baldwin—part of my goal is to track the status of this culture of sacrifice and the gendered virtues it rests on. We would do well to keep Walker's depiction of the treacherous slave woman in mind as we consider whether each conception of politics and the political is capacious enough to encompass the testimony and lived experience of enslaved women—the most abject and circumscribed group from the point of view of the norms of citizenship, but, arguably, the most crucial population for any "colored citizenry" worth its salt.

2

"Glorious Revolution" in the City of Mastery

Frederick Douglass on the Corruption
of the American Republic

It has been frequently remarked that it seems to have been reserved to
the people of this country, by their conduct and example, to decide
the important question.[1]

The American people have been called upon, in a most striking manner, to abolish and put away forever the system of slavery.[2]

For when I have said all, the half will not then have been told.[3]

Frederick Douglass is widely recognized for his heroic antislavery political activism and for his brilliant rhetorical powers. His struggles for
human dignity, social justice, and multiracial democracy serve as a
potent moral example. Admirers and critics alike have described him as "the
most articulate former slave who ever lived," the "preeminent black leader of
the nineteenth century," "one of America's greatest Statesmen," "a superstar
intellectual," and "the soul of honor."[4] In addition to holding these indisputable titles, Frederick Douglass, I argue, was also an insightful theorist
of politics.

One way to appreciate the distinctiveness of Douglass's political thought
is to contrast his political vision with that of David Walker. As noted in the
previous chapter, Walker charged that American civil religion was an intox-
icant that sustained an illicit public happiness. In his view, the imaginary
of the City on the Hill helped to construct a mirage of public well-being

by providing white Americans with a self-congratulatory theologico-political ideology that licensed public habits of moral evasion. In particular, American civil religion masked from America's citizens the parasitic relationship between American prosperity and the systematic dehumanization of black people under American slavery. In the face of this narcotic effect, Walker argued that the only exceptional thing about America was the gravity of its crimes and the peculiar moral pathology that underpinned its moral evasion. The thinker who was arguably the first political theorist of black America counseled the cultivation of martial virtues and habits of character commensurate to the necessary task of battling an insouciant and pernicious white supremacist republic.

Roughly thirty-five years later, Frederick Douglass would also attempt to mobilize martial energies among blacks. In his view, however, these energies should be directed against neither the republic nor its civil religion. Instead, Douglass insisted that these energies should be limited to destroying the rogue and rebellious "slave power" and its political representative, "the slave party," a deformed, malignant, and increasingly ascendant regime that, according to Douglass, had insinuated itself into the heart of the republic and corrupted it from its original and true aims.[5] The word "regime" captures Douglass's understanding of the personal and institutional supports of American slavery as a comprehensive political formation—a formation of political actors, with their beliefs, interests, and desires—as well as an institutional apparatus of governance and administration.[6] For Douglass, authoritative regulative practices generated by the apparatus of governance and administration not only informed and delimited the beliefs, interests, and desires of political actors within the regime, but also structured the kind of politics that proliferates within its jurisdiction.[7] By insisting that the regime of slave power contradicted the original and true aims of the American polity, Douglass rehabilitated the constitutive principles and fundamental commitments of America's founding documents, which, in his reading, supported the abolition of slavery and the incorporation of blacks into the American body politic as citizens. Douglass's attempt to facilitate and redirect martial energies among blacks was, then, a political project in service of a critical theory of the "slave power." He offered not simply a partisan brief against a contingent political malfunction, as is often supposed, but an engaged theoretical explanation of a degenerate yet formidable political way of life. In this regard, Douglass's political theory builds on ground cultivated by Walker. His project, similar to Walker's, seeks both to provide answers to theoretical questions about the nature and origins of American slavery and white supremacy and to articulate a conception of politics that would facilitate black freedom.

Where Walker had developed a theory of the American will to mastery, Douglass offered an alternative set of analytical tools. Walker had sought to expose the "natural enmity" between blacks and whites as a historical, socially constructed, yet objective relation between black slaves and white masters. This relation was a complex political achievement involving the perversion of Christianity, systematic repression of black intellectual development, and organized efforts to isolate free blacks from enslaved blacks, thereby undermining the emergence of black solidarity and political leadership. In identifying the will to mastery as a political phenomenon causally tied to unrestrained greed, Walker offered few arguments to explain the political origins of this greed or to illuminate the institutional forms that organized and sustained it. By contrast, Douglass sought to demonstrate how the values of mastery had refigured public ethics and organized oppressive politics within and beyond the community of masters. Douglass explained the political development of the will to mastery as a form of corrupt sovereignty, a degenerate and disfiguring principle of political rule. In his view, the ethical commitments and normative orientations of the "slave power" supervened commitments to natural rights and political equality and manifested themselves as a will to mastery over America's "other." Adding depth to Walker's notion of the will to mastery, Douglass explored the dangerous allure and the destructive and imperializing authority of mastery. Rather than reducing the motives for mastery to the operations of greed, as Walker had, Douglass examined how the commitments to slavery and white supremacy eviscerated commitments to natural rights and political equality by perverting notions of interest, obligation, and reciprocity.

Like Walker, Douglass illuminated and politicized the evil of American slavery. Viewing this evil as a perversion of true American political principles, however, Douglass provided a genealogy of American slavery that tracked its contingent historical development. Analyzing the will to mastery as a form of corruption, Douglass complicated Walker's static model by attending to historical change. He transcended Walker's monocausal account of greed by investigating the complex ways that pseudo-ethical forms produce and sustain immoral practices. Although Walker and Douglass were united in their concern to explain the nature and effects of mastery and identify the enabling conditions of black freedom, they approached these issues in very different ways.

Douglass built on Walker's attack against the Aristotelian view that masters and slaves share a common interest by virtue of the master's natural fitness for rule and the slave's natural fitness for obedience.[8] Both insisted that the true relation between master and slave was one of natural enmity.[9]

However, although Douglass agreed with Walker that master and slave were natural enemies, he did not accept Walker's conclusion that America was an enemy combatant against whom blacks must prepare vigilantly for battle. As a contested normative ideal and an imperfect assemblage of republican political institutions, America was, for Douglass, more complicated than Walker acknowledged. Blacks faced a merciless and vicious enemy, but their true enemy was neither the entire American political community nor its powerful civil religion sustained by the imaginary of the City on the Hill.[10] Rather, the true enemy of blacks was the formidable and retrograde "slave power." For Douglass, this degenerate regime—comprising the institutional ensemble of American slavery's social, political, and personal relations—was distinct from and opposed to the regime imagined by the American founders and set forth in the public principles of the American republic. In Douglass's view, the commitment to slavery and white supremacy had become the ruling principle of southern life. It functioned as both the organizing principle that animated its public institutions and private social relations and the tribal ethos that sustained a specious political equality among wealthy planters, middling farmers, and poor whites. Distinguishing between the "slave power" and the original design and proper *telos* of the American republic and between the "spirit of slavery" and America's civil religion was critical to Douglass's argument that the "slave power" had dragged the northern states into a corrupting union and caused them to violate the regime specified by American founding principles.[11]

Although Walker's educational project of inculcating martial virtue as the principle normative and programmatic aim of black politics may have appealed to Douglass's own masculinist conceptions of resistance and political freedom,[12] Douglass rejected the concept of a war between the races as a frame for black politics. According to Douglass, blacks were fighting neither a defensive war against America nor an offensive war for national liberation. Instead, he advocated that blacks make common cause with the Union. For reasons of expedience, morality, and symbolism, enslaved and free blacks, Douglass argued, should enlist their martial capacities and energies in the Union's larger cause of vanquishing the "slave power's" rebellion.[13]

Douglass assured his predominantly white audience that the substance of black energies and capacities was not naturally or latently bellicose, as Walker had suggested, but was emblematic of an authentic, if still nascent, democratic character. The ultimate aim of these energies was not the founding of a black public, as Walker had threatened. On the contrary, black political aspirations coincided with the true purposes of American republicanism. Indeed, Douglass maintained, blacks were quintessentially American, despite having been denied the protections and blessings of America. Although there are significant parallels between Douglass's antebellum arguments about the desperate need to politicize free blacks after years of disenfranchisement, cultural marginalization, and exclusion and Walker's effort to found a black public,[14] Douglass rejected Walker's idea that American white supremacy was ultimately incorrigible.

Because Douglass continued to believe in the dream of a multiracial American republic, he could not embrace black political institutions as anything more than a pragmatic and temporary organizational adjustment to white supremacy.[15] Douglass agreed with Walker that black political institutions were good insofar as they provided an appropriate and necessary organizational form to defend and promote black political interests in a stubbornly racist political environment. He also agreed that black political institutions provided a critical vehicle to cultivate and practice black political virtues. Yet, unlike Walker, Douglass insisted that the institutions of black political insurgency were temporary, rather than permanent, forms, and he argued that they were instrumentally, rather than intrinsically, good. According to Douglass, enslaved blacks—in their aspirations for freedom, everyday forms of resistance, and all-too-infrequent but no less consequential insurrections—fought against the corruption of American political principles and institutions and struggled for the best in America itself. If free blacks were beleaguered and depoliticized, then their dispiritedness derived from the frustration of their desire for citizenship within the republican political community. The aim of black politics, Douglass explained repeatedly, was to force America to become the exemplary republican political community that the founders originally envisioned and that the true civil religion of America required.

As a political theorist, then, Douglass made two central contributions. He provided a profound analysis of the complex political evils of American slavery, and he articulated a compelling vision of authentic American political purposes that featured black freedom as a central constitutive element. To comprehend these contributions, it is important to examine both the content and form of Douglass's writings in the context of nineteenth-century abolitionist struggles and in relation to Enlightenment constructions of natural law and theories of moral sentiment.

Situating Douglass: History, Genre, Theory

Frederick Douglass escaped from slavery in 1838 and gave his first antislavery lecture in 1841. He came of age intellectually fourteen years after David Walker's death in a social and political context altogether different from the world in which Walker wrote and thought. Unlike Walker, Douglass found and enjoyed a receptive and increasingly energetic audience in a broader abolition movement that embraced and assisted him (albeit problematically) in the cultivation of his already impressive intellectual powers. He also found in the abolition movement an organizational apparatus that would promote his political ideas. Douglass struggled against demeaning and dispiriting racism within American abolitionism,[16] which he concisely captured with the observation that "Opposing slavery and hating its victims has come to be a very common form of Abolitionism."[17] Nonetheless, he consistently enjoyed access, mobility, and prestige within an organized network of politically sympathetic white persons that did not exist for Walker.

Douglass's literary career spanned five decades during some of the most dramatic transformations in American history. Over the course of his career, Douglass forged alliances with various factions of the abolitionist movement as his political views grew and changed. Early in his career, under the influence of William Lloyd Garrison, Douglass initially repudiated the Union as "a covenant with the devil," suggesting (much as Walker had done) that the U.S. Constitution was a document that *guaranteed* slavery. Yet even when advancing the view that the Constitution was "a pro-slavery instrument" that he could "not bring himself to vote under or swear to support," Douglass could stake his claim on the terra firma of political and personal support provided by white American allies within the American Antislavery Society. After 1850, Douglass turned from the Garrisonian doctrine of principled withdrawal from all civic institutions complicit with slavery to embrace political abolitionism—the commitment to abolish slavery through the political process. An energized and organized movement against slavery provided support for Douglass and helped him to envision a wider range of possibilities for racial coexistence in America's political present and future.

Douglass's creative contributions to the theorization of American slavery and American politics emerged within and were constrained by a particular literary genre: the slave narrative.[18] The first of his three autobiographies, *Narrative of the Life of Frederick Douglass, an American Slave, Written by Himself* (1845), is the best known and best selling of Douglass's writings and was written for a predominantly white audience. The slave narrative afforded former slaves an opportunity to recount their horrifying experiences under the peculiar institution. However, the primary purpose of the form was to quicken the conscience of a potentially sympathetic white audience rather than to engage the intellects and experiences of a black public or to mobilize its passions.[19] The form, thus, placed strictures on which experiences former slaves could disclose, which emotional responses they could reveal, and which private interpretations of these experiences slaves could share with their white readers.

As a number of scholars have pointed out, former (and often fugitive) slaves' characterizations of slavery were designed to shock their audience into moral outrage. To do this, ex-slave writers had to anticipate and negotiate the ethical and normative sensibilities of a nineteenth-century white audience predisposed to doubt their moral and intellectual fitness.[20] The ideal audience, then, for the slave narrative consisted of a discursive community that had not simply failed to develop the linguistic and conceptual frames needed to interpret the complex injuries of enslavement but one that had actually developed elaborate tactics to disavow and conceal these injuries. As Saidiya Hartman has shown, nineteenth-century law, prescriptive literature, travel narratives, and popular entertainment worked in concert to restrict white recognition of slave humanity and to support popular representations of blacks as inherently reprobate. The humanity of slaves—including the power of will and the capacity to formulate human purposes and impose self-restraint—was recognized only in the law's prohibitions against and penalties for a slave's crimes.[21] Within a cultural milieu that effaced the human attributes of slaves—the very attributes necessary to trigger human empathy—Douglass and other authors of slave narratives confronted an enormous challenge. The configuration of a transgressive black agency—legible only insofar as it was imagined as degenerate, invasive, or seductive—rendered slaves' experiences of violation not simply invisible but unintelligible to the nineteenth-century reader. If audiences thought black men were childlike and cowardly, except for a natural predisposition for theft, it would be difficult for them to imagine them grieving the theft of their bodies, their loved ones, or the products of their labor.

Moreover, sentimental literature, proslavery tracts, and even abolitionist writings regularly represented the agency of the slave in obverse relation to the slave's powerlessness.[22] These cultural texts attributed to slaves "powers of weakness," an ability to influence, if not dominate, their masters through their manipulation of paternalist affections. The twinned signification of the slave as person and as property allowed the relationship between the master and slave to oscillate between reciprocity and submission, between intimacy and domination. The odd duality of the legal, cultural, and political relationship between master and slave affirmed both the master's use of violence against slaves and the obligation to protect them. By figuring black agency in this manner and by figuring the slave as a hybrid form of personhood and property, the political and popular culture of antebellum America made it exceedingly difficult for most whites to perceive or imagine the boundaries of black moral selfhood. Apprehension of a moral violation of the other requires that one perceive (or imagine) the other's moral boundaries. However, recognition of this kind requires that one see the other's capacity to formulate legitimate purposes, which implies the existence of boundaries to legitimate interference. The kinds of interference deemed intolerable as an unambiguous moral violation when directed at oneself must be recognized as equally intolerable for the other. In the absence of this kind of imaginative reciprocity, a moral agent might perceive the pain of the other and perhaps feel disturbed or burdened at the sight of it. Even so, this agent may not apprehend the moral significance of this pain. Thus, it was exceedingly difficult for most whites to comprehend violations of the moral boundaries of black selfhood as akin to comparable white experiences of personal disgrace, demoralizing injury, and debilitating trauma.

Uncorrupted human nature might feel pity at the at the sight of the suffering of any sentient being, as Rousseau famously hypothesized, and the growth of liberal democracy might even extend this passion at the expense of more discriminating political judgments, as Alexis de Tocqueville worried, but the effects of white supremacist conceptions of black subhumanity prevented white Americans from apprehending the moral meaning of slaves' suffering.[23] Douglass was keenly aware of the imperviousness of most white Americans to the evils of slavery, and, in particular, to the moral significance of black pain. "Our white fellow-countrymen do not know us. They are strangers to our character, ignorant of our capacity, oblivious of our history and progress, and are misinformed as to the principles and ideas that control and guide us as a people."[24] In his view, most of his white contemporaries were both unable and unwilling to appreciate the magnitude of the marvel that so many blacks had managed to survive the sheer personal catastrophe of enslavement. Where Walker had used a rubric of avarice to account for this failure on the part of white Americans, Douglass sought a more complicated explanation, one that could resolve the patent contradiction between widely shared notions of natural law and their pervasive moral aphasia.

Originating in a philosophical tradition dating to classical antiquity, natural law posits the fundamental freedom, equality, and rationality of all human beings. Embedded in the version of liberalism framed by John Locke and encoded in the Declaration of Independence by Thomas Jefferson, the modern theory of natural law posits objective moral principles that are universally valid and are immediately grasped by human reason. Natural law then is an intelligible normative order available for discernment by all rational individuals. It guides private action and public moral and legal codes. Legitimate governments are those that recognize and secure the space for the peaceful and competent exercise of the freedoms and responsibilities ordained by natural law.

Douglass incorporated the tenets of natural law within his claims about individual character and social order.[25] He suggested that human societies tend naturally toward harmonious order ordained by natural law. Moreover, Douglass intimated that our common nature is predisposed toward recognition of the natural rights of others and outfitted with faculties of reason and conscience. These faculties guide us in the apprehension and performance of our natural duties, obligations that, given in nature, we have to ourselves and to other human beings. We are not only predisposed to recognize the dignity of other human beings and the freedom required for the exercise of that dignity but also predisposed by nature to hold ourselves accountable when we fail to treat human beings with the adequate measure of respect. Conscience, according to Douglass, is the internal registry that enforces each individual's compliance with natural duties to other human beings.

Accepting these tenets of natural law, Douglass confronted two problems: (1) how to make sense of slavery within a moral order that posits equal freedom for all; and (2) how to explain white Americans' apparent cognitive incapacity to grasp the mandates of natural law pertaining to enslaved and free black persons. Slavery was, for Douglass, a glaring violation of natural law not only because it violated natural law's mandate of equal freedom but also because mastery appeared to corrupt the human faculties of reason and conscience. Clouding reason and subverting conscience, mastery did grievous harm to masters as well as slaves. Whites' imperviousness to the harms of slavery depended on a subversion of natural reason and the unmaking of conscience, two forms of corruption that posed a serious danger to social order. As a political theorist, then, Frederick Douglass's primary contribution lies in providing a comprehensive account of the manifold evils of slavery that illuminates the magnitude of the harm done to the slave population, the slave owners, and non–slave owners, and to the moral values and political institutions of the nation.

Slavery and the Evils of Mastery

Douglass used his autobiography to illuminate the peculiar evils of slavery and demonstrate that white Americans had the power to eliminate these evils. Similar to other authors of slave narratives, Douglass depicted slavery as an actionable injustice, a grave evil that white readers could eradicate. To elicit abolitionist activism, slave narratives did not portray the horrors of slavery as an irremediable evil for its victims because this kind of depiction might lead to paralysis or despair among white readers. Nor did they aim, in most cases, to underscore moral complexity, because complexity might lead to contemplative inaction or indifference. To evoke a sense of urgency and possibility, the narratives often dissembled about the most painful but central truths concerning slavery. Deploying melodramatic representations of good and evil and appealing to austere moral sensibilities, the narratives sought to mobilize moral outrage among white readers, while eschewing white fantasies of black depravity. To grasp Douglass's systemic critique of slavery, then, it is necessary to read his autobiographical narratives against the grain.

Throughout his writings, Douglass consistently argued that slavery was a "system of wickedness," a systematic project of moral and political evil that simultaneously corrupted the souls of individual masters and disfigured the bodies and souls of slaves. As he argued repeatedly and emphatically, "The slaveholder, as well as the slaves, is the victim of the slave system." He also insisted that "under the whole heavens there is no relation more unfavorable to the development of honorable character, than that sustained by the slaveholder to the slave."[26] Douglass mapped three dimensions of slavery's harm. First, slavery violated the laws of nature. The violent assault on the humanity of the slave defied what Douglass took to be universal and objective standards of (and rights to) decent treatment of human beings. Second, enslavement did harm to undeserving persons: It aimed to disfigure slaves and was too often successful. Third, mastery ultimately contravened its own most often-stated goals. In contrast to its avowed aim to secure leisure for slave owners to enable them to cultivate and enjoy higher human activities and pleasures, mastery unleashed tyrannical power and disfigured the souls of masters. As masters attempted to vindicate their abusive practices, they corrupted their own rational and moral capacities, conflating the perversions of tyranny with ethical necessity. I consider each of these arguments in turn.

Douglass insisted that slavery was a flagrant violation of American morality and authentic Christianity, as well as an open embarrassment of the principles of natural rights articulated in the Declaration of Independence. As he said often to antebellum white audiences, "Your fathers have said that man's right to liberty is self evident. There is no need of argument to make it clearer. The voices of nature, of conscience, of reason, and of revelation proclaim it as the right of rights, the foundation of all truths, and all responsibility."[27] As the right of rights, the foundation of all truths and all responsibility, liberty is not simply a principle hallowed by American tradition. Liberty is the precondition for action according to reason, conscience, duty, and religious piety. Moreover, liberty is recognized by reason, conscience, and various religions as a privileged and foundational value, an essential ingredient for a fully human life. Slavery was evil, then, not simply because it violated the rules of morality, reason, and religion but also because denying liberty to slaves abrogated the slaves' free exercise of their faculties. As a result, enslaved persons could neither develop self-sanctioned attachments nor cultivate the skills necessary for enjoying recognizably human lives. In short, slave societies practice and legitimate dehumanization.

With one important qualification, Douglass anticipated the theory of slavery formulated by Orlando Patterson's *Slavery and Social Death*, his groundbreaking and definitive comparative sociology of slavery. Examining historical, anthropological, and literary evidence from ancient, medieval, and modern slave societies, Patterson concluded that, despite the extraordinary social and cultural differences distinguishing these slave systems from one another, the transhistorical phenomenon of slavery involves a form of "social death." In those societies in which the labor power of slaves is extracted for the benefit of others, the social existence of the enslaved entails "the permanent and violent domination of natally alienated and generally dishonored persons."[28] According to Patterson, there are four essential features that distinguish slavery from other forms of institutionalized domination: First, slavery is extreme in the routinization and normalization of the violence necessary to sustain the absolute personal domination of a master over a slave; second, this relation of violent domination is permanent and subjects the enslaved person to the absolute domination of a master for life; third, the enslaved person is denied ties of birth both to ancestors and to progeny as a means of producing absolute submission and total dependence; and fourth, the enslaved person is denigrated and dishonored as a disgraced or disgraceful social outcast.

Douglass's descriptions of regular and arbitrary beatings, his account of his masters' demands for unquestioning acquiescence, his analysis of being stripped of his "manhood," and his pained recollections of the destruction of his familial relations to his mother and siblings foreshadow Patterson's theory of social death. However, Douglass also describes a political dimension of the practice of mastery, an aspect that Patterson's account omits. He explores the normative and creative dimensions of mastery as a practice of statecraft and soulcraft, suggesting a structural relation between particular types of regimes, the institution of slavery, and the character of citizens. Defining extreme violence, dishonor, and natal alienation as constitutive elements of the institutional and ideational structure of slavery, Douglass also suggests that these practices of power produce in masters certain habits of the heart and mind and a misguided conception of the good life. In his view, a fully adequate theory of slavery must make sense of the ways that American political life had incorporated the principles and practices of mastery. For Douglass, American slavery was a robust institution because mastery generated a particular set of social and political relationships that corrupted moral and rational sensibilities and thereby provided the institutional and existential supports for slavery. Douglass understands slavery to be the consequence of the exercise of mastery, a political relation of domination that, in turn, corrupted the principles and practices of the American polity and generated the retrograde political project of the slave power.

To appreciate the important difference between Douglass's political theory of mastery and Patterson's sociology of slavery, it is helpful to contrast Patterson's controlling notion of social death with Douglass's claims concerning the essential purpose of mastery. Patterson defined the life of the slave as social death. Compelled to be an appendage of the master's will and a victim of extreme violence, alienation, and dishonor, the slave, for Patterson, is a living person who is rendered dead to the social, moral, and political protections of the community. Although Douglass uses metaphors that liken slavery to death—referring to "the tomb of slavery," and slavery's "death-like stupor"—he insists that, as a mode of domination and an unnatural and corrupted misuse of authority, mastery "unmakes" human nature and turns human beings into brutes. It perverts human possibilities as its necessary condition of existence. Mastery's transformative power is productive precisely because it makes defective humans of not only the enslaved but also the masters themselves and their non-slave-owning fellow citizens.

Although social death is a rich and evocative metaphor, it does not interrogate the mechanisms of mastery. Douglass, however, provides an account of mastery that analyzes its dynamics and explores its implications for those who, neither enslaved nor slave owners, tolerate mastery in their polity. In doing so, Douglass provides a theory of slavery in relation to mastery within American liberal republicanism that ties the systematic production of black subjection to the nature and fate of the American experiment in self-government. Writing as a political actor as well as a theorist, Douglass advanced a theory of the interconnections of mastery, slavery, and polity, a theory designed to provoke political transformation.

A Political Anatomy of Dehumanization

Douglass argues that mastery seeks to obliterate the personhood of slaves through the categorical denial of human recognition. Whippings, destruction of family ties, severe circumscription of movement, forced labor, institutionalized dishonor, commodification, sexual exploitation, and coerced reproduction were practices designed to dehumanize those who were subjected to them. The systematic exposure to these practices, masters hoped, would eradicate a slave's inherent capacity to comprehend natural law. By undermining slaves' rationality and conscience through violence, dishonor, and alienation, masters sought to create defective humans, so enfeebled intellectually and spiritually that they would come to perceive the master's authority as legitimate. Yet slave masters also recognized that they must preserve sufficient rationality to enable slaves to carry out the complex purposes of their masters. Historian of American slavery David Brian Davis resolves this peculiar paradox by describing the construction of slaves as "human animals" as the ultimate goal of slavery. The practices of slavery "[focus] on and [exaggerate] the so called animal traits that all humans share and fear, while denying the redeeming rational and spiritual qualities that give humans a sense of pride of being made in the image of God, of being only little lower than the angels."[29]

Davis's characterization of this paradox, however, misses a key dimension of the phenomenological distinctiveness and peculiar utility of human slaves over domesticated animals. Douglass acknowledged that domestic animals might be made to perform a wide variety of simple tasks, but they could not be made to apprehend and implement the complex purposes of a master. Animals could not be made, through either repetition or threat of constant violence, to execute the complex tasks routinely expected of slaves—for instance, to rise at a specified time every morning despite their level of fatigue and to conduct themselves of their own accord to a work space where they perform specific tasks in accordance with the specifications of a master or overseer. Nor could animals devise and implement a regimen of social reproduction that might rejuvenate them enough to show up for another day of excruciating and exploitative labor. Moreover, the fact that masters sexually exploited slaves, sought intimate nonsexual companionship from them, and elicited pleasure from the theatrical and musical amusements of slaves suggested that masters recognized the "human" over the "animal" as the salient dimension of the slave category.

Douglass noted that "slaveholders of America resort to every species of cruelty" to transform slaves into this peculiarly human mode of instrumentality, but he insisted that "they can never reduce the slave to willing obedience."[30] Contrary to the hopes and designs of mastery, "the natural elasticity of the human soul repels the slightest attempt to enslave it," and contrary to prevailing beliefs, "the black slaves are not wholly without that elasticity; they are men, and being so, do not readily submit to the yoke."[31] Using the metaphor of "elasticity," Douglass suggests that, despite their masters' abuses, slaves retained their inner conviction that their own aims and interests were separate from and in opposition to those of their masters. However, the tension embedded in his recognition that slaves "do not readily submit to the yoke" indicates that Douglass was keenly aware that American mastery stretched this "elasticity" to a breaking point, even if it did not invariably result in a complete dehumanization. Douglass's narratives of his own experiences with enslavement illuminate the damage done to the "elasticity" of the souls of slaves by routinized and extreme practices of mastery.

Few examples demonstrate this issue more dramatically than Douglass's struggle to represent the explosive problem of slaves' sexual vulnerability and humiliation.[32] Consider Douglass's description of the first of the many beatings administered to him by the notorious slave master Covey who "had acquired a very high reputation for breaking young slaves."[33] Covey's virtuosity as a slave breaker derived from his devotion to his art and his rigorous self-discipline in organizing his entire personal life to accommodate the demands of mastery. In all three biographies, Douglass insists that his ability to deceive his slaves by controlling and manipulating the context within which slaves lived and labored and providing relentless physical torture were the two great techniques that marked Covey's "superior efficacy as a slave-breaker." As Douglass explains in the *Narrative*, "Everything [Covey] possessed in the shape of learning or religion, he made conform to his disposition to deceive. He seemed to think himself equal to deceiving the Almighty."[34] Douglass characterizes his own ability to break through this deception, "essential to the relation of master and slave," as a "glorious revolution" of individual resistance, "the turning point in his career as a slave," a development so momentous that it "revived [his] manhood, recalled [his] departed self confidence, and inspired [him] again with the determination to be free."[35] In *My Bondage and My Freedom*, his second biography, Douglass characterized this breakthrough as a "rekindl[ing] in my breast the smoldering embers of liberty." Before that victory, however, Douglass admits that Covey succeeded in initiating him into a world of deception and violence so systematic and relentless that Covey temporarily "broke" him.

During the first of many beatings that temporarily "transform[ed] [him] into a brute,"[36] Douglass reports without much fanfare that Covey commanded him to remove his clothes: "[Covey] then went to a large gumtree, and with his axe cut three large switches, and, after trimming them up neatly with his pocketknife, he ordered me to take off my clothes."[37] Douglass implicitly acknowledges that there was something odious and disarming about this particular command and uses it as a point of resistance.

When a particularly savage beating commenced, Douglass notes that he stood motionless and refused to remove any of his clothes. Douglass discloses no further details about why he insisted on remaining dressed and no details about why, of all the dreadful violations he would have to endure as a slave, removing his clothing before being beaten induced such a display of resistance. Having made multiple requests to Douglass to "strip [himself]," Covey rushed at him, Douglass reports, "with the fierceness of a tiger, tore off my clothes, and lashed me till he had worn out his switches, cutting me so savagely as to leave the marks visible for a long time after."[38] Although Douglass does not explain explicitly what he thought or felt about this event, his narrative takes a suggestive turn. As if to direct the reader's attention away from Covey's exposure of his naked body, Douglass quickly concludes his discussion of this incident with a generalization: "This whipping was the first of a number just like it, and for similar offenses."[39]

In his second biography, *My Bondage and My Freedom*, Douglass's report of this incident was more introspective and revealing. He notes that he had regarded the order to remove his clothes—rather than the actual beating itself or the frequency of these beatings—as the singularly galling and unreasonable aspect of the entire sordid episode: "To this unreasonable order I made no reply, but sternly refused to take off my clothing. If you will beat me thought I, you shall do so over my clothes." Without explicitly tying Covey's command to purposeful sexual humiliation, Douglass conveys that, whatever Covey's purposes might have been, Douglass's own sense of bodily integrity demanded his conscious resistance to this particular humiliation.[40] In *The Life and Times of Frederick Douglass*, his final biography, Douglass returns to this scene, but adds an explanation for his resistance. He explains that he was immobilized by the command precisely because he had not *understood* Covey's order to remove his clothing. In this final account, he emphasized his assertive, unyielding, and *instinctual* internal resistance to Covey's command: "This done, he ordered me to take off my clothes. To this unreasonable order I made no reply, but in my apparent unconsciousness and inattention to this command I indicated very plainly a stern determination to do no such thing." Douglass then repeats his thoughts verbatim from *My Bondage*: "If you will beat me, thought I, you shall do so over my clothes."[41]

Vacillating from incomprehension to willed resistance only to return to putative incomprehension, Douglass's varying accounts over time of this encounter provide hints of the pathos and depths of personal catastrophe that Douglass experienced as a slave. Covey's command and subsequent violent disrobing of Douglass can be interpreted in many different ways. Minimally, he wanted to remove all barriers to Douglass's flesh. Either he believed that exposed flesh registered injury more readily than clothed flesh, or he knew that exposed flesh enabled him to calculate the precise amount of violence he could administer before the slave's body would be rendered unproductive. Alternatively, Covey may have been economically motivated. Perhaps he sought to avoid the cost of replacing damaged clothes when he ordered Douglass to disrobe in advance. Within these interpretive frames, Covey is ruthlessly economical. He uses a mental calculus to avoid the risk of additional costs from damaged clothing, just as he calculates the precise limits of physical and emotional violence that could be deployed against Douglass's body before it would be rendered unproductive.[42] Covey's virtuosity as a slave breaker, then, is enhanced by a calculative and acquisitive rationality, according to some of modernity's champions, a distinctively modern civic competence typically associated with industrial productivity rather than slave production.[43]

Covey's violent tactics might also be read in the context of torture and the unmaking of a world such as that analyzed by Elaine Scarry in *The Body in Pain*.[44] By intensifying the experience of bodily pain, Covey may have sought to heighten Douglass's sense of dependence on him by obliterating his consciousness of everything except his body in pain and his relation to Covey's power over him. Ties to a larger world—of slaves, other associates, and even earlier masters—would be sundered in this moment of excruciating trauma, as Douglass's autonomous will was unmade and remade as an extension of Covey's. In this sense, Covey's command that Douglass strip off his clothing might be interpreted as a deliberate action that is not as narrowly instrumental as maximizing laboring capacity or minimizing clothing costs.

Perhaps a more revealing way to understand Covey's command is to regard it as the performance of an initiation ritual orchestrated to specify and confer the meaning of the particular identities of master and slave prevailing on the plantation. Rituals serve a variety of purposes, but one of their important functions is to generate and sustain a particular system of value among a group of actors. Rituals constitute identities by encouraging participation within an elaborately structured and tightly organized performance of meaning-producing symbols.[45] Formalized social practices may orchestrate symbolic performances to unsettle old identities and transform them into new ones. The symbolic production of new identities may also generate new meanings, knowledge, obligations, and privileges for particular participants within ritual. In short, ritual action can inscribe fundamental human commitments on the identities of human beings. Interpreted as ritual, these two acts, Covey's command to Douglass to remove his clothes and his execution of the savage beating that followed, constitutes a rite designed to inculcate a shared but nondiscursive and nonreciprocal understanding of the powers and forms of powerlessness, these relations of honor and extreme dishonor obtaining between master and slave at Covey's plantation.

Covey's command that Douglass remove his clothes might also be interpreted as a matter of routine. That is, Covey may have required all of his slaves to remove their clothes before being beaten as a matter of habit. Habitual rather than reflexive action also has theoretical significance in ancient, modern, and contemporary discussions of political philosophy. Aristotle, for example, argued that one's character developed through habituation rather than through the application of rationally derived principles or moral rules. Similarly, the great skeptic David Hume argued that custom and habit, rather than rational deliberation, structure human perception, organizing experience to make it useful. Hannah Arendt also construes habit as a complex activity rooted in some originating action so pleasing (or intoxicating) for an actor that he or she thoughtlessly repeats it. In this view, repetition over time removes the context of the habit and its originating action from consciousness.[46] Interpreting Covey's command as a mode of habit, then, suggests that a master's routine exercise of absolute power over the slave's body shapes character, perception, and behavior in powerful and fundamental ways. Whether understood as economic calculation, applied torture, self-conscious ritual, habit, or some combination of these, this revealing encounter encapsulates and allows Douglass to interrogate the processes of dehumanization under slavery.

Douglass's various accounts of his experiences of enslavement also provide insights into the complex *effects* of brutal violation on both the soul and the body of the slave. At one point, he discusses a low but revealing moment during his life in slavery, a point at which he found himself "regretting his own existence." During this moment, his "soul was roused to eternal wakefulness" about the utter futility of his life as a slave. Between thoughts of suicide and hopes for freedom, he noted, "I have no doubt but that I should have killed myself, or done something for which I should have been killed."[47] This brief and elusive reference to "something for which [he] should have been killed" is puzzling. It seems to indicate that Douglass believed he was momentarily capable of committing an outrage that exceeded vengeance, retribution, or justifiable rage—intelligible responses to the violations he had suffered. In his despair, then, Douglass contemplated performing an act that was beyond the pale of intelligible moral defense, one that could be judged as a kind of senseless, gratuitous, or nihilistic transgression.[48]

It is important to distinguish such an act from forms of violence that Douglass condoned. His graphic depiction of the intensity and variety of mastery's sustained violation of his person made a powerful case for his (and all slaves') right to self-defense. It was, after all, during his decisive physical battle with Covey that he pierced through the "tomb of slavery" to claim a human authority he believed he was morally entitled to at every moment during his life in bondage.[49] In later writings, Douglass celebrated the Haitian Revolution, the successful defeat of French colonizers by former slaves, as a strike for human freedom no less spectacular than the American or French Revolution. Utterly convinced of the moral equivalence of slave rebellion and democratic revolution, Douglass wrote the *Heroic Slave*, a novella depicting the unbroken continuity between the heroes of the American Revolution and Madison Washington, a slave who led a successful revolt by commandeering the slave ship *Creole* to British territory. "The name of this hero has been by the meanest of tyrants suppressed," Douglass wrote of his fictional character. "Such a man redeems his race. He is worthy to be mentioned with the Hoffers and Tells, the noblest heroes of history."[50] Defensive violence against masters, then, would not, in Douglass's view, justify his death. Given that he explicitly referred to suicide as the alternative to this elusive something that would have earned him death in the *Narrative*, the most reasonable interpretation of this cryptic reference would seem to be unprovoked violation of innocent others—either other blacks who had not harmed him and who were also victimized by slavery, or other whites who were not masters, their defenders, or their beneficiaries—that is, white persons who opposed slavery on principle.

Operating within the constraints of the genre of slave narrative, Douglass was under considerable pressure to present his life as an indubitable case of uncorrupted human dignity, a dignity menaced by the inherent brutalities of slavery. Even a cryptic reference to a degree of corruption so debasing that it provoked contemplation of nihilistic violence, then, is telling. Even the most virtuous forms of violence would be reprehensible for some abolitionists, particularly those such as William Lloyd Garrison, who were also pacifists. We might read this veiled reference as Douglass's attempt to push back against the expectations of his audience and command a broader license than his audience may have been willing to grant him. Douglass may also have included this reference to press upon his readers a disturbing point: that mastery had the ability to destroy the inherent moral capacity of slaves to know and comply with the dictates of natural law. Contrary to masters' claims that their regulation of slaves produced moral benefit, Douglass gestures toward a far more dire truth. Through their brutality, masters were in danger of producing amoral nihilists. Although Douglass moves quickly away from this intimation to reassert the human dignity of slaves and emphasize the restorative possibilities of abolitionism, his *Narrative* nonetheless provides tantalizing clues to a fuller range of emotional, intellectual, and moral effects of enslavement.[51] If mastery leads slaves to the temptation to commit gratuitous violence, then it is a system of domination without redeeming value.

In another essay, Douglass sketched the physical effects of enslavement: "He stands before us, today physically, a maimed and mutilated man. His mother was lashed to agony before the birth of her babe, and the bitter anguish of the mother is seen in the countenance of her offspring. Slavery has twisted his limbs, shattered his feet, deformed his body and distorted his features."[52] Such physical degradation might well be accompanied by the impairment of moral judgment. In the *Narrative*, Douglass noted that "to make a contented slave it is necessary to make a thoughtless one. It is necessary to darken his moral and mental vision, and, as far as possible, to annihilate the power of reason. He must be able to detect no inconsistencies in slavery; he must be made to feel that slavery is right; and he can be brought to that only when he ceases to be a man."[53] To produce a happy slave, then, would require a refashioning of human sensibilities with profound moral implications.

For Douglass, slaves reduced to a debilitating view of their suitability for slavery had internalized a belief far more pernicious than their individual inferiority to a particular master or group of masters. More damaging even than this internalized belief, the slave degraded in this fashion also conceded the inferiority of the entire race of blacks to the race of whites and the collective impotence of all who shared (or could be reasonably presumed to share) their common predicament.[54] Such a belief undermined the possibility of collective action of any kind, whether large or small in scale, and thus exaggerated the degraded slave's powerlessness. When subordinated in this way, a slave doubted not only his or her own intellectual powers and creative capacities but also the intellectual powers and creative capacities of his or her peers in the community of slaves and free blacks. Slaves who harbored such doubts might imperil any and all forms of communal action and relinquish not only individual but also collective freedom.

Slaves who were degraded in this manner transferred their powers of agency (however circumscribed) to masters to whom they attributed superior intellectual, practical, and creative capacities. They became deracinated, lacking standing and protection within any community that could affirm their humanity. Lacking individual power and social standing, and occupying a fixed place of permanent dishonor within the world, such a slave attained recognition only through forms mediated by mastery. Reduced to the purposes specified by the master, this ideal slave possessed the "excellences" of servility and slavishness and fulfilled the ideal of non-personhood at which mastery aims. By detailing this predicament, Douglass pointed out that slavery was more than a status or a juridical identity; it was also a political project aimed at creating a particular kind of human. It was a project to create beings, as Tocqueville admitted candidly, who not only anticipated and fulfilled the complex and multiple needs of their masters but also replaced their own needs with those of their masters.[55] In devoting their agency to satisfying the needs and interests of masters, ideal slaves abandoned their capacity for moral discernment. Once again, Douglass pointed out that the effect of slavery—even for those who appeared content—was to impair the slaves' inherent capacity to recognize violations of the laws of nature. "The time was, when we trembled in the presence of a white man, and dared not assert, or even ask for our rights, but would be guided, directed, and governed, in any way we were demanded, without ever stopping to enquire whether we were right or wrong."[56]

Even so, Douglass argues that, for most slaves and free blacks, rather than indicating deep cultural deficits or native deficiencies, this impulse resulted from the habits and practices of acquiescence that were actually strategic responses to mastery. Furthermore, as responses to brutal practices of mastery, strategic acquiescence revealed quite a bit about masters, but very little about the true character of slaves. As Douglass noted, "We feel that the imputations cast upon us, for our want of intelligence, morality, and exalted character, may be mainly accounted for by the injustice we have received at your hands."[57]

Challenging the popular justifications that slavery was morally uplifting for enslaved people, Douglass notes that overcoming the effects of enslavement could be a very long process: "Degradation, mental, moral and physical, ground into the very bones of a people by ages of unremitting bondage, will not depart from that people in the course even of many generations."[58] Nonetheless, he argues that most slaves had managed to maintain a moral compass, manifested in their sense of the cruel injustice of their enslavement, despite the intensity and variety of assaults that perennially menaced their lives. Masters' awareness of the prevalence of this sense of injustice among enslaved people, according to Douglass, had led them to devise elaborate ruses to "disgust slaves with their freedom." By indulging slaves with alcohol on holidays, for example, masters sought to "carry off the rebellious spirit of enslaved humanity."[59] As early as 1848, Douglass suggested that these ruses were becoming less effective and that enslaved and free blacks were beginning to see through tactics of intimidation and manipulation: "This sentiment has nearly ceased to reign in the dark abode of our hearts; we begin to see our wrongs as clearly, and comprehend our rights as fully and as well as our white countrymen. This is a sign of progress; and evidence which cannot be gainsayed."[60] The habits and practices of strategic acquiescence were contingent, then. Perfectly understandable and predictable responses to mastery, they could be transformed under changing conditions.

Where white supremacists alleged fixed deficiencies in black moral character, Douglass traces the mechanisms by which masters sought to pervert the moral capacities of enslaved people. Where white racism posited inherent intellectual deficiencies, Douglass illuminated pragmatic and contextually specific attempts to solve concrete and immediate problems caused by the brutality of mastery. By emphasizing the depths of degradation and the possibility for moral regeneration, Douglass also sought to debunk exaggerated claims about the achievements of mastery and to affirm black resiliency and creativity. For all its violence to the slave, the mechanics of mastery, according to Douglass, had only partially succeeded. Despite the intellectual and cultural degradations suffered by too many victims of slavery, precious few were so thoroughly beaten down that they experienced slavery as anything other than a bleak and tortured existence.[61] The very experiences of pain, trial, and desolation bore indisputable witness to the unconquerable humanity of even those persons most disfigured by slavery.

To construe mastery as a near-divine power to unmake the natural constitution of the slave would be to unwittingly affirm the master's fantasies of omnipotence. Instead, Douglass argues that mastery's quest to unmake human nature—a quest to acquire and wield divine power—was an indication of hubris, and thus, another manifestation of the evil involved in the exercise of mastery. Illuminating the manifold evils intrinsic to the processes and purposes of mastery and assessing their effects on the American polity are central to Douglass's political theory.

Mastery's Corrosive Effects on Masters

The morally reprehensible and largely unsuccessful effort to unmake the personhood of slaves was, however, only one dimension of the evils of mastery. Douglass also demonstrated that mastery had a corrosive effect on masters and on those who tolerated mastery within a political community. The most famous example of mastery's power to corrupt its practitioners was Douglass's account of the moral degeneration of his mistress, Sophia Auld. According to Douglass, Auld was originally "a pious, kind and tenderhearted woman," whose disposition under the influence of slavery "became stone [and] gave way to tiger-like fierceness."[62] After learning from her husband that responsible mastery precluded teaching any slave, let alone one as pre-cocious as young Douglass, to read, Auld not only stopped instructing him but also became wholly absorbed with preventing him from learning to read.

Denying literacy to slaves was a cardinal rule of American slavery, codified into law in many jurisdictions and, in some extreme cases, punishable by death. Unlike ancient forms of slavery, where literate slaves were seen to pose no danger, American mastery enshrined the principle of forced illiteracy as an essential institutional support. When she denied Douglass literacy, Auld did not merely acquiesce to a practical rule; she became wholly invested in upholding the principle of mastery. Within the American context, masters withheld literacy to slaves on the grounds that literate slaves posed a danger to themselves, the community of slaves, and the community of masters. Masters feared that literate slaves might not only reinterpret the Bible as a "freedom document" or imbibe the subversive abolitionist ideas circulating clandestinely throughout the South but also acquire intellectual resources that would make them self-destructive or dangerous to their masters.

Preventing literacy among slaves was more than an exercise of individual freedom, more than an indication of what Herbert Storing has described as "the radicalization" of American liberty sanctioned by the U.S. Constitution—"the ironic and terrible" liberty of southern whites to own other human beings and dispense with them in any manner they chose.[63] Rather than simply an ad hoc practice adopted by a few masters, denying literacy to slaves was a widely shared principle, more or less uniformly enforced and protected by state and federal constitutions. As an exercise of constitutionally sanctioned liberty, Auld's assent to and practice of coerced illiteracy, as Douglass described it, entailed a commitment to a system of ethical responsibilities, a structure of obligations and reciprocities honored by slave owners. Incorporated into their most fundamental conception of the good, mandatory illiteracy for slaves structured slave owners' perceptions of themselves as responsible masters. Teaching one's slaves to read was not simply imprudent; it was unethical. It did more than create an obstacle to the extraction of labor from a slave who preferred to read a book. It violated responsible masters' duties to honor and protect the system itself and, in particular, to shield their families, neighbors, and community from unnecessary or preventable malfunctions of the slave system. The responsibilities of mastery required that Sophia Auld not only cease activities she had originally believed to be proper and decent but also adopt an entirely new set of moral commitments. In adopting the responsibilities of mastery, Auld tacitly consented to become an active defender of slavery rather than its passive beneficiary, to become, effectively, a citizen of the regime of the slave power.

In *My Bondage and My Freedom*, Douglass examined the way that Auld's new ethical commitment to the responsibilities of mastery undermined and eventually eviscerated her conscience. In ceasing to instruct him, Auld had to silence and do violence to her former self. Her new commitments violated her original moral inclinations—inclinations that not only *seemed* right, according to Douglass, but also were objectively right, according to natural law. As someone who had been reared to respect the precepts of natural law, particularly the ideal that "nothing but rigid training, long persisted in, can perfect the character,"[64] Auld had to find some means to justify her changed behavior. It was difficult for her to "cease to respect that natural love in [her] fellow creatures." To comply with the dictates of the ethics of mastery, then, Auld required intensive counter-socialization: Auld's conscience had to be unmade.

Douglass sketched the process though which Auld abdicated her natural duty. Before heeding her husband's advice, Auld had to be convinced of the ethical propriety of mandatory illiteracy. She delved into ongoing contestations concerning how masters ought to treat slaves. After immersing herself in this "the great debate," Douglass reports, she became "riveted to her position . . . becoming even more violent in her opposition to my learning to read than was her husband himself. She was not satisfied with simply doing as well as her husband had commanded her, but seemed resolved to better his instruction."[65] For a proponent of natural law such as Douglass, the transformation of Sophia Auld required explanation. How exactly did the ethics of mastery seduce her away from the self-evident tenets of natural law?

An account of Auld's immersion in the ethics of mastery and the subsequent evisceration of her conscience surfaces obliquely in Douglass's works. Although he does not provide an explicit theoretical account of this process in any of the autobiographies, an indirect account can be derived from his antebellum writings and speeches. In one of his most famous speeches, "What to the Slave Is the Fourth of July?" (1852), Douglass succinctly framed the central issues. Following the precepts of natural law, Douglass depicted slavery as a clear and self-evident evil that all morally competent people should naturally and immediately apprehend as a manifestation of natural law. His powerful rhetoric conveyed his moral indignance: "What, am I to argue that it is wrong to make men brutes, to rob them of their liberty, to work them without wages, to keep them ignorant of their relations to other men, to beat them with sticks, to flay their flesh with the lash, to load their limbs with irons, to hunt them with dogs, to sell them at auction, to sunder their families, to knock out their teeth, to burn their flesh, to starve them into obedience and submission to their masters?"[66] To even entertain such a challenge, Douglass insisted, "would make [him] ridiculous, and offer an insult to [the] understanding. There is not a man beneath the canopy of heaven that does not know that slavery is wrong for him." Because slavery was so self-evident an evil, and because no moral reasons, however hypothetical, could ever be adduced to justify slavery, the only possible function and outcome of a debate about the putative morality of slavery would be to weaken or corrupt the moral constitution of slavery's defenders. Deliberation about the ideals and purposes of mastery were nothing other than a demoralizing inquiry into the techniques and purposes of political evil. In Douglass's view, these debates were a form of moral masquerade, lending specious ethical cover to the corruption of moral reason. As such, these specious debates were potentially toxic to the moral health of any decent person and to any society that professed allegiance to Christianity or republicanism.

By taking part in "the great debate," Sophia Auld had placed her conscience at the mercy of abominable questions. Seduced by evil, she had become "fierce," "anxious," and "hard." Auld's moral corruption had allowed her to believe she was doing Douglass a service by denying literacy to him. Adopting commitments to preserve the institutional stability of slavery, she had fallen prey to the preposterous delusion that she had acted with concern for Douglass's good rather than the good of masters as a class. Deliberating the ideals of mastery situated evil within a *faux* moral framework that conflated the abuses associated with mastery with a strategy to advance human welfare. Under the guise of moral deliberation, mastery advertised the violation of the slave's humanity as a means to secure the good of its violated victims. For morality's sake, then, it was important, according to Douglass, to refuse the seductions of "the great debate."

In addition to explicating the corruption of Sophia Auld's conscience, Douglass analyzes mastery's perversion of the natural duties and affections between parents and children. He is particularly concerned with the perversion of the affections between white fathers and their slave children.[67] Douglass begins the *Narrative* with the admission that his father was a white man and proceeds to reveal something even more scandalous: "It was also whispered that my master was my father."[68] Douglass was never able to confirm the truth or falsity of this rumor and ceased to mention it in his latter biographies, an omission that has led scholars to wonder whether Douglass believed it to be true.[69] Yet the extent of the problem of white male parentage of slave children, as well as the moral significance of this problem, remained a core concern of Douglass. In the *Narrative*, Douglass notes that the sexual exploitation of enslaved women and the subsequent birth of mixed-race enslaved children were extensive: "Every year brings with it multitudes of this class of slaves."[70] In *My Bondage and My Freedom*, Douglass states even more pointedly that "thousands are ushered into the world annually, who like myself, owe their existence to white fathers, and most frequently to their masters, and master's sons."[71] In taking up questions concerning mastery's corruption of natural affections, Douglass is attentive to the multiple dimensions of moral license among masters. He carefully documents the manifold corruptions of white masters who sire slave children.

One of the prerogatives of mastery was unimpeded access to the bodies of female slaves. Absolute power over women slaves consisted of not simply the power to coerce their labor but also the power to coerce them into sexual relations. In other words, masters claimed both the productive and reproductive labor of enslaved women.[72] Douglass notes that the law that the enslaved status of mothers determined the status of their offspring was contrived by masters "too obviously to administer to their own lusts, and make a gratification of their wicked desires profitable as well as pleasurable."[73] This fundamental law of American slavery gave official license to male masters to violate slave women and gain property through each enslaved child born as a result. More than regulating the movement of property, the law of slavery authorized the fabrication of human property by condoning masters' sexual exploitation of slave women and then securing the chattel status of the fruits of this exploitation. Fulfilling Aristotle's prediction about "natural slaves," who are marked from the hour of their birth for slavery, American slavery devised a means to transform unrestrained sexual license among masters into the production of new generations of slave labor.

In *My Bondage and My Freedom*, Douglass depicts the economic benefits of masters' sexual license and the horrifying political economy of slave women's vulnerability. Within a system that idolized and de-eroticized white women and simultaneously debased and eroticized black women, Douglass intimates that, for a range of sexual purposes, "slave women are preferred in many instances" to masters' wives.[74] As scholars have amply documented, the cult of chastity and domesticity among white women went hand-in-hand with the social construction of black women as sexual temptresses, a construct that not only facilitated desire for enslaved black women but also, quite usefully, reversed the causal order of predation: White men rather than enslaved black women became the victims of these encounters.[75]

Douglass's bold and provocative admission that the "slave woman is at the mercy of the fathers, sons or brothers of her master," coexisted, however, with his reticence about the content of this exploitation. He did not specify whether or to what extent these episodes of sexual humiliation and exploitation involved acts of "rape" or forms of sexual coercion considered less egregious. In refusing to distinguish sexual violation as "rape," his accounts paralleled the recognition given enslaved women under the law—which did not consider the crime of "rape" to encompass the sexual abuse and violation of enslaved women (or any man). As Saidiya Hartman notes, "In nineteenth century common law, rape was defined as the forcible carnal knowledge of a female against her will and without her consent. Yet the actual or attempted rape of an enslaved woman was neither recognized nor punished by law."[76] When discussing the sexual vulnerability of slave women in *My Bondage and My Freedom*, Douglass avoids a precise characterization of this exploitation and concludes his provocative thoughts with an evasive rhetorical shorthand: "The thoughtful know the rest."[77] In so doing, Douglass concludes his discussion of slave women's sexual vulnerability with an appeal to self-evidence. The simple but grotesque fact that slave women were at the mercy of any white man who desired them, he suggests, should lead every reasonable person to comprehend the precise nature of this vulnerability. Anyone with sense and a reasonably informed view of the character of mastery, in other words, should be able to infer the moral consequences of this vulnerability.

Even when speaking to an all-black audience, Douglass characterizes the enslavement of black women as the "sale [of black women, principally] for the purpose of pollution."[78] In failing to make public the particular crimes suffered by enslaved women at the hands of masters, Douglass conforms to Victorian literary and social conventions, which sought to inculcate bourgeois gender norms in the middle-class reading public. Even women's rights advocates such as Douglass and a number of his abolitionist colleagues ascribed to at least some aspects of what historians have termed the "cult of domesticity" governing gender relations in middle-class households. As Douglass and other slave narrators were well aware, a reader's ability to extend empathy to the enslaved population hinged on the moral and sexual propriety of enslaved women and the extent to which they could be refigured as wives and mothers with a grievance.[79] Thus, Douglass's references to the sexual violation of enslaved women leaves both the crime and the victim in the domain of the "private," where it could be easily digested in the public imagination. In privatizing the most intimate abuses of the regime of mastery, Douglass forces questions about his depiction of slave women's experiences and the uses to which these anecdotes are put.

In what is perhaps his most famous account, Douglass recounts the trauma he experienced when witnessing the beating of his Aunt Hester, who suffered torture and sexual humiliation for the express purpose of her sexual domination. When she disobeyed Captain Anthony's command to refuse the advances of another slave named Lloyd's Ned, Aunt Hester was stripped

naked to the waist. Her hands were tied, and she was suspended from a raf-
ter in the ceiling and beaten mercilessly by Captain Anthony as he screamed
racial and gendered obscenities. Douglass notes that this "was the first in
a series of such outrages" where "[he] was doomed to be a witness and a
participant."[80]

Although this highly provocative account is purposefully vague about
both the consummation and termination of the outrages committed against
Aunt Hester, Douglass is quite clear that these outrages were of a sexual
nature. He notes that Aunt Hester was repeatedly tortured precisely because
she was considered beautiful. Captain Anthony sought to exercise his
monopoly over Aunt Hester's body, and he punished her brutally when she
attempted to deny his prerogative by associating with a man of her choice.
Yet Douglass does not tell us whether, during one of these dreadful episodes,
Captain Anthony violently asserted his masterly prerogative by raping Aunt
Hester, whether she eventually yielded to Captain Anthony's commands by
consenting to sex with him under duress, or whether these beatings persisted
until she finally ended her association with Lloyd's Ned. Nor does Douglass
specify the nature of his "repeated participation" in these outrages. Douglass
captures the intricate interplay of the master's sexual lust and license with
punitive caprice and capricious punishment, relying on an appeal to the self-
evident evil of this sexual violence to evoke appropriate moral condemnation
from reasonable readers.

He also makes his Aunt Hester into a powerful and literal body of evidence, a titillating spectacle for readers hungry for descriptions of abuse. In
this sense, he sacrifices the dignity and integrity of a black female body for
the purpose of extending and dramatizing the abolitionist cause.[81] As we
saw in Chapter 1, Walker feminized treachery to frame his (masculine) conception of citizenship. Here, Douglass feminizes powerlessness to frame his
(masculine) conception of agency. In an important respect, Aunt Hester is a
foil for Douglass as he grasps after his own sense of agency. We might fruit-
fully compare this scene to his account of the beatings he would suffer at
the hands of Covey. Whereas Aunt Hester is stripped naked as a matter of
course and her voice is reduced to a series of mind-numbing shrieks, Douglass responds to the command that he remove his clothing with an articulate
defiance. Furthermore, over the course of his life, he reflects on and revises
his account of the internal dialogue that ensues. The discrepancies in these
two accounts reveal how the regime of mastery shaped Douglass's gendered
theorization of agency.

If moral relations governing sexuality were corrupted by mastery, so
too were natural parental affections. In the *Narrative*, Douglass notes that

masters typically treated the slave children they sired more cruelly than other slave children in their possession, often selling them away. He attributes this callousness to the resentment of the master's wife, suggesting that wives insisted that their husbands disavow these children and their mothers as proof of their lack of emotional attachment. As "a constant offense to their mistress," the children of these unions suffered greater hardships, according to Douglass, not only because the betrayed mistress "is never better pleased than when she sees [these slaves] under the lash,"[82] but also because the mistress held inordinate power to enact her resentment. "When a slaveholding woman hates, she wants not means to give that hate telling effect."[83] The understandable anger that betrayed wives felt—to say nothing of their disgust and shame at what, to white supremacist sexual norms, could only have appeared to be depraved sexual behavior—made paternal concern rare, if not altogether impossible. Douglass found the predicament of these unfortunate children (a predicament he himself faced) abhorrent, characterizing the peculiar domestic dynamic responsible for this predicament as "shocking" and "scandalous."

Nonetheless, he admitted that selling these children might be a way to economize evil: "Cruel as the deed may strike anyone to be, for a man to sell his own children to human flesh mongers, it is often the dictate of humanity for him to do so."[84] If a master did not sell or brutally beat his slave children, Douglass argues, they could be subject to greater violence at the hands of aggrieved mistresses. Alternatively, the master could assign to his legitimate children the despotic responsibility to execute atrocious violence against his illegitimate children: "He must not only whip them himself, but must stand by and see one white son tie up his brother, of but a few shades darker complexion than himself, and ply the gory lash to his naked back."[85] Watching the spectacle of his legitimate child beating a sibling was not the only horror that confronted licentious masters; a master might witness vicious incest in the form of a legitimate son's sexual violation of a sister or brother. Situating the sale of illegitimate children within an economy of evil, Douglass suggests that selling such children away from the plantation may be more merciful for the children, helping them to avoid greater harm over time. Invoking the "dictate of humanity" to account for these sales, Douglass also suggests that the master's calculation should be evaluated according to the terms of natural law, which purportedly supports the moral choice in favor of a lesser evil to avoid a greater one. Douglass, thus, demonstrates how twisted and ethically unsavory the moral reasoning of masters had become.

In a later autobiography, Douglass returns to the corruption of moral sentiments created by masters' sexual transgressions against enslaved women and to the ethical dilemmas posed by the children born of these unions.

Although the resentment of mistresses continued to play a role in this later account of the mistreatment of the enslaved progeny of the master, Douglass devotes far more attention to the immorality of the offending men. He suggests that the mistreatment of slave children conceived by their masters should be understood in relation to the offending master's guilt. "A man who will enslave his own blood may not be safely relied on for magnanimity. Men do not love those who remind them of their sins—unless they have a mind to repent—and the mulatto child's face is a standing accusation against him who is master and father to the child."[86] In this depiction, the intensity of the master's guilt overwhelms his sense of natural duty, making it impossible for him to love or care for his slave children. Douglass uses the language of sin in this instance to encompass something broader than adultery, suggesting that masters' sexual exploits with slave women violated multiple moral principles and duties. In addition to transgressing the vows of marriage and the natural duties of parents to their children, masters' sexual dalliances with enslaved women violated their commitments to the moral code of mastery, which included the principle that slaves were not quite human. As manifested in the ethical duty to deny slaves literacy, the duties of mastery included a mandate to view slaves as subhuman and to act in accordance with that view.[87]

Fathering children by slave women, whether or not sex was coerced, embodied a perverse form of human recognition. As Douglass pointed out, it was a common assumption that masters often found enslaved women more attractive than their wives, an implicit recognition that female slaves were human beings capable of eliciting the master's desire. Brazen contravention of the doctrine of black subhumanity through practices as various as sexual predation and education threatened to undermine the stability of the slave system. If masters repudiated this central justification for slavery by their own behavior—witnessed by non-slaveholding whites, abolitionists, free blacks, and slaves themselves—then the principled case for slavery would wither from within. The fact that masters continually undermined the principles of the slave system by engaging in such blatantly hypocritical practices might also incite slaves to revolt. Defenders of the doctrine of black subhumanity argued that the safety of the entire community was placed at risk by any recognition of the humanity of blacks. Nonrecognition was a principle of right conduct within a community that required amoral conduct as a condition of its possibility. Sexual relations with slave women that resulted in the birth of children made visible the master's violation of his duties to his wife and legitimate children, his duty to uphold the integrity of the "superior race," and his duty to maintain the stability of the slave system.

The economy of evil that shaped the master's decision to minimize harm by selling his slave children appears to coincide with utilitarian ethics. However, this apparent concurrence is yet another testament to the corrosive effects of the ethics of mastery on the natural capacity to comprehend and comply with natural law. The master's humane gesture was formally correct but substantively evil because it entailed action on a commitment to the code of mastery, which itself violated the precepts of equality and freedom essential to natural law morality. The reciprocal duties that characterized the "ethical relations" among masters were better understood as a compact of mutual protection for the express purpose of corrupting humanity. From the vantage point of natural law, this was a criminal contract that violated the minimal duties humans have toward one another. The fact that the ethics of mastery could so debase the consciences of its proponents provided decisive grounds, according to Douglass, for its unqualified repudiation. The ethics of mastery destroyed the souls of masters as well as the bodies and souls of slaves. It also had pernicious effects on the political imperatives, organizational practices, and civil religion of the American polity.

American Mastery as Political Evil

The corrosive values of mastery were not confined to the population of slave owners. On the contrary, they had permeated the American republic, shaping norms, conceptions of the common good, and behavioral practices of the non-slaveholding population. Wide circulation of the values intrinsic to mastery was crucial in preserving the social stability of the slave system and preventing both open rebellion and everyday forms of resistance. In a slave society, in which a substantial proportion of citizens lacked the resources to own slaves, masters had to devise some means to stave off resentment against their wealth, privilege, and structural advantage and to encourage non-slaveholders to acquiesce to the "slave power."[88] In various slaveholding societies, masters preserved their privilege by making concessions to non-masters, including redistributing wealth generated by slave labor (in Athens and Rome, for example) and extending enhanced civic status to non-slaveholders within the community of masters (in Rome and the United States, for example). According to Douglass, these forms of reconciliation between masters and non-masters demonstrate a political truth about slave societies: The principles of mastery become sovereign among non-masters and masters alike.[89]

On first consideration, it might appear that non-slaveholders would have little sympathy for a political project aimed at producing defective human beings. The gulf between mastery's aim and its accomplishment created an opportunity for those who were not personally invested in mastery to recognize the humanity of enslaved people. As Douglass pointed out, "It is not in the power of human law to make men entirely forget that the slave is a man."[90] Even minimal recognition of this humanity might generate ethical objections to mastery as a legitimate human practice. Douglass suggested that city life produced the contexts that might foster this minimal degree of human recognition of enslaved people. "The general sense of decency that must pervade such a population does much to check and prevent those outbreaks of atrocious cruelty, and those dark crimes without name, almost openly perpetrated on the plantation."[91] Masters tempted to use corporal punishment of their slaves would be compelled to exercise discretion rather than risk the censure of public opinion: "He is a desperate slaveholder who will shock the humanity of his non-slaveholding neighbors by the cries of the lacerated slaves; and very few in the city are willing to incur the odium of being cruel masters."[92]

Such an optimistic assessment of the power of urbanity to restrain the abuses of mastery, however, did not conform to the experiences of slaves in the cities of the South. For example, Douglass relates the story of two such slaves, Henrietta and Mary, two "fragile" young women, ages twenty-two and fourteen, respectively, whose treatment by their master was sufficient "to break a horse" and "crush the spirit of men. . . . Of all the dejected, emaciated, mangled and excoriated creatures I ever saw, these two girls—in the refined, church-going and Christian city of Baltimore—were the most deplorable."[93] Both women, abandoned to the insufficient kindness of neighbors, had been forced to scavenge for food and sometimes had to "contend for offal, with the pigs in the street."[94] Their masters added the insult of corporal punishment to the injury of starvation: Mary's neck and shoulders "were cut to pieces," and her head was regularly "covered over with festering sores, caused by the lash of her cruel mistress."

Most whites who were familiar with Mary and Henrietta's predicament were disturbed and offended by their misfortunes. Notwithstanding the derision behind Mary's nickname "Pecked," a name given by neighborhood boys for "the scars and blotches on her neck, head, and shoulders . . . Mrs. Hamilton's treatment of her slaves was generally condemned, as disgraceful and shocking."[95] The sight of these two mistreated young slave women not only upset non-slaveholders of Baltimore; it also led them to judge Mary and Henrietta's master as a wrongdoer. Yet Douglass notes that this condemnation was not accompanied by action to remedy the wrongdoing. On the contrary, the same persons who condemned Mary and Henrietta's master would also have "condemned and promptly punished any attempt to interfere with their master's right to cut and slash [their] slaves to pieces."[96] Private condemnation of particular practices of masters coexisted, then, with public support for mastery. Whole communities authorized the punishment of anyone who sought to interfere with masters' rights. In the final analysis, Douglass insists, Baltimore's non-slaveholders were defenders of masters' rights rather than mere "fellow travelers." As defenders of masters' rights, they were partisans of the regime of mastery. When forced to choose between the commands of conscience and the rights of mastery, non-slaveholders consented to the sovereignty of masters.

The rights of mastery not only took precedence over the promptings of individual conscience in a slaveholding republic but also corrupted the human competence to discern natural law conveyed to non-slaveholders and masters alike. Non-slaveholders acquiesced to the principle that there must be "no force between the slave and the slaveholder, to restrain the power of the one, and protect the weakness of the other."[97] In so doing, they allowed the rights of mastery to become the normative ground of all other public obligations. The recognition of the master's right of absolute domination was upheld by the Supreme Court in 1857 in *Dred Scott v. Sandford*. Justice Roger B. Taney, author of the majority opinion, asserted, "The only two provisions [of the U.S. Constitution] which point to [blacks] and include them, treat them as property, and make it the duty of the Government to protect it. . . . The Government of the United States [has] no right to interfere for any other purpose but protecting the rights of the owner." Speaking for the Court, Justice Taney insisted that recognizing the rights of free blacks would lead "inevitably" to "discontent and insubordination among [slaves], endangering the peace and safety of the State." Such a course would subvert the Constitution's explicit commitment to upholding the status of mastery and undermine the institution of slavery.[98]

Non-slaveholders may not have had an immediate investment in the project of producing slaves as defective humans, but in custom and in law they were committed to the practical necessity of granting masters unlimited powers to dispose of their slave property as they deemed appropriate. Beyond a respect for property rights, Douglass suggests that this commitment reflected the political insight that taking sides with a slave against a master would put the white community at risk.[99] Repudiation of the right of mastery would open the entire community to the standing grievances of all slaves. To recognize one slave's grievance as legitimate would call the right of absolute domination into question, tacitly legitimating the slaves' right to revolt. Non-slaveholders' tacit acceptance of mastery was indicative of a deeper issue than prudential judgments about order and collective safety, however. It was incontrovertible proof, Douglass argues, that the souls of white Americans had been corrupted by the principles of mastery. Thus, for Douglass, the ethics of mastery had permeated all tiers of the American republic and impaired the capacity of slaveholder and non-slaveholder alike to make correct moral choices. The imperatives of mastery had moved from the master's household to suffuse and demoralize the moral vocabulary, vision, and practice of the whole community. Once entrenched, the immoral foundations of the regime of mastery were enormously difficult to dislodge. "The ties that bind slave holders together are stronger than all other ties."[100] Indeed, Douglass suggested that "once [the human mind] disregards the conviction forced upon it by a revelation of the truth, it requires the exercise of a higher power to produce the same conviction afterwards."[101] Mastery was a mode of evil committed to the degradation and destruction of liberty and conscience, and it was both infectious and contagious.

Prophetic Critique at the Twilight of the New Republic

Over the course of his long life, Frederick Douglass witnessed the long-awaited "jubilee" of emancipation that emerged from the cataclysmic Civil War. He saw his extravagant hopes for the redemption of the United States dashed in 1877, when the federal government terminated its reconstruction policy and returned home rule to the South. After defending his own version of American exceptionalism for half a century against black leaders such as Martin Delaney and Henry Highland Garnett, who were the intellectual heirs of David Walker, the aged ex-slave wrote a letter of praise to Ida B. Wells-Barnett, a young black woman from Mississippi who had just completed "Southern Horrors," her controversial study of American lynching. This courageous and astute analysis of American terrorism seemed to vindicate the political theory of Walker far more than it did that of Douglass.

In his final years, Douglass acknowledged that his political analysis and vision had been flawed in some crucial respects. Although he had once believed that white supremacy was the epiphenomenal dross of mastery that would dissipate after emancipation and concerted governmental effort to secure the rights of freedmen, he lived long enough to see the appallingly short duration of this effort. He saw the growing national fatigue with matters of race and the explosion of national hopes for sectional reconciliation. He lived long enough to witness the political and judicial chicanery that facilitated the emergence of the racial caste system of Jim Crow and the resurgence of racial terror that would accompany it. Near the end of his life, Douglass began to talk about the problem of white supremacy in the same terms that he had used to describe slavery. In his letter to Wells-Barnett, Douglass referred to lynching in language identical to that used to describe his claims concerning the political evil of slavery: "But alas! Even crime has the power to reproduce itself and create conditions favorable to its own existence. It sometimes seems we are deserted by earth and Heaven yet we must still think, speak and work, and trust in the power of a merciful God for final deliverance."[102]

Douglass's final works raised doubt about the adequacy of his explanatory framework. He had argued that the will to mastery constituted the chief foundational evil, producing white supremacy along with other oppressive practices. He had drawn inspiration from the promise of emancipation that doing away with the slave power would put the United States back on track toward achieving the City on the Hill. However, if white supremacy survived the eradication of mastery, then other forces would have to be invoked to explain it. The nature of white supremacy became the focal point of investigation for a new generation of black intellectuals. W.E.B. Du Bois, a young sociologist trained at Harvard and Berlin, took up Douglass's unresolved conundrum. It is to the political theory of this freeborn, Ivy League–trained black scholar that we now turn.

3

Aristocratic Strivings in the Gilded City

The Political Theory of The Souls of Black Folk

Let the ears of a guilty people tingle with truth, and seventy millions sigh for the righteousness which exalteth nations, in this drear day when human brotherhood is a mockery and a snare.[1]

It is, then, the strife of all honorable men of the twentieth century to see that in the future competition of the races the survival of the fittest shall mean the triumph of the good, the beautiful, and the true.[2]

When night falls on the City of a Hundred Hills, a wind gathers itself from the seas and comes murmuring westward. And, at its bidding, the smoke of the drowsy factories sweeps down upon the mighty city and covers it like a pall, while yonder at the University the stars twinkle above Stone Hall.[3]

Veiled behind erudite evocations of Greek myth and Roman monumental history, W.E.B. Du Bois's aristocratic critique of the City on the Hill is so subtle it is easily missed.[4] Formulated in the highly wrought prose of "Of the Wings of Atalanta" and placed within the fifth chapter of *The Souls of Black Folk*, Du Bois's critique seems, at first glance, scarcely more than an exquisitely learned (if not pretentious) sermon against the moral dangers of commercialism for the segregated futures of black and white America. However, a careful reading of this chapter alongside the writings of David Walker and Frederick Douglass reveals Du Bois's deeper and more complex engagement with the political imaginary of the City on the Hill than one would suspect. Beneath the elegant veneer of romantic pictur-esque,[5] Du Bois launches an aristocratic philosophical critique of American oligarchy and lays the groundwork for a thoroughgoing theoretical refor-mulation of the conceptual, social, and political transformations required to revive the political imaginary of the City on the Hill as a compelling politi-cal vision for America.

Du Bois's critique and reformulation of the idea of the City on the Hill is informed and burdened in important ways by the intellectual predilections, gender investments, and class aspirations Du Bois held at this early stage of his intellectual and political development. As is well documented—and as Du Bois later admitted—he had yet to integrate the insights of Karl Marx's critique of political economy or the penetrating insights of Freud's analyses of the subconscious into his political and social theory.[6] Although Du Bois would later develop a sophisticated and hard-hitting critique of patriarchy, the language and conceptual framework that Du Bois employs in *The Souls* betray his deep-seated investments in masculinism.[7] Nonetheless, this early engagement with the political imaginary of the City on the Hill represents a remarkable effort on his part to grapple with four distinctive post-emancipa-tion political realities, new challenges peculiar to his epoch. He contended with the resentment, grief, and exhaustion of white Americans in the after-math of the unprecedented destruction and loss of life during the Civil War.[8] He confronted a deepening chasm of public cynicism regarding the efficacy and legitimacy of state intervention on behalf of blacks, a cynicism caused in part by the heightened visibility of political corruption at the highest levels of government and in part by an equally dispiriting spectacle of corporate pre-dation and greed.[9] He witnessed the ascendance and consolidation of racial extremism in the institutionalization of Jim Crow and the escalation of racial violence, including widespread lynching and urban race riots. Du Bois also contended with the virtual hegemony of Booker T. Washington's politics of appeasement as the appropriate response to these developments.[10]

In addition to the challenges posed by pervasive fatigue, widening pub-lic cynicism, escalating racial terror, and Washingtonian appeasement, Du Bois faced a broader American politics of "reunion." Proponents of reunion practiced a mode of sectional reconciliation premised on the articulation of whiteness as the essential attribute of American national identity and effectively reframed the quest for social justice for freedmen as the "Negro problem."[11] Du Bois's engagement with the City on the Hill is best under-stood, then, as part of a larger theoretical effort to comprehend, explain, and subvert the resurrection of white supremacy and racial violence in the new regime of Jim Crow America.

Athens, Rome, and Atlanta: Rhetoric and Theory in "Of the Wings of Atalanta"

Du Bois's critique of the City on the Hill in "Of the Wings of Atalanta" (hereafter, "Wings") evades easy detection for two principal reasons. First, Du Bois's subtle and complex argument issues from within an ostentatious but genuine quarrel with commercialism. Second, the dense invocation of ancient mythology in "Wings" tends to obscure his trenchant political critique within a form that is itself undertheorized and subaltern. Du Bois deploys two different sets of myths for two very different argumentative purposes in "Wings": the ancient Greek myth of Atalanta and the civic myth of the founding of the Roman republic. Du Bois evokes the myth of Atalanta to frame his thinking about the problem of commercialization, and he uses the legend of the founding of Rome to frame his thinking about the American political imaginary.

Du Bois worried that "the dream of material prosperity" was increasingly becoming the ethico-political norm for the post-Reconstruction South, a norm increasingly embraced by Northerners as well as by Southerners. He also feared that the ascendance of Booker T. Washington's program reflected the embrace of this dream on both sides of the "color line," by whites as well as by blacks. Specifically, he worried that the untroubled facilitation of commerce without regard for (or with willful disregard for) clear evidence of economic exploitation was quickly becoming the "touchstone of success" for those debating the "Negro problem."[12] Independent of any serious consideration of the new structures of exploitation developing between races and classes across the South, most white and some black Americans (North and South) uncritically championed commerce as the answer to the complex problems of black dislocation.[13] Most Americans embraced the quest for wealth as an honorable pursuit and regarded commercial redevelopment as an obvious improvement both to the anachronistic slave economy of the antebellum South and to the postwar economic disorder that replaced it. To disrupt the deep-rooted veneration of commerce and the seemingly indisputable prudence of replacing the old Southern order with modern capitalist institutions and practices, Du Bois sought to identify and help create a constituency that could think critically about commerce as the answer to the South's problems.

Du Bois's meditation on the ancient Greek myth of Atalanta constituted his early attempt to summon and mobilize a cohort that would be drawn to a higher and nobler purpose in life than the mere quest for wealth and that could conceive of racial uplift as such a purpose. The Greek myth of Atalanta tells of a "young maiden who defiles the temple of Love." Having promised to marry the man who could best her in a foot race, her quest for a worthy suitor derails when she is seduced by the golden apples placed in her path by her wily pursuer Hippomenes. Thus distracted, Atalanta loses the race to Hippomenes and is forced to marry him. However, because their bond grew out of Atalanta's lust for gold and Hippomenes's venal manipulation of Atalanta's weakness for shiny metals, it is irrevocably tainted. According to Du Bois, "The blazing passion of their love profaned the sanctuary of love, and they were cursed."[14] By referencing this myth, Du Bois not only probes and problematizes the postwar commercial renaissance underway in Atlanta, Georgia, but also assails the idea that economic growth, improved standards of living, and Southern prosperity could be an adequate answer to the problems bequeathed by slavery.

In 1903, Atlanta was widely regarded as the model city of the "New South" because it seemed to have turned away from antebellum ideals of mastery and toward more enlightened ideals of commerce and industry. Such an optimistic view of Atlanta's enlightenment, however, concealed the truth about the complex history and character of the city. The true source of Atlanta's industry, Du Bois insisted, was the Confederate war machine. From the seeds of war, "the city rose like a widow and cast away her weeds, and toiled for her daily bread; toiled cunningly, perhaps with some bitterness, with a touch of reclamé and yet with real earnestness, and real sweat."[15] The commercial dynamism of Atlanta stemmed not from its recent turn from its past but from its mobilization in support of armed rebellion to protect the rights of mastery. Atlanta's economic revitalization was far more complex, according to Du Bois, than an enlightened choice for modern industrial life over the anachronistic and despotic seigniorialism of the old regime. Although the old forms of American mastery had been shattered by the turn of the century, it was not at all clear to Du Bois that Atlanta's deep commitments to the purposes of mastery fueling the Confederate war machine had been extinguished or replaced. Like Atalanta, the city of Atlanta, Georgia, had once enjoyed a bucolic autonomy, sleeping "dull and drowsy at the foothills of the Alleghenies."[16] In the same way that the "sanctuary" of Atalanta's and Hippomenes's love was profaned by the love of gold, Atlanta's material prosperity had been profaned or corrupted by the city's lust for mastery.

With the myth of Atalanta, Du Bois exposes the ignoble roots beneath Atlanta's New South veneer. However, Du Bois draws on another ancient myth, the myth of the Roman founding, to locate someplace within Atlanta, this symbol of the commercial ethic, to anchor the possibilities of black freedom and national regeneration. Like Atlanta, the city of ancient Rome was founded on crime, a crime motivated, as St. Augustine reminds us, by the lust for mastery.[17] Romulus, the founder of Rome, murdered his brother Remus because he sought to eliminate Remus as a rival for rulership within the new polity. Between the period of its founding and the period of its imperial excesses and ultimate decline, however, Rome exemplified a model of republican political excellence that inspired generations of political thinkers, including the American founders and their African American critics, such as David Walker and W.E.B. Du Bois. Evoking ancient Rome as the city of seven hills, Du Bois christens Atlanta, Georgia, the city of one hundred hills, a city, Du Bois writes, that "stretched long iron ways to meet busy Mercury in his coming."[18] In spite of Atlanta's excesses, Du Bois struggles to invoke the glories of ancient Rome to appeal to what he hopes are the anticommercial sensibilities of his patrician audience. As we shall see, Du Bois shows how the descendants of abolitionists and slaves managed to preserve one of those hills in particular as a space where these old ideas could continue to flourish.

More than mere rhetorical gestures, Du Bois's classical allusions provide a foundation for his political theorizing. In "Wings," Du Bois demonstrates that the pursuit of wealth could not function as "the panacea of all social ills," unable as it was to "overthrow the remains of the slave feudalism" or to address the problem of poor and undereducated whites, whom Du Bois, quoting the derisive language of elite whites, called the "'cracker' Third Estate."[19] Furthermore, the focus on commercialism as panacea masked the toxicity of commercial norms and hid the oppression of beleaguered black communities behind "the veil." Indeed, the nation's failure to acknowledge and confront the structural entrenchment of black impoverishment, the rise and legitimation of neo-slavery under new guises of peonage, crop lien credit, and other fraudulent economic practices, and the political disenfranchisement of blacks through terror and other forms of repression proved to Du Bois that the material well-being of blacks was never a genuine priority of the polity. In contrast to those who uncritically valorized commerce as the solution to black problems and to the larger problem of reconstituting the South, Du Bois appealed to alternative values often associated with the patrician view, values such as a reverence for lineage and a scorn for philistinism. Specifically, he characterized blacks' historic quest for freedom and the abolitionists' quest to end slavery as a noble and glorious political inheritance at risk of dissolution. "Must . . . that fair flower of freedom which, despite the jeers of latter-day striplings, sprung from our father's blood, must that . . . degenerate into a dusty quest for gold—into lawless lust with Hippomenes?"[20] Du Bois entreats his patrician readers not to abandon the blood-soaked and tear-drenched struggle for freedom and justice undertaken by generations of slaves and their descendents.[21] If the pursuit of wealth were allowed to eclipse this "crucial legacy of striving," the nation would abnegate its responsibility to a venerable political tradition and deprive the republic of the spiritual depth it so desperately needs.[22] "The transformation of the fair and far off ideal of freedom into the hard reality of breadwinning and consequent deification of bread" troubled Du Bois deeply.[23]

Du Bois's quarrel with commercialism in "Wings" has political as well as moral roots. "Wealth is [increasingly seen] as the end and aim of politics," as "legal tender for law and order," Du Bois argued, evincing a classical disdain for commercialism. More ominously, in his view, wealth had displaced "Truth, Beauty, and Goodness" as "the ideal of the public school" and had invariably enervated principles of morality and concern for the common good.[24] To mitigate against such consequences, Du Bois insisted that the higher principles of "Truth, Beauty, and Goodness" be inculcated in schools, affirmed and reinforced by law, and lived by citizens through their participation in just political actions.[25] Commercialism's encroachment on these three key spheres of education, law, and politics threatened the very foundations of political life.[26] Commercialism posed a particular threat to the knowledge, freedom, and citizenship claims of freed persons and their descendents.

In offering his critique, Du Bois placed himself in the midst of a long-standing philosophical debate. Classical republican thinkers had stressed the threat that commercial norms posed to the moral and spiritual constitution of a people and to the integrity and character of communal forms and public practices.[27] By contrast, modern defenders of the commercial republic argued that industry and commerce provided a sound foundation for the establishment of a new and distinctively modern polity. Commerce, they insisted, introduced enlightened norms of self-interest to republican political life, thus softening the intrinsic bellicosity and intractable imperial logics endemic to ancient republics. Far from threatening republican political life, commerce provided it with a worthy foundation because it linked the self-interest of individuals to the establishment of domestic political stability and the facilitation of international peace.[28] Seeking to address the problem of slavery and its lingering effects on former slaves, freed persons, and their heirs, Du Bois exceeded the aristocrat's proverbial distaste for illiberal pursuits. In this important theoretical debate about the political implications of commerce, he articulated a perspective that neither classical republican thinkers nor modern defenders of the commercial republic had any reason to consider.[29] Du Bois introduced the novel insight that the political toll of commerce could not be adequately assessed unless the experiences of people who had themselves been objects of commercial exchange were taken into account. Having lived as chattel property and having been excluded from civic protections and liberties that constituted the consensual basis for the "social contract," formerly enslaved persons and their heirs provided a unique lens for evaluating the effects of commerce.[30]

Classical republican writers regarded property as a resource that was morally and politically significant only insofar as it provided a means for the exercise of other virtues, such as liberality, magnanimity, and moderation. The experience of former slaves and their direct heirs revealed the underside of a wealthy master's putative virtues: illiberality rather than liberality, meanness rather than magnanimity, and decadence rather than moderation. With their direct experience of being objects of commerce on domestic and international slave markets, enslaved persons held intimate knowledge about a global system that was anything but enlightened, peaceful, or stable.[31] Moreover, the experiences of blacks after emancipation revealed that the logics undergirding the slave economy persisted into the present. "Even the white laborers," Du Bois maintained, "are not yet intelligent, thrifty, and well trained enough to maintain themselves against the powerful inroads of organized capital. But among the black laborers all this is aggravated, as I have said before, by the wretched economic heritage of slavery. With this training it is difficult for the freedman to learn to grasp the opportunities already opened to him, and the new opportunities are seldom given him, but go by favor to the whites."[32]

Du Bois's view counters conceptions of property that link capital accumulation to pious pursuits that were being put forward by such modern thinkers as Max Weber. In Weber's view, the habits and practices necessary for accumulation resemble (if they do not replicate) religious practices of moral conscientiousness and worldly asceticism, and large-scale accumulation could be interpreted as a sign of divine favor. As former objects of property, freed persons knew intimately that a master's wealth, rather than offering proof of the master's hard work and moral desert or evidence of divine election, testified primarily to the backbreaking labor of his slaves. As Douglass had made clear, mastery often entailed severe bodily violence and deprivation for slaves, forms of exploitation that hardly warranted divine reward. Furthermore, racial barriers to property ownership, many of which assumed similarly violent form, persisted into the Jim Crow era, carrying forward the deprivations of slaves to freed persons and their descendants.[33] According to Du Bois, persons who had been held as property and their descendants could level a powerful critique against elaborate claims connecting market success to divine election, moral conscientiousness, and asceticism.[34]

Du Bois reserved special critical attention for labor policies associated with market freedoms, ideals, and practices that seemed "progressive," especially when compared with enslavement and indentured servitude. Pointing to the inferior quality of products issuing from a system in which laborers have little stake in the process and the unfortunate excesses of violence required to force enslaved persons to submit, theorists who adopted the free market paradigm typically characterized slave labor as an inefficient, unsustainable, and morally costly mode of production.[35] By comparison, they understand the market to be a morally and economically superior system because it appeals to the individual freedom to pursue self-interest, meets the demands of necessity, and guarantees more efficient and productive labor. Motivated by a fear of starvation and a desire for commodious living, workers retain their capacity to choose what kind of work to undertake and are able to discipline themselves.[36] Replacing the individual exercise of mastery with the impersonal operations of the market allows wage laborers to live honorable lives. In short, the market's invisible hand organizes human nature productively and preserves the dignity of workers.

In theory, a worker's experience in slavery should present few challenges to the proponents of the virtues of free labor. Because the formerly enslaved felt their bodily needs in the same way as laborers who had always been free, they would have no alternative but to report for work promptly and punctually if they hoped to survive. Moreover, former slaves should be attracted to the honorable nature of free labor and the prospect of enacting their freedom through work. Free labor theorists, then, should have no problem incorporating blacks into the postbellum economic as equals. However, as Du Bois suggested, there was, from slavery to freedom, far more continuity in modes of economic coercion than proponents of free labor tended to acknowledge.[37] New forms of post-emancipation economic exploitation resembled the old order in important ways, and new forms of terroristic violence were gruesome in ways that may have even exceeded older forms of violence against blacks. While he acknowledged that freed persons would certainly prefer market freedom to slavery, Du Bois was doubtful that the capitalist market would foster the kinds of virtues necessary for black politics. More likely, commercialization of the black world would simply inculcate "petty passions" and "sordid aims," "woo[ing blacks] from a strife for righteousness, from a love of knowing, to regard dollars as the be-all and end-all of life."[38] Commercial values would disseminate egoistic, short-sighted, and nihilistic aims that were incompatible with social reciprocity and the forms of organization required for African American communal uplift.

Du Bois especially emphasized the manifold threats that commercial values posed to public education and advanced a trenchant critique against vocational training as the exclusive paradigm of instruction for black youth. It is tempting, therefore, to read "Wings" solely in relation to Du Bois's repudiation of Booker T. Washington's educational program. However, Du Bois's primary concern was to illuminate the fragile existential predicament of blacks just thirty-eight years removed from slavery and to demonstrate that the commercialization his rival championed would likely exacerbate their intricate problems. Du Bois pointed out that, despite enslavement and marginalization under the old regime and oppression, exploitation, and physical threat under the new order, blacks had managed to devise, cultivate, and sustain communal ideals of moral righteousness and political justice. Although they were often unlettered and outmoded, religious leaders and educators had cautioned against egoistic and anomic behaviors and fostered communal forms that propagated the values of individual integrity and collective security to an oppressed black community. Commercialization threatened these leaders and these values. Where once, according to Du Bois, the "Preacher and Teacher embodied once the ideals of this people, the strife for another and juster world, the vague dream of righteousness, the mystery of knowing; but to-day the danger is that these ideals, with their simple beauty and weird inspiration, will suddenly sink to a question of cash and a lust for gold."[39] Far from promoting virtue in the black community, Du Bois suggested, the spread of commercial values into education, law, and politics would render blacks unfit for American citizenship and for effective moral and political struggle against Jim Crow.

Du Bois's argument in "Wings" builds on a critique made earlier in *Souls* that linked the practices of commercialization to structures of racial articulation and signification.[40] As an authoritative discourse about material prosperity, commercialism tied income and wealth to hard work and merit and thereby legitimized visible leisure as earned reward. It promoted a discursive logic that obscured the historical experiences of blacks (and other nonwhites) who had been consigned to nonremunerative labor and denied the right to profit from their work. The rhetoric of commercialization further supplemented and reinforced the rhetoric of white supremacy. Further, the pursuit

of materialism by blacks was taken by whites as proof that blacks had relin-
quished the quest for higher values and thus demonstrated black unfitness for
citizenship and civilization. Through a peculiar circularity, whites assumed
that blacks who restricted themselves to commercial or vocational endeav-
ors "voluntarily surrender respect, or cease striving for it" and hence "are not
worth civilizing."[41] Du Bois argues, then, that commercialization contributed to a larger process by which "whites shift the burden of the Negro to the
Negroes' shoulders and stand aside as critical and pessimistic spectators."[42]
In this respect, white Americans perceived blacks as a problem people rather
than a people with problems,[43] misattributed responsibility for black problems to blacks, and absolved themselves of culpability for black suffering.

Throughout his work, and particularly in "Wings," Du Bois implores
blacks to rely on the hard-won knowledge they gained at the hands of their
masters, as traded commodities, and as victims of Jim Crow, and to contest the public zeal for their segregation, disenfranchisement, and degradation. Du Bois also sought to alert sympathetic American elites to the nobility
of the souls of black folk and to the deep content of their knowledge of
and investment in U.S. history. However, Du Bois was by no means operating within a vacuum of black leadership on these issues; the public stage
was almost completely occupied by Booker T. Washington, whose commercial ethos and endorsement of racial segregation fit squarely with the nation's sensibilities. In making his case, then, Du Bois had to contend with
Washington's formidable presence and popular message. Du Bois placed
Booker T. Washington's emphasis on vocational training within this system
of racial signification and showed how Washington's emphasis on practical activities and his devaluation of purely intellectual pursuits inadvertently
sustained white supremacist constructions of blacks. By demonstrating that
Washingtonianism, as a strategy of black political leadership, ran contrary to
long-term black political interests, Du Bois was able to put forward his own
political philosophy and identify what he believed to be the proper aims of
black politics.

Republican Politics and the Problem
of Booker T. Washington

Booker T. Washington's political program sought to make blacks indispensable to the economic redevelopment that was underway in the South and
therefore vital to the nation as a whole. As Washington explained in his autobiography, *Up from Slavery*, "I think that the whole future of my race hinges
on the question as to whether or not it can make itself of such indispensable

value that the people in the town and state where we reside will feel that our presence is necessary to the happiness and well-being of the community."[44] In his Atlanta Exposition address, the famous 1895 speech that confirmed his status as the preeminent black leader, Washington urged black and white Southerners to "cast down [their] buckets" where they were and forge an interracial economic and commercial mutuality. Washington insisted that the most urgent political question facing blacks was whether they or European immigrants would profit from this commerce, and he stressed the complementary, if not identical, aims of Southern blacks and whites as they attempted to "progress" upward from the "misfortune" of slavery.[45] "To those of the white race who look to the incoming of those of foreign birth and strange tongue and habits for the prosperity of the South, were I permitted I would repeat what I say to my own race, Cast down your buckets . . . among the eight millions of Negroes whose habits you know, whose fidelity and love you have tested in days when to have proved treacherous meant the ruin of your firesides." This reminder of black trustworthiness (as laborers) was juxtaposed against the questionable loyalties of immigrants,[46] some of whom were suspected of fomenting labor unrest in the North. Blacks had proven their "loyalty to you in the past, in the nursing of your children, watching by the sick-bed of your mothers and fathers, and often following them with tear-dimmed eyes to their graves." Washington insisted, "In the future, in our humble way, we shall stand by you with a devotion that no foreigner can approach."[47]

Although Washington depicted a deep interracial knowledge and intimacy, he was careful not to convey support for social integration. He assured his Atlanta audience of the proper limits governing his vision of interracial mutuality: "In all things that are purely social we can be as separate as the fingers, yet one as the hand in all things essential to human progress."[48] This formulation confirmed the thrust of American law. In the civil rights cases of 1883, the U.S. Supreme Court had ruled that the Civil Rights Act of 1875 was unconstitutional and that Congress lacked the authority under the Fourteenth Amendment to outlaw racial discrimination beyond that perpetrated by state and local governments. With the Supreme Court decision in *Plessy v. Ferguson* (1896), the year after Washington's Atlanta Exposition speech, the permanent segregation of the races became official policy of the American polity.[49] In an important respect, Washington seemed to provide the language for the majority opinion of the court, showing that "separate" could indeed be "equal."

Washington's balancing act of promoting economic mutuality while ensuring social separation required that he find ways to appease white anxieties and confirm white superiority publicly. Washington routinely regaled his white audiences with "darkie jokes" that affirmed whites' perceptions about black incompetence. Presenting himself as an affable and entertaining confidant, he released whites from their disagreeable passions (e.g., fear, shame, rage) by making black struggles literally a laughing matter. Washington did not simply dispute the value of higher education for blacks. He publicly caricatured the very idea of liberal arts university education for the sons and daughters of freed persons. "One of the saddest things I saw," Washington lamented, "was a young man, who attended some high school, sitting down with grease on his clothing, filth around him and weeds in the yard, engaged in studying French grammar."[50] Washington's conspicuously sentimental reminder to Southern whites that blacks were loving and faithful during slavery and the Civil War sought to banish memories of slave resistance and slaves' aid to Union armies, as well as more recent efforts by blacks to exercise and consolidate their political and civil rights during Reconstruction. He congratulated Southern whites above all other white Americans for their effective management of race relations: "Only in the South is the Negro even given a fair chance." Preparing his audience with racial flattery and reassurance, Washington skillfully extracted patronage from white donors.

As surprising and disarming as they were, the claims Washington made absolved whites of any responsibility for rectifying the "Negro problem." Without any hint of irony, Washington acknowledged that racial prejudice was a pitiable misfortune for the racist. He suggested, moreover, that a good deal of Southern hostility toward blacks stemmed from two perfectly understandable causes: the impatient and unreasonable black demands for civic equality and the lingering revulsion of cultured whites at the possibility that they might be coerced by outside forces to embrace black people as intimates.[51] "Ignorant and inexperienced," in the aftermath of what he elsewhere described rather too euphemistically as "the school of slavery," blacks had sought "to beg[in] at the top instead of at the bottom;" they had foolishly believed "that a seat in Congress or the state legislature was more sought than real estate or industrial skill."[52] Washington's speech urged blacks to adopt norms of deference toward Southern whites and to embrace racial apartheid as a legitimate probationary arrangement. Suggesting that blacks had antagonized whites by demanding political equality without establishing their equal desert, Washington implied that blacks were responsible in important respects for the growing racial hostility they faced. To reverse this escalating hostility, Washington counseled blacks to abandon their demands for the right to vote and to acknowledge the deficiencies in their professional skills and cultural competence.[53]

Washington argued that the chief "danger" that blacks faced was not disenfranchisement, repression, or exploitation, nor was it the stirrings of white supremacist violence that would soon congeal into the organized terror of lynching. On the contrary, the singular and most grave threat that blacks faced was the result of their own crude sensualism, unsurprising naiveté, and predictable gullibility. "Our greatest danger is that, in the leap from slavery to freedom, we may overlook the fact that the masses of us are to live by the productions of our hands, and fail to keep in mind that we shall prosper in proportion as we learn to dignify and glorify common labor and put brains and skill into common occupations of life."[54] As persons whose freedom was to be found in the glory of labor, the real dangers that blacks faced, according to Washington, were their own vices of frivolity, pride, and sloth. Frivolity would lead blacks to overvalue vain pursuits and give short shrift to the menial arts; pride would give rise to the exceedingly destructive fantasy of self-importance, a fantasy Christian moralists have always insisted was the fertile ground for all other human failings; and sloth would prevent the development of ingenuity and devalue the significance of labor by encouraging a fantasy of entitlement to ease and comfort. Washington assured his listeners that they need not fear the proliferation of vices in blacks that would be so debilitating to their regional economy.

Having perceived that racial hostilities toward blacks were hardening and gaining new legitimacy throughout the United States, Washington prudently surmised that a strategy of conciliating whites might diffuse the extreme dangers blacks faced as an impoverished and stateless pariah group. Conciliation might also be an effective means of enticing white support for his efforts at institution building.[55] Washington suggested that blacks would be an economic resource only if white elites—business owners, investors, entrepreneurs, and philanthropists—acted their part by supporting the sober and practical program he was attempting to implement through institutions such as Tuskegee.[56] Washington sought to establish the principles of his educational model—self-reliance, thrift, and industriousness—as the normative orientation and public face of black America.[57] By cultivating these skills and competences among blacks at Tuskegee and similar institutions, Washington sought to help create a durable structure of black business and property owners, professionals, and workers to deliver the goods and services that blacks could not count on receiving from whites in a segregated society.

Washington's predecessors, such as Walker and Douglass, and his contemporaries, such as Du Bois and Ida Wells-Barnett, agitated for rights, which were understood as entitlements to official protections and backed up by the collective coercive force of the political community. They demanded that the American polity enforce the protections blacks were entitled to by virtue of their humanity and, after the passage of the Fourteenth Amendment, their citizenship. In a shrewd calculation, Washington neutralized and reframed these demands. "It is important and right that all privileges of law be ours," Washington argued, even though, he maintained, "it is vastly more important that we be prepared for the exercise of these privileges."[58] Seeking to create interracial goodwill favorable to economic interdependence, he carefully construed black rights as "privileges of law" and requested that the polity remain open to grants of special recognition for exceptional blacks at some unspecified future date. Pointing to his own sobriety and impeccable judgment in lifting himself up by his own bootstraps from the dark abjection of the peculiar institution, Washington offered himself as evidence that blacks could improve themselves, learn from their mistakes, and deserve such privileges of law. He deflated the historic claims of equal citizenship for blacks by soliciting a gift that a white American polity might bestow on particular blacks at its own discretion.

In Du Bois's opinion, Washington had done the unthinkable. Unlike Walker, Douglass, or any other black leader at any time in American history, Washington had managed to accomplish the "well-nigh impossible" task of "gaining the sympathy and cooperation of all the various elements that comprised the white South." With this speech, he had managed to become a leader of the South, whose greatness, Du Bois insisted, in all seriousness, was second only to that of Confederate President Jefferson Davis.[59]

Du Bois understood that Washington's Atlanta Exposition speech sought to carve peaceable social space out of escalating racial tension and create economic opportunity within white supremacist structures that were committed to permanent black subordination. He understood that Washington was trying to lay the foundation for gainful black economic activity, which entailed keeping philanthropic money flowing from Northern elites to Tuskegee and similar institutions. He also understood the strategic advantage of Washington's efforts to convince white Americans that blacks would gratefully accept and dutifully perform the menial work that no Americans, other than desperate immigrants of unproven loyalties, would accept. Du Bois acknowledged the sophistication of Washington's statesmanship and paid tribute to Washington's powers of political calculation. "Mr. Washington knew the heart of the South from birth and training. So by singular insight he intuitively grasped the spirit of the age which was dominating the North."[60]

Du Bois also understood and agreed, to some extent, with Washington's insistence that most blacks needed to acquire the market skills and cultural capital requisite for employment, entrepreneurialism, and eventually, ownership—a program that Du Bois maintained was not original. "The free Negroes from 1830 up to wartime had striven to build industrial schools, and the American Missionary Association had from the first taught various trades."[61] In his own time, the most thoughtful educated "blacks advocate with Mr. Washington a broad system of Negro common schools supplemented by thorough industrial training."[62] Far from being opposed to vocational training institutes such as Tuskegee, Du Bois argued for a complementary relationship between industrial educational institutions and the liberal arts colleges and universities he prized. "Teach the workers to work and the thinkers to think; make carpenters of carpenters, philosophers of philosophers, and fops of fools."[63] Du Bois also agreed with Washington's endorsement of property and literacy requirements for voting rights, insisting only that such restrictions ought to apply to all, without respect to race. Du Bois was loath to see "ignorant black men vote when ignorant whites are debarred, or that reasonable restrictions in the sufferance should not be applied."[64]

Ultimately, however, Du Bois's concessions to the Washingtonian position cleared the ground for his devastating and multipronged critique. Du Bois found Washington's coercive power and his capacity to squelch black opposition and criticism especially worrisome and felt that Washington's leadership dishonored the race and posed significant dangers to black political interests and spiritual needs.[65] Washington had claimed, "The wisest among my race understand that agitation of questions of social equality is the extremest folly," particularly for those who were morally and culturally unfit for full rights.[66] In response, Du Bois insisted that most thoughtful blacks would never abandon black freedom, "know[ing] as the nation knows, that relentless color-prejudice is more often a cause than a result of the Negro's degradation."[67]

Du Bois analyzed three contradictions that contributed to a "triple paradox" in Washington's program. First, Washington "insist[ed] on thrift and self-respect, but at the same time counsels a silent submission to civic inferiority such as is bound to sap the manhood of any race in the long run." In other words, Washington's social ethics promoted the very servility they were meant to counter. Second, Washington "advocate[d] common-school and industrial training, and depreciate[d] institutions of higher learning," but, as Du Bois pointed out, "neither the Negro common-schools, nor Tuskegee itself, could remain open a day were it not for teachers trained in Negro colleges, or trained by their graduates." Thus, Washington failed to understand the degree to which his own educational model rested on and required the very kinds of elite education he so publically eschewed. And third, in advocating economic development over political and civil rights, Washington did not understand that political and civil protections were necessary to make property and work secure. In Du Bois's view, advocacy of any one of these contradictory views should cast serious doubt on the quality of Washington's leadership. Advocating all three at once provided indisputable proof of Washington's incompetence and illegitimacy.

To Du Bois, Washington's reawakening of the memory of the trustworthy slave, his surprising defense of white supremacy and black deference, and his deft fabrication of political capital by assuring white audiences that blacks would know their place within the social world amounted to nothing less than self-imposed dishonor. In the antebellum period, free blacks, such as David Walker, had demanded that thoughtful blacks hone their critical skills and refute slaveholders' claims of black inferiority, and Walker labored to counteract the moral effects of slavery by providing models of honor and glory. Fugitive and former slaves, such as Frederick Douglass, had insisted on human dignity under slavery and affirmed the slave's struggle for freedom as the highest expression of America's founding principles. By contrast, Washington offered assurances of black inferiority and sought to institutionalize black submission, thus betraying the very legacy black Americans had to offer to the world.

Washington's failure to discriminate between the best and worst among black students constituted a second unforgivable failure of leadership, in Du Bois's view. If the brightest of black students were provided with only technical training in menial arts, they would be unlikely to progress from the subservient roles assigned to them within a highly competitive and racially stratified political economy. Deprived of the opportunity to pursue edifying and life-affirming work, the best students might easily succumb to nihilistic ways of life. Furthermore, no sound educational strategy for black progress "can rest on any other basis than that of the well-equipped college and university."[68] Du Bois insisted that higher education was foundational for even the most resolutely practical of educations promoted by Washington. In his less restrained 1903 essay, "The Talented Tenth," Du Bois pointed out that, in declaring a liberal arts education to be irrelevant for blacks, Washington disavowed not only the talents of the college-trained blacks he employed as teachers at Tuskegee but also the training of his own Fisk-educated wife, "a woman," Du Bois noted, "who read Virgil and Homer in the same class with me."[69]

The final unpardonable failing of Washingtonianism, according to Du Bois, was that it did not recognize the direct link between black economic prosperity and black civil and political rights. Washington sought to create the conditions for black material prosperity and black property ownership without acknowledging, as Du Bois did, that the security of property depended on legal protection and the willingness of the state to deploy force to uphold it. From the end of Reconstruction to the passage at the Civil Rights Act, roughly 1877 to 1965, blacks had little reason to hope that the polity's force would be exercised on their behalf. Black property could not be secured on the basis of the polity's grudging recognition and enforcement of formal guarantees to protect black lives, property, and liberty alone. If liberty were construed simply as the freedom of blacks from seizure of their property, arbitrary restrictions on their movements, and freedom from violation of their bodies, then economic security would continue to elude them. Du Bois insisted that property accumulation presupposed political liberty as well as civil liberty. "Washington is striving nobly to make Negro artisans business men and property owners; but it is utterly impossible, under modern competitive methods, for workingmen and property owners to defend their rights and exist without the right of suffrage."[70] Even if their chief political good was to amass property, blacks needed the right to advocate for their interests within the corridors of political power as well as the right to represent their interests in the offices of governance. By these means, blacks could adjust the aims and activities of black politics to dynamic historical circumstances. This was true for any legitimate minority interest, Du Bois argued, but it was especially true when the group in question was a permanent, marginalized, and dishonored minority group. Washington's neglect of this critical fact represented, to Du Bois's mind, a monumental failure of political vision.

When he stepped back and surveyed the breadth of Washington's paradoxical commitments—especially his blindness to the inextricable link between economic prosperity and effective political agency—Du Bois concluded that Washington's political incompetence held an ominous, self-serving quality. Washington had orchestrated a consensus around his program among Southern whites and Northern philanthropists. He had masterfully leveraged this consensus to fund Tuskegee and other ventures that met his approval. When Washington managed to extract jobs and other spoils from white elites, he continually distributed them among his lieutenants and other supporters. In these accomplishments, Du Bois perceived Washington to be no less than a demagogue. As the "great malefactor" of black America, Washington was, in the eyes of Du Bois, a despotic political boss who ruled in his own personal interests and effectively silenced those who opposed him. Du Bois warned, "The hushing of the criticism of honest opponents is a dangerous thing. It leads some of the best of the critics to unfortunate silence and paralysis of effort, and others to burst into speech so passionately and intemperately as to lose listeners."[71]

Du Bois and the Talented Tenth

In repudiating Washington's program, Du Bois vowed to be neither silent nor intemperate, and he insisted that his devastating critique represented the views of a new generation of black leaders, a "class of thinking Negroes" who were singularly qualified to represent and steward black interests on behalf of black folk and the American polity as a whole. Situating this group within a larger tradition of black political thought and activism, Du Bois constructed a genealogy of black political response. He traced a line of "adjustment and submission" from "mulatto immigrants from the West Indies" to Washington, whose demagoguery constituted an unprecedented development within this tradition.[72] He traced a line of "revenge and revolt," born out of "the disappointment and impatience of the Negroes at the persistence of slavery and serfdom." As exemplified by Nat Turner, Denmark Vesey, and Gabriel Prosser, this tradition included notorious slave rebellionists and some contemporary black preachers. Du Bois worried that this tradition threatened to become hegemonic for many dislocated black migrants to the North. Dispirited by "harsh competition and color discrimination," and guided by the fiery black religion of Northern black churches, black migrants were, according to Du Bois, "intellectually quickened and awakened." "What wonder," he muses, "that every tendency is to excess—radical complaint, radical remedies, bitter denunciation or angry silence."[73] Finally, Du Bois traced a line of intellectual and spiritual descent from "the great form of Frederick Douglass," who had died in 1895, only months before Washington delivered his Atlanta Compromise, to his own "thinking class of Negroes."

When confronting evils stemming from human sources, such as opinion, convention, custom, and habit, the oppressed respond in one of three ways, corresponding to the three genealogical strands of leadership.[74] They "attempt to adjust and accommodate thought and action to the will of the environing group," they develop desires and tactics for "revenge and revolt," or they set themselves to the task of "self realization within the group, despite the environing group."[75] As members of this last thinking class, Frederick Douglass and his direct descendants offered a tradition of black resistance and a response to slavery and white supremacy grounded in literacy, self-education, and deliberate and principled political engagement. In his previous essay, the "Talented Tenth," Du Bois had created a pantheon of activists, critics, and revolutionaries that blurred the distinction between rebellionists and self-realizers. This move enabled him to isolate the tradition of adjustment and accommodation, barring it, specifically, from inclusion in his "talented tenth" of black leadership, while welcoming the heirs to the other two prominent lineages. Despite different historical contexts and corresponding differences in vision and tactics among the many black political figures, all of them, except the accommodators, according to Du Bois, were exceptional among their peers and, thus, fit to lead.[76]

It is important to note that Du Bois had no deep democratic commitments at this stage of his intellectual development. He held no commitment to the intrinsic value of political participation as a constitutive element of a fully human life. While Du Bois insisted that black voting rights were necessary inasmuch as the "[commission] of its own leaders" would provide blacks with a "peculiarly valuable education," he was not committed to rights of participation as an effective means of redistributing political and social power.[77] As a patrician, he was perfectly comfortable with various voting restrictions, as long as they remained race-neutral. Lacking deep democratic commitments, the early Du Bois nonetheless held firm and unambiguous liberal convictions. That is, like the theorists John Locke and John Stuart Mill, he was committed to a liberal conception of political justice that grounded the legitimacy and fairness of the polity's basic political institutions and practices on a stratified conception of political equality. Criteria for membership in such a polity and the distribution of honors, offices, and protections rested, for him, not on an arbitrary distinction among persons but on a broad set of competences presumed to be attainable by all. By linking political legitimacy and fairness to widely accessible standards of competence, Du Bois attempted to rule out arbitrary exclusions while ensuring that "reasonable exclusions," based on such indicators as age, moral turpitude, education, or property, remained available to the polity. By contrast, unreasonable exclusions, such as religion, philosophical conviction, personal expression, race, and gender, reflected social distinctions deriving from cultural and historical circumstances rather than natural or permanent differences. Ideally, in his view, one's competence for rights to political participation should be based on excellences of mind and character and a sense of civic obligation to the nation as a whole.

Blacks who aspired to leadership roles, Du Bois argued, should possess the character strengths necessary to represent and advocate for black political interests at the highest levels of the American polity. They should constitute a "talented tenth," a special "aristocracy of talent and character."[78] For Du Bois, what distinguished this "thinking class" of persons from everyone else in black America was not primarily their relation to a mode production, their consumption patterns, or their visibility and status within the black community, as has too often been supposed in regard to this formulation.[79] Rather, the defining characteristic of the "talented tenth" was identification with the freedom dreams of slaves and victims of white supremacy, coupled with a passion for a public life.[80] Because Washingtonian accommodators and others who advocated "fainthearted compromise"[81] lacked the means, opportunity, or will to publicly oppose slavery and white supremacy, Du Bois considered them unfit for political leadership. Creating this stark opposition between accommodators and the principled leadership of the "talented tenth," Du Bois proclaimed, "The Negro Race, like all races is going to be saved by its exceptional men."[82]

By contemplating the political acumen and accomplishment of the Wizard of Tuskegee, the Sage of Great Barrington, as Du Bois would come to be known by his admirers, gained an important theoretical insight into the nature of political agency within American political modernity. This insight illuminated a distinctive form of white supremacist republicanism and the kinds of political skill that enabled one to thrive within this peculiar political configuration. Within a white supremacist republic, Du Bois discovered that all distinctions of status and interest ordinarily dividing whites evaporated where the "Negro problem" was concerned. Whites enacted a desire to live unmolested by the Negro problem, to be done with the Negro problem once and for all, and Washington exploited this desire with consummate skill. Because he suggested that blacks were content to remain "in their place," he was richly rewarded with unprecedented influence over whites and virtually unlimited power over blacks. Du Bois's "thinking class of Negroes" sought to disrupt the white supremacist complacency that Washington refused to trouble. "It is wrong," Du Bois wrote, "to encourage a man or a people in evil-doing; it is wrong to aid and abet a national crime simply because it is unpopular not to do so." His "class" of black leadership demanded rights, protections, respect, and the immediate and permanent cessation of racial intimidation. Such a course would require that whites reconceive their supremacist project to create space for black men and women as political and social equals, a ceding of power that whites would be unlikely to undertake lightly or by choice.

Taking up such daunting political objectives in the era of Jim Crow America required of black leaders an impressive strength of character and courage. If national reconciliation "is to be marked by the industrial slavery and civic death of . . . black men, with permanent legislation into a position of inferiority," Du Bois argued, "then those black men, if they are really men, are called upon by every consideration of patriotism and loyalty to oppose such a course by all civilized methods, even though such opposition involves disagreement with Mr. Booker T. Washington."[83] In "Of the Sons of Masters and Man," Du Bois stated the point more forcefully, using the social Darwinist language of his day. His "thinking class of Negroes" held no less than the future of "civilization" in its hands: "It is, then, the strife of all honorable men of the twentieth century to see that in the future competition of the races the survival of the fittest shall mean the triumph of the good, the beautiful, and the true; that we may be able to preserve for future civilization all that is really fine and noble and strong, and not continue to put a premium on greed and impudence and cruelty."[84]

Challenging his peers to take up the Negro problem anew, Du Bois sought to demonstrate a kind of aristocratic nobility, hoping that, by his singular example and masterful grasp of the origins and ends of America, he could awaken a patrician class identity around an alternative resolution of the Negro problem. In an attempt to awaken, consolidate, and mobilize a patrician class identity around high ideals, Du Bois showed his preference for the political vision of the ancients. Unwilling to pander to white supremacy, the very best that this exceedingly talented black man could do was to appeal to his peers and hope they would heed him. In doing so, Du Bois made a special place for the university, the institution where, as a graduate of Fisk, Berlin, and Harvard, and a professor at Atlanta University, he probably felt most comfortable.

The Political Office of the University

In "Wings," Du Bois subtly articulated his aristocratic conception of the political through his analysis of the nature and office of the university within a well-ordered polity and the role of the "genuine scholar." As an aristocrat of the intellect and spirit, Du Bois insisted that the maintenance of a civilized polity's highest ideals (its intellectual achievement, aesthetic standards, and moral foundations) required that the public recognize and support the foundational and, indeed, the sovereign role of the university. It was within the permanent and publicly recognized space of the university that the leading lights of a community crafted the souls of the community's future leaders and played a critical role in the advancement of civilization. As the proliferation of factories, mills, and other commercial ventures in Atlanta made clear to Du Bois, institutions dedicated exclusively to the production of wealth reauthorized a will to mastery and insinuated the philistine spirit and leveling practices of oligarchy into the very foundations of contemporary political culture. He believed that "a withering of the South's ancient university foundations"[85] constituted a monumental obstacle to black cultural and civic development and signaled a larger crisis within the republic itself.

Like many political theorists before him, Du Bois believed that a well-ordered polity was one in which truth and rationality prevailed over ignorance and superstition. The triumph of valid knowledge could be achieved, then, only by ensuring that enlightened leaders were at the helm. Organized around the production and preservation of knowledge, the university was uniquely situated to help guide talented persons toward truth. It also was well positioned to provide leadership for those whose experiences, misfortunes, poor training, or inadequate abilities left them with insufficient powers of comprehension and cognition to lead themselves. Although Du Bois had serious reservations about the meaning of historical progress, he believed that the university must enjoy an esteemed place within the polity so it could fulfill its leadership mission and help maintain optimal constitutional order. Empowering the university in this way constituted a "secret of civilization" essential to the cultivation of character and courage. For Du Bois, then, the university was neither a purely cultural institution operating in the private sphere nor a politically neutral institution operating within civil society. Properly understood, the university was a preeminently political and architectonic institution within the civic life of the community.

"The function of the university," according to Du Bois, "is not simply to teach breadwinning or furnish teachers for the public schools, or to be a centre of polite society; it is above all, to be the organ of that fine adjustment between real life and the growing knowledge of life, an adjustment which forms the secret of civilization."[86] For Du Bois, the term "adjustment" referred to the method by which a polity negotiated internal and external contingencies and the term "organ" indicated the durable structure of purposive human action arising from a polity's organization of "adjustments." As an "organ of fine adjustment," then, the university exercised a political office because it was an institution capable of mediating the many and disorderly individual and group responses to historical contingency. Only the university (as opposed to the church, the family, or even the Constitution) could facilitate the "adjustment" of a direct encounter between the "growing knowledge of life and real life." The scholar's "quest for wisdom" was essential to the successful mediation of various and conflicting experiences of life. Reiterating classic views of the tension between knowledge and opinion, between philosophical wisdom and civic virtue, Du Bois invoked a debate reminiscent of Plato's argument for the rule of philosopher kings. Conceding that the wisdom that reposed in the university was provisional, however, Du Bois implied that the findings, discoveries, or truths guiding a civilized polity's "adjustments" should be open to revision. As Du Bois well understood, the kinds of contingencies a polity might face were legion, encompassing internal and external conflicts pertaining to race, class, and gender; corruption; natural disaster; or enemy attack, for example. By opposing "real life" and the "growing knowledge of life," Du Bois suggested that the intractable tension between the genuine experience of life and the conflicting opinions about life that arise from the diversity of human experiences constituted a permanent source of contingency and posed an elemental and enduring challenge for political life.

In "Of the Dawn of Freedom," another chapter in *Souls*, Du Bois models the function of the university when he grapples with the tensions in the contradictory cultural and spiritual inheritances of masters and slaves. The "growing knowledge" of Southern life that prevailed in the politics of sectional reconciliation hinged on the national public's acknowledgment of the fundamental honor of the Southern "way of life." In the national imaginary, the postbellum plantation was a picturesque place, where happy former slaves—faithful retainers and dutiful mammy figures—and Southern gentlemen coexisted in mutual harmony, each certain of his or her "place." Booker T. Washington happily accommodated this public knowledge by effacing the violence of American mastery, domesticating the injuries slaves had suffered in slavery, and abetting the rehabilitation of mastery that was occurring within U.S. culture under the auspices of sectional reconciliation. Washington's assurances to whites that freed blacks would be content to inhabit separate social worlds effectively formalized and raised the stakes of Douglass's privatization of some of the most unseemly traumas of slavery, especially the traumas that enslaved women incurred when sexually violated by their masters. Seeking to subvert Washington's accommodation, recover the traumas of slavery from the black private sphere, and convert them into serviceable categories for political mobilization, Du Bois stages the various central conflicts on the postbellum plantation, specifically, the moral, spiritual, and political confrontation between an archetypal freedwoman and her former master.

Deploying the figure of this violated ex-slave woman as a symbol of the inheritance of slavery, Du Bois explains, She is "a form hovering, dark, and mother-like, her awful face black with mists of centuries." Of this woman's violation, Du Bois continues, "She had aforetime quailed at [the] master's commands, had bent in love over the cradles of his sons, and closed in death the sunken eyes of his wife—aye, too, at his behest had laid herself low to his lust, and borne a tawny man-child to the world, only to see her dark boy's limbs scattered to the winds by midnight marauders riding after 'damned Niggers.'"[87] Du Bois's depiction of this formerly enslaved woman recovers the trauma of her sexual violation from the obfuscation of Douglass and Washington and the disavowal of Northern and Southern whites. In contrast to Douglass's intimations, which stopped short of explanation, and

Washington's deafening silence, Du Bois's words provide a depiction of rape that is artfully subtle, but nonetheless clear. The woman "laid herself low [to her master's] lust." However, her submission is forced, and she submits from fear, "quail[ing] at her master's commands." Moreover, even if sentimental and somewhat strained, Du Bois's depiction of the violated ex-slave woman portrays an agent who is capable of exercising moral discernment. Outwardly, she performs the duties of the loving mammy, but internally, she seethes with a hatred that follows her to her grave. Nonetheless, her ability to care for her master's children and show due regard for the master's dead wife reveals a capacity for distinguishing perpetrators from bystanders and innocents.[88]

By contrast, Du Bois artfully subverts the image of mastery by depicting this woman's violator as a failed patriarch. This former master is a "grey haired gentleman, whose fathers had quitted themselves as men, whose sons lay in nameless graves; who bowed to the evil of slavery because its abolition threatened untold ill to all; who stood at last, in the evening of life, a blighted, ruined form, with hate in his eyes."[89] Although Du Bois may go too far in bestowing honor on this failed patriarch (and perhaps even expose the excesses to which his aristocratic commitments led him), Du Bois subtly recasts the will of "the grey haired gentleman" from prideful self-assertion to slavish submission, thereby undermining the rehabilitation of mastery that was occurring within American political culture. In the same way that the enslaved woman quails in fear at the commands of her master, Du Bois suggests, the "grey haired gentleman bows to the evil of slavery." In contrast to the enslaved woman, who exercises moral discernment, her former master remains incapable of either acting or judging. Fearing that abolition of "the evil of slavery" will result "in untold ill," the "grey haired gentleman" simply defends the status quo of a decaying and corrupt way of life, thus failing to live up to the model of the Southern gentleman so prevalent in contemporary political discourse. Like the ex-slave woman who cannot protect herself or her son from the ensuing racial terror, the "grey haired gentleman" is not able to live up to the patriarchal ideals of his anachronistic fathers or to protect his white sons from the fate of their decadence.

By deploying these two figures, Du Bois has succeeded in his vocation of the genuine scholar. He facilitates a powerful "adjustment" between his understanding of black persons' experience of life and the growing body of public knowledge regarding that experience so central to the political imperative of national reconciliation. Some scholars have argued that this depiction of the enslaved woman's experience reveals Du Bois's investment in patriarchy.[90] Understanding the sexual agency of enslaved women to be a fraught and complex notion, particularly for those who are forced to make compromised choices for the sake of their relative well-being and that of their children, I do not charge him with so drastic a crime in this important passage.[91] However, I do suggest that, in the process of making her experience available as a "figure" to the genuine scholar, Du Bois, to some extent, sublimates the vulnerability and violation of enslaved women, making the experience something other than the harsh reality that it was. This process of sublimation might be considered a further violation of the humanity of enslaved women. Nonetheless, his sublimation of these two figures forces deeply submerged truths to the forefront of public discussion, where they could meet and do battle with Washington's and others' representations of the legacy of slavery and of contemporary black life.

Rather than focusing on the old Platonic question concerning which members of the polity knew the venerable truths, entitling them to rule, Du Bois raised different questions illuminated so brilliantly by his depiction of the hateful aged ex-slave woman. What happens, Du Bois wondered, when the polity's most esteemed truths are no longer believable to particular segments of the nonphilosophical populace? What happens to the nonphilosophical populace when they grow certain of the untruth of the polity's philosophical certainties? What happens within the souls of persons who are in, but not of, the polity when their own bitter experience reveals the true character of the polity? As Du Bois notes, "Of nine millions of the Negroes in this nation, there is scarcely one out of the cradle to whom these arguments do not daily present themselves in the guise of terrible truth."[92] Capturing the poignant epistemic situation of black Americans, these questions had important implications for the linked fates of blacks and whites in Jim Crow America.

"Even today," Du Bois wrote, "the masses of the Negroes see all too clearly the anomalies of their position and the moral crookedness of yours. You may marshal strong indictments against them, but their counter-cries, lacking though they be in formal logic, have burning truths within them which you may not wholly ignore."[93] If Southern commercialization was simply the most recent incarnation of the will to mastery, as Du Bois suggested, and Southern blacks understood this with the undeniable certainty born of their own bitter experience, then how were they to live with that knowledge? In Du Bois's view, blacks possessed philosophical, but unaccredited, insight into the nature of America. In spite of the lack of institutional accreditation afforded these insights, Du Bois sought to preserve and disseminate them. He sought to prevent blacks from succumbing to deep and dispiriting nihilism in the face of an intransigent racist majority. How, he asked, might they avoid having their knowledge manipulated by demagogic leadership that sought to divert them toward futile and demoralizing ventures? Who among us, he queried, possesses a sufficient degree of nobility and greatness of soul to assume responsibility for our fundamentally American problem?[94] Evoking the Biblical story of Ezekiel, Du Bois summons his talented tenth: "Today the ferment of [black] striving toward self-realization is to the whole world like a wheel within a wheel. . . . Few know of these problems; few who know notice them; and yet there they are, awaiting student, artist, and seer—a field for somebody to consider sometime." He asks his patrician readers and his thinking class of black leadership: What, if anything, can be done to redeem, revise, or re-enchant black people's profound and unsettling insights into the heart of American darkness?

The Aristocratic Strivings of the "Genuine Scholar"

Through the example of his own political intervention in *The Souls of Black Folk*, Du Bois suggested that the "genuine scholar," the figure who truly understood the civic dimension of an intellectual's vocation, would treat the tenuous and provisional character of this knowledge as a real and weighty responsibility. Du Bois realized that it would be futile and foolhardy for any modern polity to attempt to prevent or root out skepticism from among its citizenry. As he noted, "The price of culture is a Lie."[95] Nonetheless, Du Bois also believed that, through prudent leadership, a polity might be able to forestall the onset of widespread public cynicism and political nihilism. The university and the public intellectual had key roles to play in such an endeavor. If the polity could maintain a public conviction that the university is, and must forever be, the sovereign "organ of adjustment" for the society as a whole, then genuine scholars could impart to future leaders new visions that might reanimate a new conviction among the citizenry about the origin and ultimate purposes of the polity. The privileged status of the university within the constitutional order was the necessary condition of the genuine scholar's ability to devise real solutions to difficult political problems. Even though a scholar's wisdom might be tenuous, an intellectual and cultural elite must be empowered to think, study, and solve social and political problems. Backed by institutional power, the "genuine scholar" might impress his or her wisdom, provisional though it might be, on those who would be leaders in and of the community.

Privileging the university within the polity, however, did not completely address the vexing issues associated with the enterprise of political education itself, especially in relation to the political education of blacks. Given the acuity of black insights into the oppressive nature of white supremacy, Du

Bois did not expect this knowledge to fare well in an educational encounter in elite white universities committed, in important respects, to upholding a Jim Crow status quo. Nor, under the helm of leaders such as Washington, would this knowledge necessarily function effectively within black educational institutions. As a partisan of aristocracy, Du Bois advanced claims about the ends power should serve as well as a vision of how a well-ordered polity might conserve its power through paying attention to its educational practices.[96] This vision was far from naïve. With full knowledge of the oppressive aspects of elite white universities, Du Bois nonetheless repeatedly claimed that the role of the university was to mediate and broker the instability arising from the contingent and revisable foundations of civilization. At this early point in his career, he was persuaded that concentrating effective political power in a restricted number of the most capable hands was essential to addressing the massive problem of white supremacy. Du Bois meant what he said when he claimed, at the age of thirty-five, that "civilization would be saved by its exceptional men."

Du Bois worked out some of the implications of his views in his analysis of the unique role of Harvard University as the "first flower of our wilderness."[97] Du Bois understood Harvard, not as the crown jewel of the American system of education, but as the seed bed of the constitutional ordering of the American polity. As an exemplar of "progress in human affairs," which Du Bois described as "more often a pull than a push, surging forward of the exceptional man, and lifting of his duller brethren slowly and painfully to his vantage-ground," Harvard birthed, cultivated, and certified a genteel and principled leadership class whose political and cultural priorities included, among other things, the establishment and administration of lower-level institutions of primary and secondary education. Harvard (with similar institutions, presumably) was the "first flower of our wilderness" because it was the first thing of lasting and generative beauty to emerge from American soil. The substance of this beauty was, for Du Bois, the way the institution facilitated the discovery, rediscovery, and acquisition of high ideals, established them as priorities for the polity, and formed the class of persons who had the desire and ability to implement these priorities within the polity. In other words, the beauty of Harvard lay in its normative fecundity, spiritual efficacy, and institutional sovereignty. When the university is viewed as a social and political force operating with and against other social and political forces, such as the church or political party, for example, its politically constitutive properties come into stark relief.[98]

Beneath this generative seed bed, however, lay the Puritan vision for and practices concerning New World space and peoples, practices that were inseparable from a subterranean and constitutive configuration of violence, religiosity, and conquest. Grounded in the Puritan appropriation of New World space as the fulfillment of their covenant with God to establish a model Christian polity, Harvard was an imperfect beacon. The Puritans' New World politics of historical redemption was coterminous with the systemic displacement, disruption, and destruction of indigenous peoples of North America and Africa. From the standpoint of the dispossessed, the ignoble prehistory of Harvard and similar institutions may well have been unredeemable; nonetheless, Du Bois attempted to salvage the institution's potential as a moral, aesthetic, and political resource from this compromised foundation.

Harvard's prehistory might be viewed as a productive constitutive imperfection, a fraught and potentially unsettling philosophical truth about a polity's ignoble origins that, when theoretically grasped and prudently formulated by a wise statesman, might be pressed into the service of salutary public purposes. Harvard symbolized a common heritage, unequally borne by different persons, from which imperfect political institutions emerged. This unique heritage enabled heirs to recognize one another as members of a common—although not identical—enterprise. It engendered a distinctive spirit and trajectory of striving and laid the foundation for collective deliberation over how to address the complex mix of burdens and blessings that flowed from this complicated yet constitutive inheritance. For Du Bois, past evils could become productive constitutive imperfections if there were persons capable of grappling with such fraught questions, extracting their lessons, and embedding those insights into the institutional structure of the community.

Within this frame, Du Bois's notion of Harvard's achievement as an architectonic institution of higher learning lay in its prowess in soulcraft, a prowess developed over time and fully revisable. From ignoble beginnings, Harvard had become a durable institution committed to the discovery and transmission of high ideals that would inform the polity in useful and occasionally sublime ways. By crafting the souls of students and inculcating moral values, Harvard had produced leaders whose moral vision exceeded its own. These leaders had insisted that basic literacy for all free persons was necessary for the polity and had then used their talents to create the schools that would teach these skills. It should be noted as well that, in Du Bois himself, Harvard had cultivated the mind of a political philosopher who would challenge America's most basic assumptions by illuminating the dynamics of a white supremacist republic.

Du Bois's aristocratic conception of the nature and value of the university as a political institution was intimately connected with his understanding of higher education as enculturation. "The riddle of existence is the college curriculum that was laid before the Pharaohs, that was taught in the groves by Plato, that formed the *trivium* and *quadrivium*, and is today laid before the freedmen's sons by Atlanta University . . . but the true college will ever have one goal—not to earn meat, but to know the end and aim of that life which meat nourishes."[99] The university's unique mission required that it identify those whose gifts of intellect and character qualified them for the highest intellectual and moral cultivation. Focusing on the "thinking class," the university's principal activity was crafting the souls of qualified youth for cultural and political leadership. No other institution within the constitutional order of the American polity was equipped to perform the political functions of recruiting and crafting moral leadership as effectively as the university.

In advancing this claim, Du Bois acknowledged that the educational enterprise resembled a kind of benevolent imperialism. As his account of the founding black colleges makes clear, institution building, as with soulcrafting, was fraught with complex power relations. Originally, black colleges had been conceived as "social settlements," "homes" where the "best of the sons of the freedman came into close and sympathetic touch with the best traditions of New England."[100] Although Northern activists had acted out of a sense of philanthropy, to be sure, the creation of black colleges had also been fueled by a quest to extend and consolidate Northern political power. Through the establishment of black university education, Northerners had literally founded colonies across the South with complex evocations of foreign expeditions, annexations, conquests, and displacements. Du Bois was circumspect in his account of the founding of these institutions and, no doubt, keenly aware of the perils facing any black writer of the period who openly advocated that Northern white men colonize the South.[101] Additionally, Du Bois was under no illusions about what was required of sovereignty, even the sovereignty of the university. The relationship between the political education of blacks and the exercise of force was bound up with a prior Northern project to remake the South by "re-forming" blacks.

With a full grasp of these complex power dynamics, Du Bois maintained that the ultimate purpose of black university training was "to furnish the black world with adequate standards of human culture and lofty ideals of life."[102] Du Bois's vision of these standards and ideals raises compelling questions. How, specifically, would a people whose daily experience debunked the pretensions of America's purported commitment to equality, liberty, and the pursuit of happiness respond to social elites' efforts to impose these lofty ideals on them? At the epistemic level, would the project of "reforming" blacks within black colleges and universities involve revision, re-enchantment, or redemption?

For Du Bois, revising black people's experiential knowledge was out of the question because the knowledge they possessed about America was true. Any attempt to redeem black suffering was, to him, also morally problematic because it involved a utilitarian calculus that weighed the evils blacks had suffered at the hands of the American republic against some putative good.[103] Even if this "good" were cast in terms of the systemic transformation of America so that equality and freedom were realized for all citizens, it was not at all clear that such a good could offset the trauma of enslavement, dispossession, and dehumanization suffered by blacks in the past. Moreover, as Du Bois so cogently argued, the current climate gave no evidence that America was moving closer to the attainment of this good. Indeed, the empirical indicators suggested that, for blacks, liberty, equality, and property would continue to remain elusive. Adopting a program of re-enchantment, however, was more promising. This project required only the crafting of a new vision of American purposes that rendered black suffering intelligible. A new vision might succeed in re-enchanting American blacks if it enabled real opportunities for individual growth and communal prosperity. With this kind of project in mind, Du Bois argued that the contemporary goal of black university education was to train "Negro leaders of character and intelligence—men [and women] of skill, men [and women] of light and leading, college bred men [and women], black captains of industry, and missionaries of culture; men [and women] who thoroughly comprehend and know modern civilization, and can take hold of Negro communities and raise and train them by force of precept and example, deep sympathy, and the inspiration of common blood and ideals."[104]

After receiving this training within black colleges and universities, "broadminded, cultured men and women" were "to scatter civilization among a people whose ignorance was not simply of letters, but of life itself."[105] Here, his formulation, "ignorance of life itself," did not refer to black people's lack of knowledge about the moral poverty of the American political self-understanding, a knowledge that Du Bois believed black people possessed in abundance. As Du Bois suggested in his concluding chapter, the "Sorrow Songs" displayed a profound worldly wisdom possessed by slaves regarding questions of justice and human aspiration that rivaled that of "cultured peoples" of the world.[106] The critical ignorance that black collegians needed to dispel was ignorance about what to do with this toxic and potentially dangerous truth.[107] How should blacks comport themselves in light of this knowledge? Should they tell the truth in a world clearly built on lies? Should they restrain their passions when extravagant displays of passion (often against them or their loved ones) seemed to be perfectly legitimate for their oppressors? Should blacks bother to exert effort if the world expected little of them and took much from them without appreciation? These are the kinds of questions that a clear-sighted understanding of the black predicament elicited. The project of "scattering civilization" to dispel what Du Bois infelicitously described as "ignorance of life" would empower the sons, daughters, and grandchildren of ex-slaves to articulate and address such questions. For Du Bois, the project of black re-enchantment was intricately tied to the project of remaking America. Both projects required training talented persons, a black American aristocracy who would infuse new passion into an enlarged vision of American aims that accounted for black knowledge and who would act collectively to create a world in which ordinary black folk might fully realize their freedom dreams.

Du Bois, Demagogues, and American Aristocratic Sensibilities

Du Bois's political thought was aristocratic in another sense firmly rooted in the American political tradition. In characterizing Atlanta, Georgia, as the "city of one hundred hills," Du Bois pressed Roman monumental history into the service of a tradition of political theorizing that encompassed the Puritan roots of the American founders and the constitutional arguments of James Madison, Alexander Hamilton, and John Jay that were published in the *Federalist Papers* under the name of "Publius," the legendary defender of the Roman republic. Focusing on Atlanta, a bustling and industrializing community intent on becoming the model city of the New South, Du Bois used a long tradition of aristocratic civic republicanism to critique the American oligarchy. Du Bois sought to demonstrate that the oligarchy burgeoning in Atlanta was incompatible with a conception of a just political community in which the principal aim was to secure the common good of all of its members. Conceiving of the common good in terms of freedom from domination, Du Bois attempted to trace the manifold modes of domination perpetuated by the unfettered pursuit of wealth.[108] He objected to oligarchy, but not because it signified rule by the wealthy few. As a proponent of aristocracy, the early Du Bois, in fact, advocated political rule and cultural hegemony by a polity's best citizens as the most secure foundation for realizing the common good. Hence, he objected to oligarchy precisely because he found it incapable of promoting the common good.

Similar to the view expressed by Publius—polemicist for the new American Constitution and theorist of its distinctively New World republicanism—Du Bois's political thought in *The Souls* is saturated with anxiety about the rise of demagogic elites.[109] Publius expressed this worry as early as *Federalist 1*, where Hamilton warned of the permanent threat posed by the soaring ambitions of designing elites. Later, and more subtly, Madison, in *Federalist 10*, diagnosed the demagogic manipulation of working-class resentment as the principal and most troublesome cause of tyranny of the majority— the intractable evil endemic to republican politics. In Madison's view, natural inequality of talent and virtue was responsible for inequalities of property and social standing among citizens. However, the tendency to form factions, "sown into the nature of man," could be easily manipulated by designing and ambitious elites. If these elites were to stoke irrational resentments among laboring and poor citizens, then they would permanently imperil property, talent, and the republican political enterprise as a whole.[110] Du Bois shared the worries expressed by Publius about a tyranny of the majority. However, for him, elite manipulation of the masses was not the exclusive form that this particular problem took within the American polity. Rather, the principal form of tyranny of the majority resulted from the calm, deliberate, and normal operations of the principle and practice of white supremacy. In fact, it was precisely because of white supremacy that Du Bois worried deeply about demagogues throughout *Souls*, most notably in his critique of Washington, whose accommodationist politics sustained white supremacy, and whose demagoguery helped to popularize it.[111]

Du Bois registered a similar worry in his analysis of the office and powers of the black preacher—"the most unique personality developed by the Negro on American soil." As Du Bois explained, the black preacher was "a leader, politician, orator, 'boss,' intriguer, and idealist" because he presided over the black church, the "social center" and "conserver of morals," whose institutions had effectively become "governments of men." Du Bois acknowledged that the powers that derived from communal exigencies under slavery and continued after emancipation authorized and legitimated the office of the black preacher as the effective "centre of a group of men, now twenty, now a thousand in number." He worried that the office of the preacher could easily be pressed into the service of irresponsible and demagogic misrule. He also worried that black preachers might provide misguided moral advice and spiritual aid to the people, displacing more talented persons who were better qualified to exercise political and cultural leadership. One of the subtler political arguments that Du Bois made in *Souls* involved his analysis of the black church. He argued that university training must be made available to qualified black students because there was a clear and pressing need to inject competence, intellect, and moderation into the office of the black preacher. Yet he also noted that there was an equally pressing need to nurture and legitimate secular and enlightened leadership for the future—a leadership whose academic training might trump the black preacher's cultural and historical prestige and whose intellectual accomplishment, quality of vision, and administrative talent might ultimately displace the black preacher's authority.

Du Bois articulates his anxieties about the demagogic potential of the black clergy in "Of the Faith of the Fathers." He provides a fictionalized account of the problem of miseducation in his chapter, "Of the Coming of John," emphasizing the problems that arise when the best-educated youth are not the most promising. Du Bois's clearest statement of his worries about the rise of demagogues, however, appears in "Of the Training of Black Men." In this essay, Du Bois argues that the rise of demagogues in black America would be the clear and inevitable result of America's continuing failure to provide university education to the most promising black youth: "By taking away their best equipped teachers and leaders, by slamming the door of opportunity in the faces of their bolder and brighter minds, will you make them satisfied with their lot? Or will you not rather transfer their leading from the hands of men taught to think to the hands of untrained demagogues?"[112]

Both Du Bois and Publius elevated their concerns about demagogues to the status of an endemic, perennial, and urgent threat to republican politics. By this sleight of hand, they reified American aristocratic sensibilities and anxieties as nonpartisan civic knowledge.[113] In a polity that legitimated itself by claiming to locate sovereignty in the people, they instilled a public concern about popular abuse of political power to prevent the rise of demagogues from the ranks of ordinary persons. Citizens, they suggested, should be educated to scrutinize themselves and others for any sign of soaring political ambition. The problem, however, is that this kind of political education will not be very helpful in preventing the rise of oligarchic elites because ambition among this class is seen as normal and their superior wealth and resources allow them to dress their political ambition in the finery of competence and duty. Educated to exercise vigilance against demagogues rather than against class domination or hegemony, sovereign citizens would be unlikely to recognize the sustained exercise of inordinate power by an oligarchy until it was too late. As Plato pointed out, and as Du Bois warned in his astute analysis of the commercialization of Atlanta, oligarchs might cast themselves as the people's benefactor, seizing and monopolizing political power with popular support. Indeed, Alexis de Tocqueville had warned of those economic elites who might one day arise from within the heart of American liberal democracy, noting that if such a class were to acquire political rule, they might very well turn out to be the most heartless elite ever known to Western history.[114] By privileging the problem of demagoguery, Publius, Du Bois, and others inscribe their aristocratic priorities and anxieties on the polity, eliding problems of elite rule by encomiums to popular sovereignty.

The great irony of this particular formulation was also noted by Tocqueville, who pointed out that American liberal democracy imbued its citizens with the belief in popular sovereignty, even as it vindicated rule by a small elite. Most Americans were not and would never become political or economic elites. Without power to initiate political change as individual political actors, citizens of an American liberal democracy were not sovereign in any meaningful sense. By privileging the danger of demagogues as the political *sumum malum* of popular government, or naturalizing it as the unavoidable corollary of republican politics, Du Bois and Publius supplant the question of effective popular sovereignty within liberal democratic political institutions with concerns about how to prevent ordinary citizens from abusing their purported sovereignty. Rather than politicizing the very real difficulties concerning the effective power of ordinary citizens to pursue collective objectives, they give priority to the problem of how to ensure that the right kind of elites exercise political power.[115] Whether its source is Publius or Du Bois, this priority reflects aristocratic rather than democratic concerns.

Where Publius promoted elite rule by incorporating representative governance within the U.S. Constitution, Du Bois charged American universities with the responsibility of "sending into the life of the South a few white men and a few black men of broad culture, catholic tolerance, and trained ability, joining their hands to other hands, and giving to this squabble of Races a decent and dignified peace."[116] Publius warned that American citizens must be ever-vigilant against a class of men whose "dangerous ambition more often lurked behind the specious mask of zeal for the rights of people than under the forbidden appearance of zeal for the firmness and efficiency of government." This class of men with this "specious zeal," Publius warned, has "overturned the liberties of republics." "Beginning their careers as demagogues," they have ended them as tyrants. Similarly, a crucial part of Du Bois's project was to identify the conditions of possibility for black demagogues, to popularize a fear of them, and to enlist white support for the creation and maintenance of institutional structures capable of minimizing their harm.

Explaining the complexity of "the souls of black folk" to an audience trained to think of blacks as simple, if disruptive, aliens within the American polity, Du Bois repeatedly warned of the growing inclination of many blacks toward revolt and revenge. He also warned of the institutional supports provided to this angry black class by a black church that was not yet accountable to responsible black leadership. Du Bois warned that, because America did not know its black residents and remained blithely unaware of the complex internal strife that besets the spiritual life of black America's greater souls, it would be unable to conceive of black demagogues or to discern the implications of their rise. By articulating the dangers of black demagoguery, Du Bois attempted to come to the aid of Publius, even though he proffered a partnership on behalf of those whom Publius would more likely have considered troublesome wards than possible partners in the aristocratic governance of America.

Du Bois's Jeremiad

Du Bois solicited a partnership with Publius by clothing his reformulation of the City on the Hill in the Roman dress that Hamilton, Madison, and Jay donned when they defended the new U.S. Constitution under the pen name of a legendary defender of the Roman republic. Du Bois insisted on one final layer of subtlety in his critical re-presentation of the political imaginary of the City on the Hill. Rather than advancing a frontal attack on the glaring inconsistency between American pretension and practice, as Walker had, or casting this wickedness as the sinful, but remediable, incompletion of true American constitutional purposes, as Douglass had, Du Bois deliberately infused the idea of America as a City on the Hill with layers of irony, conveying the impression that the idea itself was silly and untenable from the very start. "Atlanta is the city of one hundred hills," Du Bois suggested, not a single city on a particular hill, or even a single part of a larger political unity set apart from others by virtue of its elevated location. With this depiction of a city built on multiple hills, Du Bois seems keener to subvert than to reconjure the idea of the City on the Hill as a plausible image for thoughtful and clear-sighted reflection. If there are one hundred hills in Atlanta, after all, which one could claim to be exemplary? Indeed, if Atlanta were simply one of many cities within the American polity, then why speak of America as though it exhibited some kind of exemplary unity? At first glance, then, Du

Bois's depiction suggests that, far from the idyllic City on the Hill, America comprised many cities that were themselves composed of many hills. Like Atlanta, much of America had devoted itself to vulgar commercialism and bellicose barbarism and, thus, presented no moral or political example to the rest of the world.

Du Bois's subversion is only partial, however. Although he criticizes Atlanta for its multiplicity of hills, whose peaks were blighted by ugly monuments to industrialization and commerce, he also points out that "the hundred hills of Atlanta are not all crowned with factories."[117] On one hill in particular, "the setting sun throws three buildings in bold relief against the sky." Within these three buildings, "students gather to follow the love song of Dido," and "listen to the tale of Troy divine." They gather to "wander among stars" and, indeed, to "wander among men and nations."[118] These three buildings were none other than Atlanta University, one of the oldest and most respected liberal arts colleges established by abolitionists to educate freed persons.[119] Linking black university education to the architectonic political purposes of the New England aristocracy, Du Bois proposed the soulcraft occurring within the walls of the university as the singularly appropriate means for re-enchanting the potentially soul-destroying but true knowledge that blacks had acquired about America. By endorsing the project of cultivating an "aristocracy of talent and character" among blacks, Du Bois suggested that Atlanta University would contribute to the formation of those who would supervise and superintend a political and social regeneration of black America consistent with an enlarged and ennobled conception of American purposes.

Du Bois's "Wings," then, was a jeremiad that offered a prophetic social critique of the failure of America's patrician class to keep faith with the noble purposes claimed, but not achieved, by successive generations of Americans. His prophetic warning was twofold: First, he cautioned that the continued failure of Americans to live up to these purposes would result in the rise of demagogic figures in black America who, in time, might mobilize them to take up arms against America. Furthermore, Du Bois argued, the rights that whites enjoyed under the white supremacist republic had deteriorated into demoralizing and publicly dispiriting license, and the failure of American patricians to recognize and remedy this problem would ultimately discredit American authority and legitimacy.

Later in his long life, Du Bois would abandon this aristocratic political project, having come to see the utter inadequacy of the aristocratic mobilization of American patricians as a means of achieving social justice for blacks. He would subsequently argue that an aristocratic conception of the political incorporated a profoundly naïve conception of the class dimension of black subordination. Furthermore, according to later work by Du Bois, this conception was wholly incapable of addressing the subrational foundations of white supremacy shared by all classes of white Americans. What Du Bois never admitted about the limits of his early political theory, however, was the irony that he had advocated an aristocratic politics at the precise historical moment that American patrician elites turned from aristocracy to oligarchy. Both Du Bois and the exemplary patrician Henry Adams, a scion of John Quincy Adams and John Adams, lamented—albeit from behind very different veils—the rise of the oligarchs who capitalized on technological innovation and inaugurated the Gilded Age.

Turning away from aristocracy and American patricians, Du Bois also later turned away from the theory and practice of the City on the Hill. As the leading black intellectual of the twentieth century, Du Bois cast a long shadow when he repudiated this tradition of thought and practice. It would be more than fifty years before a young, third-generation black preacher (ironically) from Atlanta, Georgia, breathed new life into the idea. The Reverend Martin Luther King, Jr., is regarded as the greatest practitioner of the jeremiad tradition of black politics, but the last great theoretical reformulation of this tradition came from his contemporary, James Baldwin. Baldwin had grave and settled reservations about America, the political imaginary of the City on the Hill, and the religion of the black church; however, he drew on these discourses to move the American political community beyond the limits of its vision and beyond the vicious legacy of white supremacy. It is to the political theory and civic poetry of James Baldwin that we now turn.

4

(Making) Love in the Dishonorable City

The Civic Poetry of James Baldwin

The trembling he had known in darkness had been the echo of their joyful feet these feet blood stained forever, with no continuing city but seeking one to come: a city out of time, not made with human hands, but eternal in the heavens.[1]

There it was, the great, unfinished city, with all its towers blazing in the sun.[2]

Indeed, I had conquered the city: but the city was stricken with plague.[3]

Ah. What is he doing on the floor in a basement of that historical city? That city built on the principle that he would have the grace to live, and, certainly to die, somewhere outside the gates?[4]

James Baldwin concluded his best-known work, *The Fire Next Time* (hereafter, *Fire*), with an extraordinary provocation that is arguably the most famous of his entire corpus. After boldly proclaiming that nothing less than the entire fate of the American polity was in the reader's hands, Baldwin exhorted, "If we—and now I mean the relatively conscious whites and the relatively conscious blacks, who must, like lovers, insist on, or create, the consciousness of the others—do not falter in our duty now, we may be able, handful that we are, to end the racial nightmare, and achieve our

country, and change the history of the world."[5] All of the elements of the
civil religion of America are present in this dense, hyphenated, and complex
provocation. Baldwin's call to "relatively conscious" whites and blacks resembled traditional constructions of American election. His insistence that this
favored group might change the history of the world resembled the notion
of American mission, the red herring so central to traditional invocations of
American exceptionalism. Finally, Baldwin fused these two ideas—American election and American mission—in a conception of civic duty that
looked a lot like the civil religionist's signature construction of political obligation as sacred duty. Were it not for Baldwin's metaphorical rendering of
political agency in the image of erotic love, one might mistake his concluding provocation for a rather conservative restatement of John Winthrop's
old faith. Explicating the theory behind this metaphor is one of my principal concerns in this chapter. For now, I offer the caution that to interpret
Baldwin's concluding provocation as a simple restatement of the old faith
would be an egregious error. On the other hand, we must not understand
it to be an unqualified repudiation either. Precisely what, then, does Baldwin attempt to achieve with this unwieldy provocation? What is the status of
this extraordinary provocation within the larger theoretical project of *Fire*,
and what is the status of this project within Baldwin's political thought as
a whole? Addressing these two questions leads us back to one of the central concerns of this book: to describe the shape and contours of a tradition
of African American political-theoretical reflection about America. It also
raises other questions: Can Baldwin, a preeminently literary artist, be said to
have formulated something resembling a political theory?[6] If so, where does
Baldwin's theory stand in relation to the respective interventions of his predecessors within this tradition?

There are two parts to Baldwin's provocation, one outside the hyphens
and the other inside. Outside the hyphens, Baldwin identifies, or calls into
being, the association of persons who had been chosen to achieve the country, and he locates himself within this association.[7] He describes the success
of this association as the achievement of the country and links this founding to transformation of the world. Baldwin insists that solving America's
oldest and most vexing problem of race would help the polity to avert the
creeping danger of disintegrative racial violence. If the country were able
to do this, Baldwin suggests, Americans might gain a greater depth and
breadth of experience, a reorientation of purpose from the frivolous to the
weighty, and an enlargement and refinement of civic judgment. In other
words, they would acquire the practical wisdom and existential maturity
that would enable the polity to model political excellence for the benefit of

the world. Inside the hyphens, Baldwin is just as ambitious. He deconstructs racial essentialism and insists that the proper aim to be pursued by those he called to serve is political education. Most provocatively, he suggests that erotic love, rather than Christian charity, self-interest, or unreflective patriotism, must be the principle of action. With his bold and unwieldy provocation, Baldwin rehabilitates the political imaginary of the City on the Hill in a manner at once traditional and unprecedented.

In keeping with tradition, Baldwin closes this famous essay of 1963 by exhorting readers to become involved in the effort to "achieve our country." His appeal defines antiracist political struggle as the form and content of a genuinely civic American political virtue and casts the commitment to this ideal of citizenship as a special kind of calling.[8] True to this tradition, Baldwin identifies the extirpation of white supremacy as the grand objective that must be met for America to fulfill its immanent possibilities for unprecedented human flourishing, and he locates himself within the privileged collective agency charged with interpreting and initiating the politics that this exceptional, even transcendent, calling demanded. Hence, Baldwin seems to join forces with Frederick Douglass and W.E.B. Du Bois against David Walker, embracing their critical and practical program of theoretical and practical reconstruction of American political piety. With them, he seeks to reformulate and re-signify American civil religion into a spiritually resonant political vision that placed black personhood, opportunity, and citizenship at the heart of America's collective political desire and institutional purposes. With Douglass and Du Bois, Baldwin hoped to dismantle white supremacy and bring about real opportunity for blacks to flourish. Hence, he sought, as they did, to insert, within the thought, practice, and language of American politics, the conceptual and normative categories and material and spiritual resources that would empower black agency—in itself and for others. All three writers insisted that confronting the problems of race and white supremacy was the indispensable condition of any plausible vision of America's destiny—whether this conception of destiny were to be secularly or sacredly conceived. As Douglass and Du Bois had done, Baldwin links white supremacy to American incompletion and American political evil and links black citizenship and opportunity to the fulfillment of the American mission.

However, in the tradition of Walker's *Appeal*, Baldwin underwrites his appeal to his "countrymen" to "achieve our country" with the prophetic warning of an impending political catastrophe that beckons from the future, rather than a sacred but betrayed political past. Douglass had predicted, and even encouraged, an apocalyptic battle between good and evil. However, the good called into being by the American Revolution and embodied imperfectly in the American Constitution was, for Douglass, rooted in sacred covenants made in the past, covenants whose subsequent violation and corruption by the slave power necessitated a violent cleansing that could be brought about only by civil war. Similarly, Du Bois's political theory warned of the incipient vulgarization of American civilization and the specter of demagogues, future dangers exacerbated by, but not reducible to, what Du Bois regarded as the contingent triumph of oligarchic political and cultural priorities in the present. In conceiving these, rather than other dangers, as the urgent problems of American white supremacy, Du Bois supposed not only that the imperfect vision of the American founders was simply preferable to the encroaching philistinism and nascent demagoguery threatening the republic in 1903 but also that this vision from the past was so sublime that it imposed binding obligations on Americans in the present. Thus, while Baldwin's hope that blacks could gain citizenship within a reconstructed American polity resembled the hopes of Douglass and Du Bois (as ephemeral as these hopes proved to have been for both writers), his suspicion of the impotence of appeals rooted in moral persuasion and political inspiration, and his insistence on the central role that white supremacy played in the constitution of political power in America, placed his views closer to Walker's realist theory of political power.

As Walker had before him, Baldwin seems to have suspected that, because the peculiar constitution of American racial solidarity inoculated the public from the experience of moral culpability, appeals to conscience would be inadequate. In this view, any political theory worth its salt would have to both explain the problematic character of America to itself and introduce an element of necessity into the discursive mix. In other words, it would have to introduce an element of coercive force that could chip at or destroy the bonds of white racial solidarity.[9] Like Walker, Baldwin was well aware that acts of violence by America's powerless, acts rearticulated as threats to the powerful and comfortable, constituted one of the few means at their disposal to impose political necessity on the public's agenda.[10] Neither Baldwin nor Walker threatened violence for purely strategic reasons. Both of them genuinely lamented the catastrophic upheaval that they believed was in store if America would not "perform [its] first works over," as Baldwin put it in one of his later essays.[11] Nonetheless, despite his sincerity and regret, Baldwin seems to have believed, as early as 1951, that to compel action on the problems of race in the United States, the hard power of necessity might need to be added to the gentle, if not wholly ineffectual, power of morality and inspirational rhetoric. His argument in an essay written that year came closer to Walker's conception of "natural enmity" between the races than he was probably even aware. "Americans, unhappily, have the most remarkable ability to alchemize all bitter truths into an innocuous but piquant confection and to transform their moral contradictions into a proud decoration, such as are given for heroism on the field of battle."[12] Similar to Walker, Baldwin saw the American capacity to transform unflattering facts into pleasing self-congratulation as more than simply a moral failing. It was nothing less than an instrument of national defense, an armament. Enacting this superbly ingenious form of violence held in reserve, the American polity drew criticism into itself and transformed it into source of pride that must be defended against potential wounds. Baldwin remained deeply troubled by the full implications of this peculiar capacity of Americans. In fact, *Fire* may be Baldwin's grand attempt to avoid Walker's conclusion that any serious black politics need concern itself with only the production of warriors. In an important respect, Baldwin's ambivalent entanglement in the central problem of David Walker's political theory is far more significant to the development of his political thinking than his affinities for his more "respectable" predecessors. Baldwin's innovation as a theorist of the public philosophy of the City on the Hill grew out of this complex inheritance, an inheritance that brought Douglass's and Du Bois's hopes for black inclusion into sharp contention with the clear-sighted, if not despairing, political realism of Walker.

When Baldwin exclaimed to his countrymen that their successful execution of their special duty to "end the racial nightmare" and "achieve [their] country" might "change the history of the world," he issued a jeremiad that did two things at once. On the one hand, he tried to call up the passions that Douglass and Du Bois sought to arouse by invoking America's declension from its revolutionary or patrician tradition. On the other hand, Baldwin refused to sacralize the American founding, in either its traditional and official versions or its insurgent and contraband ones. Instead, he suggested that the American polity was never achieved in the first place. The founding articulations, celebrated institutional forms, and supporting cultural formations had actually been little more than false starts, abortive efforts, and dress rehearsals. Therefore, "achieving our country" required beginning anew, returning to the denied and dishonored past to recover two things: the preconstitutional political aspirations of asylum-seeking refugees from the Old World and the freedom dreams of captives brought to the New World in chains. It was, therefore, the special "duty" of those "relatively conscious whites and relatively conscious blacks" to found the New World anew, to discover the American polity from among the ruins left behind by previous generations of proto-Americans. Hence, Baldwin invoked the political imaginary of the City on the Hill only to repudiate it, and he repudiated this theologico-political vision only to create a new version. His complex efforts raise important questions. Why would Baldwin formulate a new theologico-politics of America if the old version had proven so untenable? And, how deeply does his critique really go, if, in the end, he seeks only to replace the old faith with a new one?

The Old Faith

One of the principal themes that Baldwin pursued in his first novel, *Go Tell It on the Mountain*, was the problem of the City on the Hill as the prevailing optic of collective American self-understanding and personal self-making. In particular, he addressed the ways in which this peculiar optic promoted a sterilizing vanity at the public level and a demoralizing indifference among and between selves on the personal level. Among the many issues treated under this theme, the most subversive and unsettling was Baldwin's characterization of a peculiarly tart and double-edged irony. Despite being scattered into darkness outside the gates of "the shining city," poor, urban, black church folk—persons only a generation removed from slavery—had managed to cultivate and institutionalize a peculiarly fecund and distinctively robust form of the old piety of the City on the Hill. However, Baldwin's depiction reveals this piety to be anachronistic at best. The black community of the novel cultivates and institutionalizes the pieties of the old faith outside of "the shining city" of Manhattan south of Harlem, an opulent, if not decadent, place, where these ideals had clearly ceased to function as either an ethos or an ethics. In the "shining city," Baldwin writes, "the buildings contested God's power" and "the men and women did not fear God."[13] When the protagonist, John Grimes, sheepishly enters the "shining city," he does not see piety at all when he looks down Fifth Avenue. Instead, he sees "graceful women in fur coats," "looking into windows that held silk dresses, and watches, and rings."[14] John is tempted by the shining city, then, not simply because its apparent freedom and opulence are off limits to him but also because the "shining city" is the alternative to the stale pieties and repressive rigorism that prevail in his own community.

Baldwin's jeremiad informed Americans not only that they would find no recognizable descendents of their mythical community in this "shining city"—the ideological fiction routinely invoked to conceal the exploitative politics of American mission—but also that the real legatees of this old and unwieldy inheritance were the anonymous black people they did not see during their after-hours adventures uptown. Americans have failed to appreciate the improbable Puritanism of blacks—their direct descent from Winthrop, as it were—in part because Americans have seen black people as little more than animate objects making up the wild landscape conjured by whites to ground their adventurism. Just as importantly, Americans have failed to recognize these people as heirs to the City on the Hill because these ideals no longer mean anything to most Americans. Thus, Baldwin's story conveys a powerful lesson: The white supremacist exclusion of blacks from the life of the polity reveals the vacuity of these ideals among the citizens of "the shining city" and proves their essential impotence as effective expressions of American exemplariness. Because these ideals proliferate only within the invisible marginality of Harlem storefront churches and similar remote outposts of "the shining city," Baldwin's characters cannot claim to carry the good news anywhere beyond their own church doors.[15]

However, Baldwin's ironies cut just as deeply in the other direction. When poor, excluded, and dishonored black people—precisely those Americans whose experiences in and of America confirmed the absurdity of American piety—adopted anachronistic, but quintessentially American, practices of self-abnegating asceticism and world-less religiosity, they imposed an exorbitant cost of bitter isolation on particular members of their community. This toxic and often lethal condition, as Baldwin would go on to explain in other works, might become, in rare instances, the basis for profound art.[16] However, in *Go Tell It on the Mountain*, the final fate of the marginal person within the marginal community is left open. John Grimes submits to the ascetic life of his religious community; however, in spite of this communion (or perhaps because of it), John's decision will not provide the answers he seeks to satiate his real needs, sexual needs that the novel intimates, but John does not yet fully understand. Even though John does gain a profound, if ultimately inadequate, insight[17]—"Where joy was, there strength followed; where strength was, sorrow came"[18]—in the aftermath of the conversion ritual, he does not acquire the deep connections with others that might enable him to replicate the joy he experienced immediately after his conversion. It comes as little surprise that Gabriel, John's defeated, sanctimonious, and pitiless father, questions the depth and seriousness of his son's commitment to the faith.[19] Furthermore, the knowing pain that John's mother Elizabeth feels when she realizes that her son's choice will not answer the deepest longings of his heart[20] and John's continuing inability to solve the riddle of her profound sadness[21] make it clear that little will change between John and his family. Most revealing of all, John does not receive the affirmation he seeks from Elijah, the older boy in the church he admires and almost certainly desires.[22] As a presentiment of the tenuousness of John's conversion, the irresolution of his deepest troubles, and perhaps even the worsening dangers he will face, Baldwin has John deliver the final verdict to Elijah on the meaning of his conversion: "No matter what happens to me, where I go, what folks say about me, no matter what anybody says, you remember—please remember—I was saved."[23] As if John secretly knows he needs to arm himself for the day when this community turns on him, he implores his beloved Elijah to mark the fact and authenticity of his conversion in speech. The fact that he makes him say it out loud indicates his suspicion that, on that day, Elijah, too, might need a reminder.

In introducing these complications, Baldwin has a deeper point to make than to question the power of the religious life to combat alienation. Baldwin's first novel explores the bitter irony that the true cost of American exceptionalism is that the most marginal persons inside its already marginal and beleaguered communities are exposed to harm. More scandalous than this, however, is that these costs must be borne by persons of exceptional intelligence, sensitivity, and passion, precisely because they are exceptional and rare within these communities. Indeed, the particular sensibilities of persons such as John Grimes and, no doubt, Baldwin himself, place them in, but not of, insular and isolated communities. If the ironies of this double isolation carry the message of the novel as a whole, then John Grimes is Baldwin's figure for a specific kind of American self who is endangered by the political imaginary of the City on the Hill. What is to be told on the mountain, he implies, is not only that American theologico-politics among white Americans is meaningless, except for purposes of self-congratulation, but also that it exposes the exceptional and rare among the marginalized to harm.

Making Blackness

To arrest the decay he believed to be endemic to all political regimes, the ancient political philosopher Aristotle advised statesmen to keep citizens on a razor's edge by inventing domestic terrors. By such means, statesmen could bring "distant dangers near, in order that the citizens may be on their guard, and, like sentinels in a night-watch, never relax their attention."[24] David Walker grasped the operation of this sinister, yet quite effective, invention of ancient statecraft at work in the American republic. As an elaboration of the natural conflict between the races, arising from a pathological human convention in which racial difference and hierarchy were alleged as justification for enslavement, forced illiteracy, and expulsion, his theory of natural enmity was a profound thesis about the new republic's production of internal enemies, its generation and accumulation of destructive force by these means, and its encouragement and protection of tyrannical violence against blacks who, constituted as enemies, kept citizens on guard as sentinels. Walker's attempt to politicize this theoretical insight by circulating a call to arms among free blacks throughout the world was a bold and particular kind of response to America's production of antiblack violence. James Baldwin's political project is another.

In his masterful 1951 essay, "Many Thousands Gone," Baldwin lays out the essentials of a theory of racialization and racial violation that would inform his thinking throughout the course of his literary life.[25] This essay begins in a manner similar to Du Bois's opening chapter of *The Souls of Black Folk*, by insisting that the "American Negro" remains a stranger and an outcast in the land of his birth, yet he swiftly moves to an analysis of how blacks are systematically constituted as fearsome strangers. "It is only in his music, which Americans are able to admire because a protective sentimentality limits their understanding of it, that the Negro has been able to tell his story." Here, Baldwin insists on a categorical difference among black people's capacity to tell their stories, white people's admiration for black music, and white Americans' ability to hear and comprehend the stories contained in this music. Part of this difference resides in what Baldwin refers to as "protective sentimentality," a notion he had defined elsewhere and two years earlier as "the ostentatious parading of excessive and spurious emotion."[26] According to this earlier account, sentimentality "is the mark of dishonesty, the inability to feel; the wet eyes of the sentimentalist betray his aversion to experience, his fear of life, his arid heart; and it is always, therefore, the signal of a secret and violent inhumanity, the mask of cruelty."[27] In the later "Many Thousands Gone," however, Baldwin adopts a more generous tone, dropping the caustic explanation of sentimentality he had advanced earlier. Baldwin has a different agenda here that is no less critical. He seeks to present before the conscience of the nation the hidden and complex mechanism of American racialization, the subtle dependence of this social practice on violence and violation, and the principal modes of systematic disavowal that conceal its very existence. Thus, Baldwin neither dwells on the details that he believes are centrally constitutive of American sentimentality nor insists on exposing the vicious character that hides behind it. Baldwin's shift in emphasis suggests that, in 1951, he was beginning to think more seriously about how he might address a polity where sentimentality prevailed as an effective means of collective security. His assessments resemble those of political theorist Hannah Arendt, who arrived at an almost identical judgment about the operations of sentimentality in Nazi Germany. Arendt argued that sentimentality functioned as a prophylactic against responsibility that could be cultivated through skilled political rhetoric as a political competence among the rank and file. She credits the Nazi tactician Adolph Himmler with the discovery that, by cultivating pity for the self who violated others, he and other orators could suppress any feelings of pity that persons might ordinarily feel for victims of violence and violation. As she explains, "Instead of saying: What horrible things I did to people!, the murderer would be able to say: What horrible things I had to watch in pursuance of my duties, how heavily the task weighed upon my shoulders!"[28] As Arendt argued, the practice of sentimentality, in the right hands, could be wielded as a surgical instrument to exterminate the conscience of persons who had no strong attachments to the sinister objectives of the regime. Even though Baldwin argued that sentimentality cloaked cruelty, his chef concern resembled that of Arendt. In Baldwin's view, American sentimentality turned American violence and violation on its head. Instead of disclosing the ways in which blacks continued to be victimized by American white supremacy, white discourses about the predicament of blacks too often spotlighted white pain over black difficulties. It is not difficult, then, to see why Baldwin may have felt the need to proceed with caution.

In doing so, Baldwin attempted to lay bare the subrational processes governing racialization, to unearth its foundation in a ritually sustained symbolic grammar, and to publicize its private and public consequences for both blacks and whites. I use the term "racialization" to encompass Baldwin's description of the way in which racial identities are socially produced in the proliferation of representations of blacks by way of discourses about "statistics, slums, rapes, injustices, [and] remote violence"[29] and by way of more highbrow forms of American literature, "problem literature when written by whites and protest literature when written by Negroes." According to Baldwin, all of these representations carry a single message: "Black is a terrible color with which to be born."[30] They share "symbols," "signs," and "hieroglyphics," which constitute the black person as a perpetual outsider in the national "psyche" and produce whiteness as a normative standard of wholesomeness, national purity, civilization, and innocence. Baldwin describes this process of identity formation as subrational because it operates in silence, below conscious articulation. However, as he explains, the meanings ascribed to these identities derive from appearances that are themselves but reflections of deeper commitments and anxieties. These reflections stem, Baldwin insists, from a troublesome history that too few Americans are willing to face. "In our image of the Negro breathes the past we deny, not dead but living yet and powerful." Hence, for Baldwin, to begin to face history is to begin to examine these symbols and signs; but, for far too many, this kind of analysis would open the door to existential chaos. I explore the nature of this chaos later, but first it is important to note something about the rhetorical strategy that Baldwin pursues from this point forward in this essay. In describing the subrational processes of racialization, Baldwin is wading into deep water. He is beginning to take aim at what he takes to be the heart of darkness of American white supremacy, a minefield of deep-seated commitments that could very easily trigger the American national defense. How does Baldwin move in this dangerous space? How should any black intellectual negotiate this terrain?

In "Many Thousands Gone," Baldwin tries to secure passage by camouflaging his assault on white supremacy in the form of a withering critique of *Native Son*, the celebrated novel written by his former mentor and friend, Richard Wright. As Baldwin's biographer David Leeming notes, this was the second of Baldwin's three critiques of *Native Son*. As he suggests, Baldwin may have indulged a personal animus or an oedipal complex in which he felt compelled by subconscious forces to destroy his literary father as a condition of his own literary life.[31] As a scholar and close friend of Baldwin's, Leeming is undoubtedly more qualified than anyone else to know. I argue, however, an alternative explanation grounded in an analysis of Baldwin as a political actor. Attacking another black critic's attack on America is a plausible strategy for circumventing the American national defense. As we shall see, Baldwin later used a revised version of this strategy in *Fire*, when he discussed the limits of Elijah Muhammad's political vision. Also, this strategy had been employed, with questionable results, by Du Bois against Booker T. Washington and more subtly, but with equally questionable results, by Douglass against Walker. In "Many Thousands Gone," Baldwin pressed this strategy for all it was worth against Wright and, whether it can be said to have succeeded on a grand scale or not, it did succeed in making it impossible to celebrate *Native Son* uncritically.

Native Son and the enormous popularity it generated provided Baldwin a perfect target for exploring the ritual dynamics of blackness and whiteness. It enabled him to disarm American defensiveness by revealing the sinister operations of racialization at work in the writings of a black author. According to Baldwin, Wright succeeded in "record[ing] as no Negro before him has ever done, that fantasy Americans hold in their mind, when they speak of the Negro: that fantastic and fearful image which we have lived with since the first slave fell beneath the lash."[32] This image was captured in Bigger Thomas, the protagonist of *Native Son*, who smothers his employer's daughter Mary after carrying her to her bedroom after a night of carousing.

A young white woman understood to be innocent, Mary had committed no offense, aside from drunkenness and insensitivity to Bigger's capacity for embarrassment, other than trying to help him. Bigger's murder of Mary is a reflex reaction, not an enraged reaction to something Mary has done, but rather a panicked reaction to the possibility of being discovered by Mary's father in a compromising position with her. Bigger incinerates her body to dispose of any incriminating evidence, but from this moment of decisive non-decision to kill, Bigger comes into self-consciousness.[33] He becomes a recognizably conscious self who is, at the same time, wholly a monster. Baldwin argues that Wright's characterization of Bigger was the most sophisticated treatment yet of the national myth of blackness forming the base of white identity. When presented with Bigger's predicament—poverty, rage, dislocation, intellectual underdevelopment, and so forth—"we are [confronted]," Baldwin notes, "by a monster created by the American republic and we are, through being made to share his experience, to receive illumination as regards the manner of his life and to feel pity and horror at his awful and inevitable doom."[34] Subtly, Baldwin invokes Aristotle's definition of tragedy, the dramatic form that Aristotle approved as an aide to the polity because it could potentially purge the polity of disagreeable passions.[35] By presenting a noble character fated for ruin, the skilled dramatist could provoke passions of fear and pity in the audience and come to the aid of the founder and statesman by providing citizens a cathartic release and thus reinscribing norms of nobility. However, Baldwin invokes Aristotle only to underscore the distance between ancient tragedy and Wright's novel. Wright's novel provokes pity and fear, not to facilitate identification with a noble character fated for ruin, but to titillate white fantasies of black monstrosity. As a consequence, Baldwin argues, Wright simply strokes the sentimental self-pity of white readers at having to shoulder the burden of monsters created by the republic. Baldwin acknowledged the powerful intelligence required to conceive and execute this picture of black life. However, his assessment of the implications of Wright's gross reduction of the tragedy of black life to the fantasy of black rage led him to judge this novel in terms that resembled Arendt's judgment of Nazi rhetoric: It was a text whose outstanding quality, wittingly or not, was its power to exterminate the conscience of readers. Instead of provoking candid self-reflection about the ways in which symbolic representations of blackness facilitated violence and violation against blacks, *Native Son* actually undermined the already underdeveloped faculties of moral discernment among the very persons who had power to transform the conditions Wright took it upon himself to expose and politicize with his depiction of Bigger.

Wright attempted to put before the conscience of American public opinion the conditions of the twentieth-century proletarianization of black life in cities across the United States, conditions of grinding poverty, social and cultural dislocation, racial humiliation, and exposure to violence. What Wright did, however, according to Baldwin, was to hollow out the dense web of tradition, ritual, and interpersonal intimacy that tied blacks together into problematic, yet functional, communities. Wright also, in Baldwin's view, distorted the complex and anguished attachments that blacks had formed to America and Americans, despite never having been accepted by Americans into the national community.[36] For Baldwin, this tangle of contradictory and cross-cutting relations was the central paradox of African American life that art must illuminate. The relationship between blacks and whites in America, Baldwin argued, "is not simply the relationship of oppressed to oppressor, master to slave, nor is it motivated merely by hatred; it is also, literally and morally, a blood relationship, perhaps the most profound reality of the American experience, and we cannot begin to unlock it until we accept how very much it contains the force and anguish and terror of love."[37] Had Wright managed to present Bigger and his crime in light of this dizzying complexity of black attachments, he would have achieved something more truthful and more nearly approaching a profound and responsible work of art. "To have penetrated this phenomenon, this inward contention of love and hatred, blackness and whiteness, would have given [Bigger] a stature more nearly human and an end more nearly tragic; and would have given us a document more profoundly and genuinely bitter and less harsh with anger which is, on the one hand, exhibited and, on the other hand, denied."[38]

Hence, the scandal of *Native Son* was not simply its failure as art and reportage, but its failure as theory and politics. As politics, *Native Son* furnished the pretext for continued dislocation and isolation of blacks. Reconstituting and implicitly reauthorizing the symbol of black monstrosity meant that, when white readers encountered flesh-and-blood black people, they would either subsume blacks under the category of the monster or, as was more likely the case, perceive them as unintelligible and alien. Baldwin was concerned, not only that blacks would bear the burden of feelings of resentment at Wright's having consigned them to obscurity and anonymity by reauthorizing white fantasies about black characters, but also that many whites would bring to their encounter with blacks a hope and expectation that blacks would absolve them of guilt for the republic's creation of monsters. These concerns were political because, when whites denied individual responsibility for white power and exercised this disavowed power in their expectation of and demand for black forgiveness, this fraudulent transaction of absolution created a false equality and reciprocity that left the unjust so-cial conditions of black life untouched.

As theory, Wright's novel promoted the ritual constitution of the white self. By reinscribing a radical version of the white fantasy of black monstros-ity, Wright confirmed the legitimacy and sovereignty of the white Ameri-can self. As George Shulman has shown in his study of American prophecy, Baldwin grasped the function of race as a state of exception in the sense conveyed by contemporary political theorist Giorgio Agamben following Carl Schmitt.[39] In the United States, blackness is the constitutive exclu-sion from the normative order that provides the American order with the conditions of its possibility. In this respect, blacks are socially constituted through authoritative discourses and prevailing representational practices as the excluded other and become, thereby, the worldly referent for all that is impermissible within the moral and juridical order of whiteness. However, as the excluded other that contains the negation or perversion of whiteness, blackness becomes the enabling and constitutive condition of white iden-tity. In more concrete terms, blacks are constituted as the excluded others. The prevailing representations conjured by diverse actors involved in various kinds of discursive activities render them external to the national commu-nity. These discursive representations of blackness are grounded in an unspo-ken grammar of symbols and a spoken, but unanalyzed, set of signs. These symbols and signs are themselves part of an unanalyzed, but socially medi-ated, structure of regulative responses to sexual desire, the will to power, or the desire for destruction. Invested with these ungovernable desires, blacks become under the white gaze the visible incarnation of prehistoric human ungovernability. As such, blacks come into sight as fundamentally other, as persons whose nature condemns them to permanent outsider status within American civilization. In coming into sight as such, black bodies legitimate the versions of history that have excluded them and produced white identity. By legitimating the history in which the white self has been saddled with the responsibility for preserving civilization against ungovernable others, these representations of blacks authorize the white self as a sovereign self, a self who moves in the world in accordance with self-prescribed laws. However, this law is intelligible to the self only because the self knows when and where these laws do not apply, and these times and places are, of course, those moments when the white self encounters the black other.

Understood in this light, the unpardonable offense of *Native Son* was twofold. First, it reaffirmed the sovereign white self by upholding the gram-mar of symbols that authorized white sovereignty. Second, it contributed to the process by which black rage was generated and reproduced in the black self. In the black encounter with sovereign whiteness, the black self encountered arbitrary force and violence that were nonetheless articulated discursively and institutionally as legitimate. The price of this encounter, Baldwin explained, was rage and fear, passions that all too often in Jim Crow America resulted in a wealth of destructive consequences. What kind of politics, Baldwin asked, could possibly speak to the enormity of this predicament? What kinds of political actors would be willing and able to take up this task?

Calling All Lovers

The figure of the "lover" is the political actor designated by the concluding provocation of *Fire*, with which I opened this chapter. It describes Baldwin's normative conception of the inner condition and outward orientation of the politicized self who is competent to found a new polity. According to Baldwin, this self would be urgently committed, in thought and deed, to the immediate dismantling of American white supremacy. Yet the self committed to it as an animating and overarching aim is not so motivated because the self conceives this good as the historical fulfillment of betrayed liberal principles enshrined in America's founding documents and other constitutive articulations. On the contrary, the self pursues this good for two different reasons: first, because of the belief that antiracism is an intrinsically worthy choice for a multitude of persons whom history has formed into a multiracial assemblage; and second, because of the idea that the dismantling of American white supremacy—in all of its guises—is the proximate and penultimate good in a larger quest to found a new and genuinely American polity.[40] Hence, the "lover" would need to be a self in possession of special competences and specific sorts of purposes that would allow one to embrace rather than simply endure the arduous, exacting, and perilous work of educating others and founding the American polity.[41] These questions concerning the identity of this self and the basis for the principles of action, then, are twofold. Concerning the identity of this self, we should ask this question: What drives and purposes define this character? Or, to put it another way, by virtue of what, precisely, does this self take bearings? Concerning the principles that animate this self, we should ask these questions: Which principles or maxims of action move and constrain this self? What is the relation between these motivations and those that guide or bind persons whose conscience the self must reawaken or create? And finally, what conditions will ultimately release this political actor from these extraordinary responsibilities?

Baldwin's answers to these questions are articulated across a great many of his writings, in his novels, plays, and prose essays. However, leaving to the side for a moment his novels and plays—all of which, to varying degrees, are absorbed in some aspect of this problem—and considering only those prose writings where Baldwin makes explicit, declarative, and explanatory claims about the link between love and American citizenship, six essays stand out from the rest: "Notes of a Native Son," "Nobody Knows My Name," "The Creative Process," *The Fire Next Time, Nothing Personal,* and *No Name in the Street.*

"Notes of a Native Son" is an essay from 1955 that introduces love as a desire for the beautiful, a desire that Baldwin discovers amid an extraordinary coincidence of his father's death, his sister's birth, and the combustion of Harlem into a race riot in 1943. "Nobody Knows My Name" (1959) is Baldwin's record of his first trip to the South. In it, Baldwin records his experience of disorientation at the complexities and ambivalences of Southern white supremacy.[42] While this essay advances theoretical claims about love and citizenship, they do not reflect Baldwin's considered judgments about these matters. This essay's importance lies, therefore, in marking a moment of irresolution in Baldwin's thinking as he tries to comprehend, within his own theoretical categories, the political significance of the differences between Northern and Southern white supremacy. *Nothing Personal* (1964) is a dark, meditative piece written to accompany the photographs of his friend and former classmate, Richard Avedon. Here, Baldwin expresses his deep worries that the peculiar conditions of mid-sixties America (conditions exhibited by American popular culture) had thrown into sharp relief the urgent necessity, but increasing impossibility, of love. This essay was written shortly after *Fire,* and therefore provides something of an index of Baldwin's thinking about the fate of the project he undertakes in *Fire. No Name in the Street* (1972) is a grief-stricken assessment that seeks to explain precisely what Baldwin believes has happened to the "lover" whose politics he had devised and defended in *Fire.* Finally, "The Creative Process" (1962) is a brief but critically important explication of Baldwin's conception of the vocation of the artist and the peculiar responsibilities imposed on this important figure in America. It is in this essay that Baldwin begins to reveal his understanding of the relationship between art and politics; hence, it provides critical preparatory and introductory material for making sense of the politics of *Fire.*

The concluding provocation of *Fire* identified the activity of "creating the conscience of others" as one of the principal political tasks of the "lover." The first task was to "insist" on the conscience of others, which meant simply that the "lover" must seek to inspire others to act from principle rather than from fear, selfishness, or unreasoning fidelity to habit. Because, as Baldwin admitted, "people find it very difficult to act on what they know,"[43] the enormous task of the "lover" is to quicken the thought and enliven the spirit of persons. They must act not on the suspicion that moral principles have been extinguished from the hearts of white supremacists (in regard to blacks) but on the hope that white supremacy is a moral failing rooted in problematic societal attitudes, prejudices, and evasions. As difficult as making this distinction could be, however, Baldwin acknowledged there were other forms of arrested morality that posed an even greater challenge to the "lover," and he illustrated this by way of a story he told about a young white man he encountered in an airport bar. Explaining why he had not intervened when Baldwin and a few friends were denied service, the young man confided, "I lost my conscience a long time ago."[44] As the case suggests, it is not clear how persons such as this young man might be inspired to act from principle. He claims to have none. Even if he exaggerates in this instance, he seems to have made peace with his amoralism, a peace that presents the same problem as a lack of conscience. In such cases, there is simply too little material for the "lover" to inspire. On the other hand, one might be tempted to suppose that this problem is only illusory and to view the lack of conscience in this young man as an opportunity. Since he has no scruples, he is, in effect, the blank canvas on which the "lover" might create. However, one might object that it is precisely the temptation to find opportunity in cases such as these that points to severe limitations of Baldwin's figure of the "lover" as an ideal political actor.

Given that Baldwin never stipulates a boundary marking the distinction between the activities of "creating the conscience" and activities that are a transgression of individuals' rights to freedom of thought and expression, some may find what I have said thus far about Baldwin's conception of political engagement worrisome. Political liberalism, the ascendant political theory in the West, holds that individual rights to thought and expression—no matter how heterodox or seemingly pernicious—are necessary to any defensible political conception of human freedom. Persons informed by this theory may have reasonable concerns that Baldwin's conception of the political actor as a "lover" quietly authorizes the violation of this fundamental freedom. Specifically, they might worry that, in aiming at love, Baldwin's politics unwittingly promote a violation of one set of basic individual rights, even as they try to secure another equally basic set. There are soft and hard versions of this worry. The soft version holds that such a trade-off is grievous but necessary under the conditions of American white supremacy. Here, the trade-off is to balance the rights of blacks to freedom from violence and other egregious injustices and the rights of whites to believe that blacks are subhuman and without rights that whites must honor. Liberals who express the soft version of this worry might go on to argue that this is the best that Americans can do under the circumstances. However if, at the outset, whites acknowledge this trade-off and try to build restraint into all of their interventions on behalf of blacks, it is possible to minimize the amount of harm potentially done to whites. To put this resolution more concretely, the solution proffered by the soft version of the liberal worry is this: If Americans are aware of the violation done to whites and other nonblacks when attempting to secure the rights of blacks, there is a much better chance of acting with caution and prudence with regard to whites and other nonblacks.

The hard version of this liberal worry rejects this compromise. It holds that Baldwin's conception of political engagement can only be a dangerous program for totalitarian disregard for individual rights.[45] Precisely because Baldwin's politics assumes that it can restore persons to some earlier state of moral wholeness or, indeed, even provide a human faculty that some category of persons are presumed to lack, Baldwin's politics entail a commitment to remaking individual persons, that is, a commitment to unmaking persons and then making them over into something they are not. As those with this stronger worry might continue, Baldwin pursues precisely the program that totalitarians, authoritarians, and dictators have perfected over the past hundred years or so: invading individual persons' rights under the self-serving and preposterously arrogant supposition that they are making persons better, freeing them from themselves, or bringing them into alignment with history, nature, or God's will.

Despite the heat generated by these hard and soft liberal concerns, Baldwin was not terribly troubled that his conception of political engagement might foster violations of individual rights of either sort. His ease of conscience on this score had to do with his clear-sighted understanding that the kind of political intervention he called for aimed at a special class of persons who possessed specific competences and well-defined purposes.[46] It also had quite a bit to do with his clear and unvarying refusal to sanction violence no matter how much he understood or (as is the case with his later writings) even sympathized with the rationale for violent reprisal against white supremacy.[47] Moreover, as I discuss when I turn to his analysis of violence, power, and authority, Baldwin had a deeper sense of the vulnerability of individuals under conditions of liberal modernity than the critics who are chiefly informed by these kinds of worries. Given these provisions, Baldwin could reasonably assume that to use his political vision for purposes of coercion would be to misappropriate them. Even so, his substantive answer to both kinds of liberal worries is contained in his description of the characteristic activities of the "lover" and his theory of the specific duties inherent in the politicized conception of this figure.

For Baldwin, the activities of the "lover" were akin to the characteristic activities of the artist. This kinship might already be obvious, given that Baldwin expresses a similarity between these two figures when he suggests, at the end of *Fire*, that the task of the "lover" was the effort to create, as an artist would, the conscience of others. Tasked by Baldwin with the responsibility to create, the "lover" of Baldwin's provocation, at a minimum, creates conditions in which others might act on the principles they know. In this examination of Baldwin's elaboration of the duties of the "lover," I explore what these conditions are. The question now is whether Baldwin believes the "lover" is an artist.

Close inspection shows that, for Baldwin, the inverse is true: The "lover" is not necessarily an artist, but the artist is necessarily a "lover." To begin with, Baldwin draws a bright line distinguishing the proper activities of the artist from the normal activities of the political actor. As he makes plain, the artist is "to be distinguished from all other responsible actors in society— the politicians, legislators, educators, and scientists."[48] In an earlier essay, he had drawn an even sharper distinction: "In his endeavor to wed the vision of the old world with that of the new, it is the writer, not the statesmen, who is our strongest arm."[49] Although the statesman has a place within the social order and a duty to ensure that society's order is maintained, the office of the statesman does not encompass all of the necessary functions. Baldwin explains, "The entire purpose of society is to create a bulwark against inner and outer chaos, in order to make life bearable and to keep the human race alive.[50] The artist plays a fundamental role in this process. Because individual beings are by nature insufficient for purposes of either staying alive or thriving as human beings, we become the particular selves we are only because we live in, learn from, and are moved and sustained by a community of other selves. Yet, as Baldwin argues, for us "to become social, there are so many things we must not become, and we are frightened, all of us, of these forces within us that perpetually menace our precarious security."[51] In other words, we are required to reign in the impulses, desires, and preoccupations that are out of alignment with society's norms of right, mental health, hygiene, and so forth. Although they are inevitable, these requirements impose real costs, especially when society's prohibitions are needlessly repressive or ruthlessly manipulative. Under such conditions, society risks severing itself from the essential vitalities required to sustain human existence, or it perverts these vitalities and transforms itself into organized inhumanity. As Baldwin explains, "In overlooking, denying, and, evading [our] complexity—which is nothing more than the disquieting complexity of our selves—we are diminished and we perish: only within the web of ambiguity, paradox, this hunger, danger, darkness, can we find at once ourselves and the power that will free us from ourselves."[52] These conditions represent an acute "conundrum," to borrow one of Baldwin's favorite terms. That is, while society is the necessary ground of individuality, the needless restrictions or problematic commitments society imposes decisively shape, if not wholly determine, what forms of individuality are possible. In Baldwin's conception, the vocation of the artist is to speak to this conundrum. He explains, "The artist is present to correct the delusions to which we fall prey in our attempts to avoid [knowledge]."

Thus, Baldwin's artist is no dilettante. In calling attention to pernicious repression or ruthless manipulation, the artist must expose himself or herself to society's wrath and be prepared for a life of marginality and perhaps even hostility: "The peculiar responsibility is that he must never cease warring with it, for its sake or his own."[53] By "society's sake," Baldwin refers to the possibility for human freedom that is made legible by a collective societal decision to pursue a particular course of affairs or to revise a course of affairs that has proven itself to be repugnant, self-destructive, or no longer useful. For Baldwin, the artist is the genuine guardian of this freedom because, by virtue of this vocation, only the artist possesses the required distance and the appropriate motivations to pierce society's natural tendency to see itself as the best approximation of human possibility. Baldwin used the analogy of two lovers to capture this fraught relationship—the artist reveals society to itself in the same way that a lover reveals the beloved to himself or herself. For Baldwin, the conflict between the artist and society is "a lover's war" in which the freedom of the artist is more doubtful. According to Baldwin, the artist must continue to war with society or cease to be a genuine artist and must trust that his or her vision may one day illuminate the community. Baldwin explains that love is the motivation that drives the artist, who, in truth, has no choice. On the basis of this passion, the artist will endure wrath or suffer praise. Nonetheless, while it seems clear that no measure of love would empower the artist to transform the community into a republic of artists, it may still be possible through art to transform the community into a republic of lovers. In this respect, Baldwin provides a powerful response to the ghost of David Walker. Perhaps Walker was right that American white supremacy created the conditions of perpetual war. And perhaps he was right that blacks must arm themselves or at least dig trenches. There remains, however, the question of how a successful battle is to be waged. Is it not possible, Baldwin asked, in the case of a exploited and dishonored people with comparatively meager resources, that a battle waged at the level of the soul would provide the very best offense available? If so, there might be more to this notion of a lover's war than appears at first sight, meaning that Baldwin may be a little craftier than ordinarily supposed.

Love, Liberation, and the Covenant with Life

The Fire Next Time is a masterpiece, a classic prose essay written by a masterful memoirist, an inventive work of art composed by an accomplished novelist and playwright, and a profound and original philosophical meditation on political ethics by a committed political intellectual. Elucidating these first two dimensions of the greatness of *Fire* is straightforward because they represent widely accepted judgments about Baldwin's stature as a literary artist. Elucidating the third is more difficult because it requires that I defend a reading of Baldwin that cuts against the grain.[54] Regarding the first dimension, Baldwin is widely considered to have been one of the finest American essayists. Critics may disagree over whether "Many Thousands Gone," "Equal in Paris," or *Fire* deserves top honors in his corpus, but few doubt his place in the literary canon. Moreover, it is also fairly well established that artistic invention is often at work in autobiography and memoir.[55] Due in no small measure to the efforts of writers such as Baldwin, we are far more aware of how the historical record turns on figurative and imaginative techniques. As a result of greater awareness of the role of power in the production of history (that is, how the historical record conceals important parts of the past as a condition of disclosing those particular aspects the historian chooses to explain, how the facts available to historians are often only what historic victors have left behind, and how distortions and eviscerations of the past inevitably result from choices made by both historical actors and historians), we are more aware of the necessary invention at work in autobiography and memoir.[56] Because the autobiographer and the memoirist must simplify and stylize the past to present a particular life within a history that itself is the product of invention and simplification, the autobiographer's inventive and figurative acts need be no different or more nefarious than the historian's necessary simplifications. From these basic interpretive provisos we should be able to see that the claim to greatness of *Fire* must be a product of its inventive artistry as much as the quality of its reportage or expressive precision.

Formally and stylistically, Baldwin structures *Fire* along the lines of a love letter. There are countless models from which Baldwin may have drawn inspiration, but he seems to have been chiefly inspired by the letters of St. Paul, letters of moral, theological, and organizational instruction written by the chief architect of what would become Christian doctrine.[57] Among other things, St. Paul's letters present themselves as the authoritative interpretation of the novel and distinctively Christian conception of love. They are written by a mature lover of Christ who is concerned with explaining the new duties that this unprecedented way of life imposed on new Christians who were then organizing themselves into churches. On a basic level, Baldwin takes St. Paul as his model because he is concerned with instructing readers about the duties of love. More importantly, perhaps, Baldwin writes in the form of St. Paul because he wants to make some rather pointed assessments of the value of St. Paul's legacy. In Baldwin's view, St. Paul is the "merciless fanatic" and "wretched man" whose value as a moral and spiritual guide can be summed up by his ever-so-qualified endorsement of heterosexual marriage: "It is better to marry than to burn." As a former student of St. Paul, and a former preacher of the Gospel, Baldwin knows that it would require more to subvert the great saint than mere caricature. Effective subversion would require the creation of conditions for a new kind of conversion experience. And what more effective means are available for this project than the appropriation of St. Paul's form of literary address?

The strongest evidence in support of Baldwin's adoption of the love letter as genre is the structure of *The Fire Next Time* itself. The text is composed of two letters, "My Dungeon Shook," subtitled "Letter to My Nephew on the One Hundredth Anniversary of Emancipation," and "Down at the Cross," subtitled "Letter from a Region of My Mind." That the first letter is a love letter should not be difficult to ascertain. The essay presents itself as a letter from Baldwin to his nephew James, a letter in which Baldwin tells James that he was conceived in love and has particular duties to honor the love that produced him. When I discuss its political aim later, I make the case that the second letter is also a love letter. For now, it is enough to note that, if this political aim of Baldwin's is borne in mind, then the region of mind from which Baldwin beckons his readers is none other than the new polity he has conceived through his art. I should also note that the title "Down at the Cross" refers to Calvary, the space and time of the crucifixion, a space and time, of course, in which St. Paul was neither a participant nor a spectator. Hence, the title of this second letter seems designed not only to displace the authority of St. Paul but also to invite readers to begin the journey to the region where they must found the new polity. If this is what Baldwin intends by the title and subtitle of the second letter, then his task in the second letter is to explain to his countrymen why they must undertake this perilous journey. He must demonstrate, in other words, the ethical conditions that require them to join him. I suggest that the best way to read *Fire* is in terms of its success or failure as a case for why his countrymen must join him. This hypothesis can be stated more simply: If founding a new polity is the political aim of *Fire*, and its form is a defense and exhortation on behalf of Baldwin's conception of love, then enunciating the duties or practical requirements of love constitutes its theoretical project. I explore this idea by way of three related inquiries: First, what claims does Baldwin make about love? Second, how might the reader's recognition of Baldwin's appeal as a love letter accomplish his objectives? And third, how adequate is this category of love to the task Baldwin sets for it?

The first thing to notice about Baldwin's first letter, "My Dungeon Shook, Letter to my Nephew on the One Hundredth Anniversary of Emancipation," is that its title connects the themes of liberation and love. "My Dungeon Shook" is a verse from a slave song that takes the imprisonment and liberation of the Old Testament prophet Daniel as its subject matter. In a very real sense, the song is a work of poetry created by a slave (or probably a group of slaves improvising) to invoke liberation and liberty and to insist that these are a real possibility despite all evidence to the contrary. The subtitle indicates that this is an intimate correspondence between two black people connected through familial love. Indicating not simply a private correspondence about liberty and liberation, the subtitle also recalls Douglass's magnificent 1852 oration, "What to the Slave Is the Fourth of July?," the speech in which Douglass linked the Fourth of July to Passover and the American Revolution to the historic liberation and exodus of the Hebrew people from Egypt. Baldwin's reference to emancipation recalls this speech and its symbols to suggest not only that Douglass's project is unfinished but also that the incompletion of his grand project will be the general theme of this correspondence between the elder Baldwin and his young nephew. However, where Douglass asked, "What to the slave is the fourth of July?" the subtitle of this first letter asks, "What is the meaning of black liberation among blacks connected through bonds of intimacy, one hundred years after formal emancipation?"

Baldwin's answer to this question is simple but arresting. Not only is "the country celebrating one hundred years too soon," but also, because black liberation is inextricably yoked to white America's capacity to imagine and implement black freedom, black liberation remains the hope against the evidence that it was for the slaves who first sang of it. "We cannot be free until they are free," Baldwin concedes to his nephew. Neither race is free because both are menaced (in quite different ways, of course) by the continued operations of racialization, segregation, and American national defense. Described earlier in "Many Thousands Gone," these forces of violence and violation were underwritten by subrational processes that constituted blacks as permanent and dishonored outsiders to American society. Thus, Baldwin appears, at first sight, to be a bearer of bad news: "This innocent country set you down in a ghetto in which, in fact, it intended that you would perish."[58] And the reason for this, he explains, is quite simple. "You were born into a society which spelled out with brutal clarity that you were worthless, and you were born into this condition for no other reason than because you were black." It may seem, then, that there is little new in Baldwin's letter to his nephew, for, as I have shown, he has leveled this accusation many times in other writings. Even so, an important shift has occurred. Baldwin recalls and carries forward to *Fire*, the theory of racialization from "Many Thousands Gone."[59] However, he introduces two new categories to describe this phenomenon to his nephew: "crime" and "our country." Baldwin uses the term "crime" to describe racialization and the term "our country" to take the place of the inclusive "we," which he deployed as the addressee of "Many Thousands Gone." Though this subtle change of terms may seem rather innocuous, it, in fact, marks a fundamental shift in his theoretical perspective from literary-theoretical cultural criticism to a sharper, more theoretically aware political analysis in the tradition of Douglass, Du Bois, and especially Walker. Here, the collective subject intent on his nephew's destruction is his "country," a term with obvious political connotations that are much sharper than those conjured by the inclusive "we." The persons who comprise this collective subject are no longer figured as the naïve and anonymous consumers of a racializing grammar of symbols but rather as his "countrymen," members of a political community not necessarily equivalent to its citizens.

The nature of this enterprise, which both intends his nephew's destruction and is constituted out of the allegiances of his "countrymen," Baldwin deems "criminal," a term describing activity that has been prohibited or shunned by law and legislation. Regarding this enterprise, its intention, form, and status, Baldwin explains, "This is the crime of which I accuse my country and my countrymen, and for which neither I nor time nor history will ever forgive them, that they have destroyed and are destroying hundreds of thousands of lives and do not know it and do not want to know it."[60] Hence, Baldwin explains to his nephew that America not only intends for him to make dispiriting compromises with life, and to make peace with a demoralizing deprivation of those basic goods that American society posits as requirements for a decent human life, but also intends for all black Americans to accept this degradation. These crimes against humanity are horrible enough, but America's refusal to acknowledge the systematic character of these intentions is unspeakably worse, in Baldwin's view. Hence, what

Baldwin described in "Many Thousands Gone" as a peculiar capacity of America to transform criticism into self-congratulation, he now conceives as an achievement of a culpable collective subjectivity that wills itself to ignore the systematic destruction of other human beings, wills itself the freedom to violate the laws of humanity. To put the matter more simply, Baldwin's "country" and his "countrymen" have committed political evil.

In her magnum opus, *The Human Condition*, Harrah Arendt explicated the notion of unforgivable crime. She argued that humans can forgive only what they can punish and, hence, that what distinguished unforgivable crimes from forgivable ones was whether the offense in question could be punished.[61] Crimes such as the mass exterminations perpetrated by the Nazis and Josef Stalin, mass crimes where victims numbered in the millions and culprits were distributed throughout an entire polity, were offenses that exceeded the capacity of all duly constituted forms of human authority. Arendt argued for the establishment of international institutions that would be authorized to adjudicate and punish "this new species of crime,"[62] but her ultimate answer to this problem of unpardonable offense may well have been her theory of political freedom. Arendt insisted on the human capacity to initiate something unprecedented into the order of nature and flux of history and claimed that the West could (and, indeed, would have to) begin anew.[63] Although Baldwin never suggested an equivalence between the experience of black Americans and victims of genocide, he wrestled with the question of unforgivability. In important respects, his answer to this problem resembled that of Arendt; however, there is an important difference between these two writers on this point. For Arendt, the phenomenological basis of unforgivability was the issue of scale, the fact that Nazi and Stalinist crimes simply exceeded anything anyone or any agency was capable of adjudicating. By contrast, for Baldwin, the key issue was that of intention and will, America's will to refuse acknowledgment of its systematic intention to destroy and its will to deny the catastrophic consequences for the victims of this intention.

In light of his harsh judgment of the crime of America's will to innocence, the instruction Baldwin offers to his nephew is nothing less than shocking.

> Please try to be clear, dear James, through the storm which rages about your youthful head today, about the reality which lies behind the words acceptance and integration. There is no reason for you to try to become like white people and there is no basis whatever for their impertinent assumption that they must accept you. The really

terrible thing, old buddy, is that you must accept them. And I mean that very seriously. You must accept them and accept them with love. For these innocent people have no other hope.

This advice provokes immediate questions. How is young James to do this? And perhaps more importantly, why should he do it? As radical as Baldwin's instruction sounds, it does not lack a basis. In fact, it recalls, from "Notes of a Native Son," the two opposing principles that Baldwin claims he discovered the evening of the Harlem riot, a moment sometime between his father's funeral and the birth of his baby sister, Gloria. Describing this breakthrough, he says:

> It began to seem that one would have to hold in the mind forever two ideas which seemed to be in opposition. The first idea was acceptance, the acceptance, totally without rancor, of life as it is, and men as they are: In the light of this idea, it goes without saying that injustice is commonplace. But this did not mean that one could be complacent, for the second idea was of equal power: that one must never, in one's own life, accept these injustices as commonplace but must fight them with all one's strength. This fight begins, however, in the heart and it had now had been laid to my charge to keep my own heart free of hatred and despair.[64]

As formulated in this early essay, these two "oppositional ideas" resolved themselves, for Baldwin, as a single, personal command: He must keep his individual heart free from hatred and despair. While, individually, these two principles issue positive commands—he is commanded to accept humans as they are, and he is to oppose injustice in his individual life—the conflict between these two principles produces a compound and negative principle: He must keep his heart free from hatred and despair.

By the time he writes this first letter of *Fire*, however, circumstances have changed. It seems as though these two principles have resolved themselves dialectically in a new synthesis in which acceptance is love and love is provocation. Trying to educate his nephew about how to act, rather than formulating private principles to regulate his own conscience, Baldwin now resolves, concretely and in positive terms, the two principles he discovered twenty years earlier. Because he instructs his nephew in how to act, given the meaning of black freedom one hundred years after official emancipation, Baldwin's shifting interpretation of the meaning of these two conflicting ideas occurs in light of a change in theoretical perspective from an existentialist-literary cultural criticism to a new critical practice of political-theoretical analysis and public judgment.

Significantly, Baldwin engages this new critical practice, having recently formulated (and publicly committed to) his conception of the vocation of the artist as "a lover's war" with society, and the terms of engagement for this lover's war bear critically on the advice Baldwin gives his nephew. As he explained in "The Creative Process," the artist's vocation is a mode of critical engagement in which, as a matter of survival, the artist reveals society to itself for the sake of human freedom. The artist does this, Baldwin insists, in much the same way as the lover, at his best, reveals the face of the beloved to himself or herself. Love is, therefore, an activity of revelation, an activity in which the lover discloses himself or herself to the beloved as a condition of pushing the beloved to self-disclosure. To accomplish this revelation—which is essentially a process of removing the masks and obfuscations worn by the beloved—the lover must be prepared see through the typical modes of masking habitually deployed by the beloved. Among other things, then, the activity of love requires time and patience, a kind of acceptance that seeks to provoke growth, change, and maturity in the beloved. Baldwin's new synthesis of love as acceptance and acceptance as provocation, then, corresponds to a convergence of responsibilities in Baldwin's life that stem from his vocation as an artist and his choice to act as a mature and loving elder who must transmit moral meaning to the young. Baldwin's teaching to his nephew—that he must accept whites with love and press them to take responsibility for their complicity in crime—leaves a major question unanswered. Baldwin issues a positive command for action that, as formulated, still seems formal. Could this formal command be the extent of Baldwin's teaching to his nephew, or is this formalism merely apparent?

Easily one of the most interesting silences in scholarly treatments of *Fire* is the failure to note Baldwin's specific enumeration of the duties he insists his nephew most uphold as a condition of living a good life.[65] I already noted Baldwin's insistence that his nephew must accept whites with love, but this duty is merely one of three. Baldwin introduces the first duty rather early in the first letter, when he explains to his nephew his countrymen's unforgivable crime of the will to innocence. Baldwin's command is subtle, perhaps even purposefully cloaked within parentheses: "One can be, indeed one must strive to become tough and philosophical concerning destruction and death, for this is what most of mankind has been best at since we have heard of man. (But remember: most of mankind is not all of mankind.)"[66] Baldwin explains that, in the scale of human destructiveness, America's destruction of blacks is exceptional precisely because it is systematic, known, and denied. The operation of all three elements at once—systematicity, cognizance, and willed disavowal—constitutes the American innovation in the commission of political evil, distinguishing American political evil among mankind's expertise in human destruction. To combat the exceptional character of American destruction, Baldwin recommends an exceptional kind of wisdom: "Remember: most of mankind is not all of mankind." Thus, Baldwin counsels remembrance (of a special kind) over and against history. He insists to his nephew, as he will later insist to a select group of readers, that he remember the exceptions to human history and trust his own experience of persons and associations of persons who acted in and against history, even (and especially) when the historical evidence suggested that their actions would be futile.

Baldwin states the second duty more clearly than the first, even though, in some ways, it is more complex. Baldwin tells his nephew, "You most survive because we love you, and for the sake of your children and your children's children."[67] On the surface, this formulation may seem merely to command young James to outwit the systematic forces of destruction on the basis of another command so that he can uphold the survival of the race (a dicey proposition in a white supremacist culture, and one that requires that it remain hidden or unspoken). However, nothing could be further from the truth. Baldwin enjoins his nephew to recognize his obligations to the future, but the grounds of these obligations are in the past, and only secondarily connected with race. The true grounds of young James's obligation to the future, Baldwin explains, are the prices his forebears paid in the past. Baldwin describes the scene of these transactions. First, he tells his nephew, "I *know* the conditions under which you were born, for I was there. Your countrymen were *not* there, and haven't made it yet. Your grandmother was also there, and no one has ever accused her of being bitter."[68] Then he explains to James the conditions of his birth: "Well, you were born, here you came, something like fourteen years ago; and though your father and mother and grandmother, looking about the streets through which they were carrying you, staring at the walls into which they brought you, had every reason to be heavyhearted, yet they were not."[69] Baldwin explains to James that his parents, grandmother, aunts, and uncles had fateful choices to make in regard to how they would regard his birth. Although his family may have been obligated to provide for him, they were not, in truth, obligated to celebrate his birth. For Baldwin, their disposition to regard his birth as a unique and unrepeatable event, rather than as an accident of history or a determination of nature, reflects an act of will that was at once deeply personal and profoundly dependent on reciprocal obligations spread across multiple persons within their family. Young James, therefore, must remember these conditions and all of the individual acts of will and decision that not only constituted his arrival as a day of celebration in the past but also continue to make claims on his loved ones in the present. "We have not stopped trembling yet," Baldwin explains, "but if we had not loved each other none of us would have survived. And now you must survive because we love you, and for the sake of your children and your children's children."

Baldwin's instruction to his nephew that he must accept his countrymen with love is a provocation to young James to engage whites politically. He charges this young man of fourteen (roughly the same age as John Grimes, the protagonist of *Go Tell It on the Mountain*) with the duty to contribute to the project of revealing to his countrymen their complicity in unforgivable crime. Yet this is the last of three duties, the first being the duty of remembrance and the second being the duty of recognition of his obligations to the constitutive love acts that made his birth and life a cause for celebration. These three duties comprise Baldwin's moral instruction to his nephew and also depict a form of political education. They instruct him as to how to escape the country's intention to destroy him, but they also point beyond mere survival toward something resembling Baldwin's conception of a good life, a life involved in provocation for the sake of human freedom. This moral instruction and political education provide the answer to the question implied by the title of the first letter. What is the meaning of liberation among blacks connected by bonds of intimacy, one hundred years after official emancipation of slaves? They are honor-bound to continue the quest for liberation, and this quest will require them to engage white Americans politically and with love.

It is clear how Baldwin's project of moral instruction and political education flows from his deeply political conception of the vocation of art. Yet one might still wonder whether the project Baldwin unfolds in the first letter is really a political intervention. After all, while Baldwin allows readers to overhear a conversation between himself and a young black male, when all is said and done, his depiction is a small slice of a particular family's private life.[70] One might ask, Does Baldwin really provide us with a usable model of civic excellence? Baldwin responds to this crucial question in his second letter, "Down at the Cross, Letter from a Region in My Mind," which I analyze and evaluate in light of Baldwin's essay, *No Name in the Street*. I take this approach because, while Baldwin tries, with his notion of "authority," to provide an account of the distribution of his ethics throughout black America and attempts to provide a more general statement of the content and possible political applications of his principle of love, he does not provide the kind of epistemic explication that academic political theorists tend to demand from texts, as a condition of being taken seriously as political-theoretical works.[71] His clarification of some of these principles in *No Name in the Street* provides an effective index to his thinking in *Fire*.

Written in the aftermath of the assassinations of Martin Luther King, Jr., Malcolm X, Medgar Evers, Fred Hampton, and Bobby Hutton; the tragic death of Lorraine Hansberry and the beginning of Baldwin's coming to terms with the suicide of his beloved friend, Eugene; and in the midst of bewilderment and frustration at the imprisonment of Angela Davis, Huey Newton, and his assistant and friend, Tony Maynard, Baldwin's *No Name in the Street* reassesses the ethics and politics of love that he articulated in *Fire*. Baldwin recounts that the deepest roots of the principles of love as provocation revealed themselves to him at King's funeral. This revelation recalls an earlier moment in "Notes of a Native Son" in which his two opposing principles resolved themselves into an ethics of love shortly after his father's funeral, a funeral at which the lack of visible expressions of grief led Baldwin to comment that "it could not be called successful."[72] By contrast, King's funeral was packed inside and out, and was undoubtedly and paradigmatically successful. "Every inch of ground, as far as the eye could see, was black with black people, and they stood in silence."[73] Inside, things were somber until, as Baldwin recalls, the Reverend Ralph Abernathy asked "a long dark sister" to sing Martin's favorite song, "My Heavenly Father Watches Over Me." Baldwin reports that he was, in that instant, transported through time. "The song rang out as it might have over dark fields long ago: she was singing of a covenant a people had made, long ago, with life, and with that larger life which ends in revelation and which moves in love."[74]

In this episode, Baldwin provides his most candid and profound confession of his understanding of the deepest roots of the ethico-political duties of love. As he makes plain, these roots reach down and back to the whipping fields of American slavery. They are, he suggests, composed of promises slaves made to life and to one another, promises to live, love, and revel in life despite its nastiness, brutality, and absurdity. In sharp contrast to the notion of covenant that prevailed in early modern social contract theory, the promises made by slaves were not designed to authorize a durable and awe-inspiring power on Earth to secure order and commodious living, but rather were made to shore up battered selves so they might live in a disordered world whose only rule, it must have seemed, was their inescapable exposure to brutal violence and unchecked power. Moreover, unlike the covenant of contract theory, this covenant sought self-knowledge rather than order. Slaves covenanted among themselves to authorize life, demanding only that one day each of them would be able to tell a loved one a coherent story about the meaning of his or her individual life. With this, Baldwin provides an answer to the question about whether he has an account of the distribution and circulation of his notion of love. He also provides an answer to a deeper question concerning the phenomenological basis for his conception of love. As he explains in *No Name in the Street*, this ethic is rooted in a covenant in much the same way that the black quest for liberation *is* rooted in hope. Both are traceable to the poetic activity of American slaves, and both are expressions of love. How, then, does Baldwin begin to politicize this poetics in the second letter of *Fire*, and what are we to make of it as politics?

Achieving Our Country: Violence, Power, and Unshakable Authority

In the middle of "Down at the Cross, Letter from a Region in My Mind," Baldwin declares, "The energies that were buried with the rise of the Christian Nations must come back into the world."[75] This declaration is both a prediction and a plea. Even though Baldwin insists that America and the West must inevitably contend "with the untapped and dormant force of the previously subjugated," he is equally clear about his fear that the coming transvaluation of values and power may involve costs that are too great to bear, even as it seeks to create new conditions for human flourishing. Hence, Baldwin provokes readers to consider the very real possibility that superior economic, military, and even discursive power may prove impotent against the gathering storm: "In order to survive as a human, moving, moral weight in the world, America and all the western nations will be forced to reexamine themselves and release themselves from many things that are now taken to be sacred, and discard all of the assumptions that have been used to justify their lives and their anguish and their crimes for so long."[76] With this statement, Baldwin begins his discussion of the Nation of Islam, the black separatist religious sect founded by Elijah Muhammad, an organization thrust into national prominence by the rise of the acute, prophetic, and brilliant Malcolm X, and claiming rightfully to have facilitated the moral regeneration of black America's most wretched, from outlaws and outcasts into "warriors and maidens" in the rising city of a black God.

Baldwin attempts to explain the emergence of the genuine and increasingly formidable power that was then accumulating within the Nation of Islam; he also attempts to distinguish this power from the energies that were buried with "the rise of the Christian nations." Thus, Baldwin's analysis of the Nation of Islam is an artfully indirect analysis of the vicissitudes of Western national power. It is not difficult to understand why Baldwin would use the most feared and vilified black organization of the day to illustrate the precariousness of the American social order. Nor is it terribly surprising that he would link the rise of this organization to the rise of formerly colonized nonwhite nation states, states whose potential threat was vouchsafed by a credible Soviet power that was then contending with the United States for global hegemony. What is surprising, however, is that Baldwin uses the Nation of Islam to make a theoretical distinction that was, in form, virtually identical to a theoretical intervention that Arendt formulated at the identical moment in *On Revolution* (1963). In this text, Arendt sought to distinguish violence from political power as a means of drawing another, more pointed distinction between insurgent, insurrectionary, or rebellious violence and the violence that she conceded was undoubtedly indispensable to liberation, but not essential to genuine revolution. By means of these distinctions, Arendt tried to purify and tame the violence that too many professional revolutionists, in her view, had mistaken for politics. Such persons, according to her, had simply inflamed and perverted what may very well have been the indispensability of violence as an instrument of liberation from oppression into a conception of violence as both necessary and essential to the exercise of political freedom. Driven by a mistaken view of social welfare as political freedom, and having failed to understand that revolution, properly understood, was an act aimed at establishing institutions that would facilitate political freedom rather than economic justice, the professional revolutionists, Arendt insisted, had failed to deliver either. For Arendt, political freedom both presupposed and reproduced power, conceived as simply the energy or momentum that was produced, legitimated, and exercised in and through collective deliberation, public judgment, and concerted action. This power, Arendt argued, was a very particular store of energy generated within and for the public sphere, and it was made available only on the condition of its having arisen from speech, rather than from domination or violence. Political freedom, then, consisted of the ability to participate in these deliberations of the public sphere, and the public sphere produced the power that enabled humans to initiate something new and unprecedented into the order of nature and the contingencies of history. Therefore, for Arendt, not only political freedom but also human freedom, as such, crucially depended on this distinction between power and violence.

Without taking issue with Arendt on any number of fronts (indeed, her profound disdain for the social question is only one of a host of other troublesome commitments),[77] we can use her distinction to illuminate Baldwin's thinking on related, if not identical, matters because he also seeks in *Fire* to distinguish among violence, power, and authority. By "violence," Baldwin means what Arendt meant, although he is more clear-sighted about the violence that proliferated in American society and other Western regimes as a precondition of their public character and is clearer about the way that violence proliferated in the form of exclusions based on race, class, gender, and sexual orientation.[78] Baldwin and Arendt diverge from one another in their understandings of power. By "power," Baldwin means roughly what Arendt meant by "force" and "necessity." For him, power is what it was for Thomas Hobbes, a capacity to impose one's will (or the will of some association of persons) on another.[79] Hence, Baldwin is deeply suspicious of power and its role in social life.[80] Baldwin was not always consistent in his usage of the word "authority," sometimes blurring the distinction between authority and power. However, although he occasionally uses the word "authority" to describe the operations of power, he is conceptually consistent in distinguishing power from what he describes as a legitimate, compelling, and embodied capacity to effect changes in other persons and in the world. In his considered view, "authority" names "a human identity" whose "apprehension of life" and whose confrontation and resolution of "self-doubt, fear, sorrow, and hatred" results in a kind of spiritual resilience, intelligence, and beauty. As he explains, "That man who has been forced each day to snatch his manhood, his identity, out of the fire of human cruelty that rages to destroy it knows, if he survives his effort, and even if he does not survive it, something about himself and human life that no school on earth—and, indeed, no church—can teach. He achieves his own authority, and that is unshakeable."[81] Hence, in a manner analogous to Arendt's attempt to purify and tame the violence that she conceded was indispensable to liberation but inessential to revolution, Baldwin seeks to tame and purify the power that he believes may be indispensable to politics but inessential to love.

Love as provocation is, as we have seen, the heart of Baldwin's conception of civic virtue. It is the refinement of character necessary for the kind of political engagement that will be up to the task of founding a new polity and that will not endorse activities that seek only dissolution and disorder. Hence, this formulation depends on whether Baldwin can elucidate those spaces and practices in which authority, rather than power, prevails, those spaces and practices in which power can be made to serve the ends of love. As we have seen, love as provocation stipulates that the lover's revelation of the beloved to himself or herself is a condition of human freedom. Also, for Baldwin, love is a relation of obligation that is born from a covenant with life that is coeval if not identical with the quest for liberation. Even so, Baldwin recognized not only that power is real but also that "many things, including very often love, cannot be achieved without it."[82] As was the case with Arendt, the success of Baldwin's project of theorizing a politicized love hangs crucially on the success of the distinction he will try to draw among power, authority, and violence. That is, Baldwin must demonstrate that love as provocation is a real alternative to power and perhaps is even conceivable as a form of public authority, which is to say, quite simply, that he must convince readers that love can set them free.

Baldwin's strategy is to present a respectful, but unsparing, critique of Elijah Muhammad and the Nation of Islam. Having received an invitation to Elijah's home and having gone to meet him, Baldwin admits to genuine respect and affection for the man. In fact, he pays Elijah what would seem, for Baldwin, to be the highest compliment: He confesses that he was drawn to the man's "peculiar authority."[83] Although he is respectful to the man, Baldwin offers a piercing judgment of his political theology. Baldwin subjected a number of doctrinal and theoretical problems to withering criticism, but he reserved his harshest (and perhaps his least fair) judgment for the Nation of Islam's claim to have healed former drug addicts and criminals and regenerated the morally dissolute. "Well, in a way and I have no wish to minimize [Elijah Muhammad's] peculiar achievement—it is not he who has done it but time."[84] Although this understated piece of skepticism was devastating, going right to the heart of the Nation of Islam's most formidable claim for its practical achievement, Baldwin's respectful treatment of the organization and its leaders differed from his incisive but somewhat caustic treatment of Richard Wright's *Native Son*. The balanced, even gracious, character of Baldwin's critique of the Nation of Islam aligns his rhetorical strategy more closely with the strategy he deployed in "Notes of a Native Son" than with that of "Many Thousands Gone." In "Notes of a Native Son," Baldwin used public confession, the literary form and mode of textuality developed by St. Augustine and Jean Jacques Rousseau, both writers who, in different ways, portrayed the link between the private and personal drama of the self and the public, political, and cultural crises of their day.[85] Baldwin follows the example of these two writers by presenting his own private battle for love, authority, and self-knowledge as a grand contest against the seductions of power within a society that is itself plagued by criminal power.

As Baldwin makes plain, the temptation of power presented itself to him in the way it presents itself to most Americans, black and white alike, as the promise of safety. As needy and fragile beings fated to die, possessing drives and needs we can neither fully comprehend nor entirely domesticate, we tend, according to Baldwin, either to settle for a paltry mix of mediocre satisfactions as long as we are secure or, alternatively, to make inordinate demands for larger and more intense satisfactions than can be had without bestial indifference to others and the delusion of presumed superiority and entitlement. In Baldwin's view, the quest for security among the many and the smug license of the few are merely opposite sides of the same coin. Both are expressions of the quest for power, and both are cowardly responses to the conundrum of life. The essence of Baldwin's battle is located elsewhere: in his efforts to convey the idea that the life devoted to love as provocation is the true path of nobility and authority. And, if this were not challenging enough, if he is to fulfill his obligation as a "lover," he must also convey that the best argument for his project is one grounded in his authority and not in his representativeness as an agent of gathering forces of power. What better way to do this than to tell a beautiful story about oneself? To confess, as it were?

Baldwin's story begins in the summer of his fourteenth year and ends with his conversation with the young member of the Nation of Islam who was tapped to drive him home after his meeting with Elijah Muhammad. Baldwin explains that during the summer of his fourteenth year, he "underwent a prolonged religious crisis" and that "for the first time in my life I became afraid—afraid of the evil within me and afraid of the evil without."[86] Without warning, all of the sordid characters on the avenue—the whores, pimps, and racketeers—became a personal menace, he explains, because all of them had been produced by the same forces that produced him. His own body had become a "source of fire and temptation." Furthermore, because "school revealed itself as a child's game one could not win" and "it was clear the boys would rise no higher than their fathers," the American promise of upward mobility held little credibility.[87] In the face of an abysmal lack of options, Baldwin recounts, the cost of a single misstep would be devastating, resulting not simply in injury, incarceration, or death, but in madness, slow dissipation, and suicide. Recalling his predicament at the tender age of fourteen, he explains

> The wages of sin were everywhere visible, in every wine stained and urine splashed hallway, in every clanging ambulance bell, in every scar on the faces of the pimps and their whores, in every helpless, newborn baby being brought into this danger, in every knife and pistol fight on the Avenue, and in every disastrous bulletin: a cousin, mother of six, suddenly gone mad, the children parceled out here and there; an indestructible aunt rewarded for years of hard labor by a slow agonizing death in a terrible small room; someone's bright son blown into eternity by his own hand; and another turned robber and carted off to jail.[88]

The danger, isolation, and despair that Baldwin described in the Harlem of his youth were virtually identical to those he saw thirty years later in the "vivid," "violent," and "problematical" streets of Chicago when his young driver took him to his hotel after his meeting with Elijah Muhammad. At fourteen, Baldwin says, he discovered what all young blacks "who want to live" discover: the necessity for power, a "gimmick" "that could set you on your way" and provide "some means for inspiring fear in others," even though, as he explains, "it was absolutely clear that the police would whip you and take you in as long as they could get away with it, and that everyone else—housewives, taxi-drivers, elevator boys, dishwashers, bartenders, lawyers, judges, doctors, and grocers—would never, by the operation of any generous human feelings, cease to use you as an outlet for his frustrations and hostilities."[89] As had other young black people, Baldwin also discovered at fourteen that the distinction between power and crime was well-nigh impossible to sustain.[90] According to Baldwin, the social order that young people confronted in white supremacist America was "a criminal power to be feared but not respected." Faced with these prospects, Baldwin had joined the church just as his young driver had joined the Nation of Islam.

It is beyond the scope of this study to consider the breadth of Baldwin's fascinating and disconcerting account of his years in the church. What interests me here is the reasons he gives for leaving it, a decision that involves several telling realizations. First, he comes to see that there was no love in his church. His church was, as he explains, simply a mask for hatred and self-hatred.[91] In counseling reactive and defensive measures to deal with outsiders, the church, Baldwin realized, failed to empower him to chart a new course of association with anyone and, thus, failed to provide him with freedom.[92] The church also failed to provide him with self-knowledge, because its true principles, identical to those governing white Christian churches, were blindness, loneliness, and terror—"the first actively cultivated," he explains, "to deny the other two."[93] Finally, Baldwin explains that, when he preached to the young that they would have to "reconcile themselves to their misery," he began to feel like a criminal.[94] This last revelation may express the height of Baldwin's revulsion to the religious life he led. While he admits only to feeling regret and guilt about his sermons, he had, in effect, acted as an unwitting agent of American white supremacy by helping to reconcile these young people to their misery.

In the course of his confession, Baldwin nevertheless indicates that it is highly unlikely his young driver will come to the same realization about the Nation of Islam that he came to about his own church or, even if he did, that he would make the choices Baldwin made. Despite the perilous similarity of circumstances between the Avenue in Harlem and the contemporary streets of Chicago's South Side, Baldwin makes it clear that certain differences remain. Although there may be little new in the Nation of Islam's doctrines other than "the explicitness of its symbols and the candor of its hatred,"[95] it was under the auspices of the Nation of Islam that "African kings have come into the world out of the past, the past that can now be put to the uses of power."[96] With this observation, Baldwin means to suggest, first, that while the Nation of Islam is devoted above all to the acquisition and exercise of power, the leadership of the organization (especially Elijah Muhammad and Malcolm X) is grounded in real authority.[97] Even though they may advocate a policy that is misguided and injurious for blacks and America as a whole, Baldwin refrains from questioning the integrity of these men. More importantly, he recognizes that both men possess a sincere, devoted, and proven (if spiritually disastrous and practically futile) authority. This recognition constitutes, for Baldwin, the real and deepest problem with the Nation of Islam. In its organization, the Nation of Islam puts authority (in Baldwin's sense of self-knowledge gained from transcendence of fear, sorrow, despair, and perhaps even hatred) into the service of power. It is this sense of authority, in combination with the readings of history, Baldwin explains, that constitutes the Nation of Islam's strength and, while at odds with his own project, continues to exercise a genuine appeal to him.

For this young driver, who must survive the vivid, violent, and desperate streets of Chicago, the misguided, but genuine, authority of the Nation of Islam is a beacon. Its theology of black divinity and election has a worldly plausibility that the storefront Christianity of Baldwin's youth lacked.[98] America and the entire West have been challenged and debunked by rising nonwhite nations and brought to heel by the threat of Soviet power.[99] Whereas the idea of a black god who intended Western destruction would have once rung hollow and appeared silly, it was now possible for blacks to imagine that "all things began with the black man and that he was perfect—especially since this is precisely the claim that white people have put forward for themselves all these years."[100] The greatest difference between the young Baldwin and his young driver concerns the difference in their respective dreams. Baldwin was tempted by power through the promise of safety, but he dreamt of being a writer. By contrast, his young driver dreamt of power, Baldwin explains, in the same way his fictional character John Grimes dreamt of tyranny.[101]

> This boy could see that freedom depended on the possession of land;
> he was persuaded that in one way or another, Negroes must achieve

this possession. In the meantime, he could walk the streets and fear nothing, because there were millions like him, coming soon, now, to power. He was held together, in short by a dream—though it is just as well to remember that some dreams come true—and was united with his brothers on the basis of their color.[102]

Baldwin understands this young man's dream, has probably dreamt it himself, and has presented it in his fiction. While he sees through its practical futility and spiritual dangers, he knows that the compelling force of this dream consists of the answers it provides to deep-seated needs. One might go so far as to say that Baldwin understands that his young driver's decision to join the Nation of Islam is grounded in the will to live, just as his own decision for love is grounded in his needs as an artist.

The will to power among blacks, Baldwin realizes, is a matter of personal survival.[103] Negotiating the criminal power of white supremacy, blacks contend with insult and injury (and often worse) on a daily basis. This does not mean that they wrestle with hurt feelings, Baldwin explains. Rather, it means they contend with the internalization of power and intimidation, grapple with the confinement of the self, and manage the external forces that complicate, revise, or destroy those purposes formulated by the self. This will to power could involve the quest for pleasure, the pursuit of personal development, or simply the drive to ensure that one's children are fed and one's loved ones are safe. Yet, as Baldwin explains, once a black self comes to realize that the powers arrayed against him or her are utterly gratuitous and have nothing to do with anything he or she has done, it becomes clear that stopping to distinguish among real, imagined, intentional, and accidental injury is a luxury that can carry real dangers.[104] Under circumstances such as these, as Baldwin makes clear, the will to power is not simply tempting and perfectly rational, it is (precisely because it is both of these things) legitimate. What, then, is Baldwin's answer to the problem raised by the will to power?

Although twofold, Baldwin's most obvious answer to this question is the least important to him. The first answer simply invokes the threat implied in the title of *The Fire Next Time*, the creeping catastrophe of social disintegration precipitated internally by American blacks and externally by the confrontation of American power by other nation-states. On the basis of this increasingly likely scenario, Americans must take the necessary and decisive steps to end the discriminatory treatment of blacks in all aspects of life. They must especially address the political economy that systematically generates and reproduces the deprivation of basic social goods, such as freedom from violence, access to living wage jobs, and full protections for the exercise of voting and other political activities. If it does not take these measures, Baldwin insists, America should expect insurrectionary violence and a proliferation of the spirit of revenge among the black rank and file.

Unlike this first answer, which appeals to the calculative and instrumental rationality of readers, Baldwin's second answer appeals to "lovers," readers who are passionately driven to seek justice. To them, Baldwin puts a question that, he explains, came to him during his conversation with Elijah Muhammad. Are the ethico-political duties of love, he wonders, simply too weak a reed to contend against the will to power? As Baldwin explains, this question imposed itself on him as he tried to defend his obligations to his friends, who, although white, were nonetheless his people. These were persons whom he loved and who loved him and, as he explains, who "[struggled] as hard as they knew how, and with great effort and sweat and risk, to make the world more human." Even so, he realizes he could not have persuaded anyone at Elijah's table that these people had worth or that his sense of obligation to these persons was just, because, in truth, the white persons he loved were, in fact, exceptions to the rule, a rule confirmed, according to Baldwin, not simply by the streets of the South Side of Chicago, but by "everything stretching back through recorded time."[105] From antiquity to the contemporary streets of Chicago, "lovers" had failed miserably in their efforts to wrest change from those for whom "power was more real than love." But, in this moment of despair, Baldwin wondered, "Was this true? Had they failed? How much depended on the point of view?" Snatching victory from defeat, Baldwin recognizes an important certainty: "The world has always been made worse by those for whom power is more real than love." In doing so, Baldwin counsels his readers who are "lovers" that, while there are no guarantees, except decline and disorder, if power seekers prevail, there is a possibility, unpromising as it may be, that their efforts might initiate something new and unprecedented into the disorder and misrule of the powerful. Although Baldwin does not say so himself, one suspects that his relentless appeal to what he regards as the heroism of "lovers" stems not only from his readiness to subject himself to these same strenuous demands but also from his sense that it is precisely this kind of heroism and sublime nobility that was displayed in the covenant with life made by American slaves.

Baldwin's appeal would probably escape the notice of persons too invested in the will to power (both those whose ruling desire is for safety and those whose desire assumes some more aggressive incarnation), but it might—he believes—register as a real and genuine question to "lovers," those for whom quest, daring, and growth are more real than power. When we wrestle with the operations of the will to power in history and the indeterminacy of the effects of love as provocation, we see that Baldwin's second letter is a sustained meditation on the identity between the will to safety that is at the center of all political theologies and civil religions—whether black or white, or prestigious or disreputable—and the will to power that is at work in all political projects—whether these projects are partially defensible, as is the case with the Nation of Islam, or criminal and perverse, as is the case with white supremacy. If one has grasped Baldwin's arguments about the connection between the quest for safety and the will to power, and the connection between the cultivation of piety and the production of a power that can be called on as violence, one can understand how Baldwin's appeal for the revolutionary transformation of American society is not an invitation to avert catastrophic racial conflict and societal disintegration but an attempt to conjure the present as an opportunity to create. Baldwin's appeal is an invitation to political creation because multiracial solidarity constitutes an unprecedented beginning rather than an end. Truly actualizing this solidarity would constitute an unprecedented mode of human flourishing. If, in recognizing this invitation, the reader is moved by Baldwin's authority rather than his power, Baldwin's jeremiad has done its work as the inspiration of civic poetry rather than from a coercive pronouncement claiming privileged insight.

The End of a Tradition?

The project that unfolds in *The Fire Next Time* is, in many ways, the boldest attempt by a black writer to defend and resuscitate traditional American political ideas. In the process, Baldwin indulges some traditional American sources of blindness. For example, Baldwin's proposition that America remained an undiscovered country to be founded by "lovers" who were called into being by art was undoubtedly reckless with respect to the histories of the Native American victims of New World genocide and conquest. Moreover, as we have seen, Baldwin revived American exceptionalism, both in ascribing exceptional status to American crime and in endorsing a privileged leadership role for the American state internationally, once it had solved its race problem. Yet, bearing in mind these two serious problems, Baldwin's project in *Fire* represents a thoroughgoing attempt to reconstruct the terms of the black tradition of reflection and critique of American civil religion.

In the end, however, Baldwin would have to admit, as his predecessors had, that his project had been an abysmal failure. Not only did the polity he attempted to conjure never materialize; the old polity struck back with a vengeance that caught him off guard. Not only was he unprepared for the assassinations, expansions in police surveillance, and dramatic increases in the incarceration of black people, and especially black men; he was also caught unawares by the rise of American conservatism and, of all things, the jovial, but aggressive and knowing vindication of American innocence by conservatism's good natured strongman Ronald Reagan.

As bad as things were on this front, Baldwin also had to confront the rise and expansion of the black bourgeoisie, black people for whom professional advancement, conspicuous consumption, and identification with the American state had eclipsed the public insurgency Baldwin assumed would continue until racial justice had been achieved. This assumption, of course, was dead wrong, and Baldwin's latter work, bitter and rich, reflects an amplitude of grief and disappointment, as well as a clear recognition that "love" as provocation might continue to be a compelling private ideal, but one that was hopelessly impotent within the American public sphere. It also reflects his sad, but substantiated conclusion that Americans have little love for justice. Still, Baldwin concluded *No Name in the Street*, undoubtedly his darkest essay, with a confession about himself and black folk that recalled the covenant that he continued to believe their enslaved ancestors had made with life and with one another, and Baldwin makes this confession to a country he no longer believed was capable of honor. Finally able to reject American exceptionalism, but not black folk or America, Baldwin closed the book on this old form of political theorizing:

> To be an Afro-American, or an American black, is to be in the situation, intolerably exaggerated, of all those who have ever found themselves part of a civilization which they could in no wise honorably defend—which they were compelled, indeed, endlessly to attack and condemn—and who yet spoke out of the most passionate love, hoping to make the kingdom new, to make it honorable and worthy of life.[106]

Conclusion

Prophetic Political Critique in the Age of the Joshua Generation

The tradition of prophetic political critique has come on hard times. The once organic relation between black communities and prophetic political intellectuals has been strained, if not severed. The illuminative powers of the tradition have been vigorously contested by insightful internal critics, who have laid bare aspects of the tradition's blindness and excess. Located within a culture dominated by a political imaginary inspired by John Winthrop that continues to appeal to American exceptionalism, the prophetic critical tradition remains perennially liable to cooptation.

As the second decade of the twenty-first century begins, prophetic political critique has been both co-opted and muted by the resurgent respectability of black aspirations to the City on the Hill. The resonant oppositional consciousness that has characterized the political vocabulary of black prophetic critique seems to have given way to a messianic rhetoric of fulfillment circulating around the figure of President Barack Obama. This rhetoric is closer in spirit to President Ronald Reagan's incantation of Winthropian purposes than the critical interrogation and re-formulation of these purposes advanced by David Walker, Frederick Douglass, W.E.B. Du Bois, and James Baldwin.[1] At the same time, an intense dispute rages inside and outside of black America over the consequences of affluence. Some argue that the spectacular changes across the most important registers of material well-being for many African Americans in the post–civil rights era obviate the fundamental rationale for the tradition, while others insist that there are compelling reasons to believe that the legacies of slavery and white supremacy persist in the contemporary United States. Arguments for the continuing need for prophetic political critique are drawn from the disproportionate incarceration of African Americans (and Latinos) in both state and private, profit-driven penal institutions; the continuing structural dislocation of disproportionate numbers of African Americans outside or near the bottom of the global capitalist economy; massive and growing racial inequalities in wealth and income; and the unabated concentration of black and brown children in multiple systems of underdevelopment. Given the pervasiveness of these indicators, the transformative possibilities of black prophetic political critique seem to be needed but are nearly exhausted.[2]

Prophetic political critique appears to have been silenced despite the prolonged afterlife of slavery and Jim Crow that continues to thrive in the vulnerability of black women and men to police brutality, racial profiling, and discrepant sentencing.[3] Prophetic voices have seldom been heard to address the acute vulnerability of gays and lesbians of color to violence, violation, marginalization, and exclusion from communities of color as well as from white gay and lesbian communities. In the face of resurgent racial animosity and an ambivalent, complacent, and sometimes uncomprehending polity, prophetic political critique seems incapable of mustering a morally vigorous and intellectually robust opposition. If this once vital tradition inaugurated and sustained what Eddie Glaude has called an "exodus politics," a politics marked by its oppositional nature, it has been eclipsed by a politics of "the Joshua Generation," the nonoppositional, post–civil rights era black politics discussed by presidential candidate Barack Obama on the fortieth anniversary of the bloody civil rights march from Selma to Montgomery.[4] In the midst of intense debates over the status and well-being of black Americans, the meaning and legacy of the African American prophetic tradition are less clear than ever. For increasing numbers of Americans—black and white, Right and Left, young and old—it is unclear what work, if any, remains to be done within this political tradition. This chapter explores the legacy of the prophetic tradition of political thought and examines the constellation of political relations and historical developments that have contributed to its eclipse.

The Political Inheritance
of Prophetic Political Critique

The tradition of prophetic political critique has had many significant accomplishments, which, far too often, remain unsung. Prophetic political critique generated techniques of personal discipline that sought to coordinate individual transformation (personal overcoming) with collective political action (public engagement). Walker inaugurated this programmatic agenda, articulating a vision of black insurgency that linked the need for self-interrogation of "the slave within" to a political-theological obligation that called blacks to recognize and build on nascent prepolitical competences already extant within black America on both sides of the Mason-Dixon Line. As Walker argued, these competences were rooted in what the ancient civic republican tradition described as "courage"—citizens' willingness to die for their polity, hoping to achieve glory in a patriotic death. Douglass affirmed for his abolitionist allies the presence of this spirit among a smaller group of exceptional blacks, yet he tempered this affirmation with narratives that highlighted these individuals' resolute commitments to liberal American Protestantism and American exceptionalist, natural rights liberalism. Douglass preserved Walker's unflinching critique of black ignorance, yet he muted his predecessor's politicized conception of ignorance by construing it as African Americans' misapprehension of their true political enemies. Forsaking violent struggle for a campaign for civil rights, Douglass enunciated and performed a vision of exemplary American citizenship, a vision of egalitarian, gentlemanly individuality expressed in his commitment to secure emancipation, black civil rights, and political equality for women. Douglass reformulated Walker's project of black liberation into a vision of black self-creation and black service to the American republic. In the process, Douglass mobilized blacks to root out twin enemies—their own internalized slavishness and the unvanquished partisans of the imperious regime of American mastery. Du Bois and Baldwin embraced the programmatic agenda of the City on the Hill enthusiastically, although they defined the pathologies plaguing the black community differently and they offered alternative remedies for the issues they identified. For Du Bois, black pathologies stemmed from the anachronistic, exploitative, and dispiriting organizational forms of an un-reconstructed America. To overcome these challenges, he advocated new modes of political education conceived, executed, and modeled by skilled and honorable black political and cultural elites. For Baldwin, white supremacy and the kinds of pietistic religiosity he experienced in the church of his youth generated pathologies of existential evasion and moral cowardice, pathologies best addressed by cultivating practices of intimacy, self-confrontation, and unconditional involvement with others.

As a tradition, prophetic political critique elaborated resonant and revisable political vocabularies that enabled the comprehension and transformation of multiple and shifting manifestations of white supremacy, America's paradigmatic mode of political evil. African Americans encountered the problem of political evil in the United States as a confrontation with the absurd. They encountered both a moralistic, reformist, and experimental political culture and a systematic arrangement of cultural practices and political institutions that violated their bodies, assaulted their spirits, and demeaned their self-understanding. As Baldwin made clear in *The Fire Next Time*, individual encounters with systematic and gratuitous violence were almost always encounters with the incomprehensible. The publics constituted by the survivors of these atrocities, however, learned to make political sense of the incomprehensible. With the aid and inspiration provided by prophetic political critics, black publics developed collective perceptions, explanations, and modes of living uniquely attuned to the savage irony of America's genuine commitments to human rights, human decency, and political equality, as well as to its equally genuine and resolute commitments to violating black humanity. Prophetic political critique provided the vision that confronted and helped to manage this maddening tension. It described the catastrophic failures and horrifying atrocities of American liberal democracy as the expression of fallen, but not wholly incorrigible, selves who could still be brought to a moment of decision. The tradition of prophetic political critique also developed resonant re-descriptions of blacks as the burdened but blessed (or fated) beings who had been chosen to bring the crisis of decision to a head.

In addition, the tradition articulated modes of responsible and effective political agency that recognized the energetic passions of political desire, the powerful calling to political life, which the American founders feared and described as "political ambition," and which Max Weber described as a "vocation" and a casualty of modernity's professionalization of politics. Within American political thought, African Americans' passion for the political life has been overlooked, maligned, or misunderstood. Constructed as inherently inferior, "second-class citizens" at best, blacks have been denied any desire for a way of life dedicated to acquiring and exercising public power, appearing in public, and struggling with and for their peers. In the rare instances when this inner calling of black political agency has been taken seriously as a political motivation, it has been treated as a malformed priestly desire for hypervisibility or as the otherworldly service of saintly heroes. Du Bois may be as responsible as any for the first misunderstanding, while the grand, weighty, and genuine example of the Reverend Martin Luther King, Jr., continues to foster the second. Indeed, King was only the most visible of a coalition of black preachers who provided crucial leadership and organizational talent during the civil rights movement of the mid-twentieth century.

I do not wish to engage Du Bois or those under his influence on whether and why preachers have acquired "undue political influence" within black America. Nor do I wish to question the saintly service of genuine heroes such as King. I frankly acknowledge some black preachers' historical excesses and King's mortal limits and ethical blind spots, even as I note the crucial role black preachers have played under markedly oppressive conditions in American society. I would like to suggest, however, that African Americans' quest for political agency is not exhausted by the quest for citizenship, although this historic quest has been the guiding preoccupation, outstanding contribution, and unfinished project of prophetic political critique. Beyond the grand quest for equal rights, the struggle for African American political agency has also been manifested in the prophetic political critic's vocation for political leadership. To illuminate the nature and import of this form of political agency, I turn to the insights of Weber. His shifting formulation of the political role of the prophet helps clarify some of the crucial tensions in the prophetic thought of Walker, Douglass, Du Bois, and Baldwin.

Faith and Desire: The Dignity of Prophetic Political Critique

In *Ancient Judaism*, the final work in his pioneering sociology of religion, Weber argued that the prophet's vocation was a political office inasmuch as "the prophets stood in the midst of their people and were interested in the fate of its political community."[5] The internal esteem and public authority of this vocation, however, was essentially religious. "The dignity of the prophetic calling was rooted in the prophet's habitual possession of consciously clear and communicable interpretations of Yahweh's intention."[6] Prophets demanded from their audience complete humility and total faith in God, yet they sought neither to found a new cult nor to impress their audiences with their elevation from sin or their ability to perform miracles. As devout members of an ancient community that was imperiled externally by imperial predation and beset internally by monarchial excesses, as members who nonetheless were committed to the belief that "[God] was an intelligible interlocutor who visited military disasters on the enemy and allowed Israel to suffer," prophets could not help but become "'politicians' of a sort."[7] Although Weber acknowledged the important political dimension of prophecy in *Ancient Judaism*, his conception of the dignity of the prophetic vocation accentuated the religious dimension of prophetic faith and muted the political character of prophetic desire. For Weber, the prophet was institutionally articulated as a political actor because he stood in the midst of his people. This stand remained only derivatively political, however, because the prophet's political concerns and desires were simply implicit within a fundamentally religious sense of mission.

In a later work, Weber amended this distinction in important ways. In *The Profession and Vocation of Politics*, the lecture explicating his theory of the modern state and the accompanying crisis of political action given modernity's professionalization of politics, Weber broadened the political dimension of the prophetic vocation. Fearing that the rationalization and professionalization of modern politics enervated the spirit that would be necessary to sustain the modern self against the immensity and variety of modern political problems, Weber sought alternative historical foundations of political authority. Weber analyzed these political foundations as historically specific forms of political rule that flowed from the authority of tradition, the authority of *charisma*, and—increasingly in the modern world—the authority of legality or statutory validity.[8] According to Weber, charisma, or the personal power of the inspired or heroic genius, provided the basis for the rule of "the chosen warlord," "the plebicitarian ruler," "the demagogue," and "the prophet."[9] Providing pre-modern leaders an inner justification for the exercise of power over others and subjects a justification for their deference to leaders, charisma was a normal source of rightful political rule in the pre-modern world. This "right to rule" presupposed an intersubjective recognition by leaders and their subjects of a formal and substantive inequality between them. Whatever reciprocity may have prevailed within these unequal relations of power, its basis was not subjects' reasoned and voluntary assent to the normative validity of a leader's claim to rule. Nonetheless, charisma provided a meaningful claim to political leadership that was personally captivating for the leader and communally valid for subjects.

Addressing political, rather than religious, concerns in *The Profession and Vocation of Politics*, Weber shifted from his earlier preoccupation with the political implications of prophetic faith to a new question about the political character and power of prophetic desire. Seen from the vantage point of political theory, prophetic practice functioned identically to other forms of pre-modern political leadership. The spirit that animates the charismatic prophet is akin to, though not identical with, the kinds of desires that constitute the sphere of politics. As Weber famously noted, power is the animating spirit within the political sphere. "Anyone engaged in politics is striving for power, either power as a means to attain other goals (which may be ideal or selfish), or power 'for its own sake,' which is to say, in order to enjoy the feeling of prestige given by power."[10] Weber stopped short of collapsing prophetic activity into politics by sustaining his earlier distinction between prophetic faith and prophetic desire. By providing a foreground for the political role and character of prophetic desire, however, he amended his earlier notion of the dignity of the prophetic vocation. Within this new frame, the dignity of the prophetic office was inherently tied to interdependent, albeit distinct, intensities of faith and desire. The prophet's faith in possessing clear interpretations of God's message provided one powerful mode of being in the world. Yet the prophet's will to deploy the power of public critique to create the conditions of faith provided a distinct and different mode of being. The prophet's faith was concerned with the ultimate source and truest ends of communal action and with ensuring compliance with these ultimate commitments as an end in itself. By contrast, the prophet's desire was civic— concerned with instrumental means—in a twofold sense. First, the prophet sought to influence compliance with ultimate ends as a means of respecting those ends. Second, the prophet attempted to generate power through cultural and political critique as a means to ensure prophetic influence.

Weber's distinction between faith and desire provides a means for distinguishing the religious impulse from political agency within the African American prophetic tradition. While there is no question that this tradition grew out of and responded to Winthrop's faith-based conception of the City on the Hill, it also provided a vehicle for the articulation of distinctly political desires of black Americans in a polity that denied them opportunities for equal political aspirations.

Walker's prophetic faith consisted in his decisive belief that blacks throughout the New World could be convinced that submission to slavery was worse than death and that American whites could be convinced that black uprising was worse than conceding dignity and the right of self-determination to blacks. His prophetic desire sought to destroy blacks' belief that American military and economic might was founded on Providence, or "the law of grace," as Winthrop described it. Instead, he sought to craft a new law, "wrought in the heart" of blacks that American might was the provocation that set the stage for eventual African American self-determination and glory. Walker's political desire was to be a lawgiver, one who destroys old laws and legislates new ones to found a new people. Although his rhetoric appropriated religious discourses, his project was altogether political.

Douglass's prophetic faith consisted in his belief that white Americans could be brought to choose the human rights commitments of the American Constitution over the imperious tyrannical commitments unleashed on the American polity by the unwritten constitution of American masters. His faith also consisted in a belief that the trauma of African Americans' experiences of slavery would be mitigated as freedom enabled the progressive development of African American personal excellences. By qualifying blacks to be equal partners in American self-government, these newly acquired excellences would also inaugurate a new order of individual black existence. Douglass's desire was to be a statesman whose courageous stands against the regime of masters would help give birth to a new multiracial republic where he and other blacks would be full citizens. Daring to reconceive the new world political imperatives of Winthropian political aspirations as the contingent failing of an otherwise praiseworthy project, Douglass desired to carve out a space for African Americans in a polity founded on the sacred dignity of individual rights. In inspiration and aspiration, this too was a profoundly political project.

Du Bois's prophetic faith was lodged in unhopeful (but not hopeless) hope that Northern elites would choose nobility over vulgarity and genteel, reformist liberalism over the racial despotism of philistine and anachronistic oligarchy. Du Bois's political desire sought to empower black intellectual elites to solve American problems of race and to disseminate these solutions across the land. He recovered and reframed the political imperatives lurking within the Winthropian ideals of America that had been artfully obscured by Douglass. By recasting these imperatives as constitutive imperfections, however, Du Bois recharacterized Winthropian aspirations as a noble, but unfinished, legacy, imperiled by exploitative commercialism and demagogic misrule. He harnessed his extraordinary scholarly acumen to serve as a statesman, whose prudence consisted in clarifying the highest virtues available to those he took to be patricians. Envisioning a new form of political leadership that drew on liberal faith in the power of education and aristocratic notions of a natural elite, Du Bois committed himself to the thoroughly political project of recruiting and training a new generation of political leaders.

Baldwin's faith lay in art as a social power that could facilitate individuals' decision to choose courageous self-examination rather than succumb to the proliferation of death-dodging myths and catastrophic crimes. This faith moved Baldwin to silence his initial skepticism about the capacity of black and white America for social and political justice. His desire was to articulate a vision that would enable Americans to abandon myths created to deny the fearful, sorrowful, and shameful experiences that accompanied colonization and nation building in the New World. Baldwin sought to destroy the political imperatives of New World modernity and to found the New World anew. A poet who cast himself in the role of revolutionary and founder, Baldwin adopted a political role with impressive similarities to the role Walker had embraced so enthusiastically almost a century and a half earlier.

All four writers struggled against the Winthropian vision of sacrifice that authorized practices of mercy among white Americans that devastated the lives of black Americans. They advanced probing critiques of the rhetoric of American election, mission, and exceptionalism, and sustained reverent attachments and gratitude for the constitutive sacrifice made by ancestral forebears. They sought to disrupt the political imaginary that bound white Americans to a deeply problematic polity constituted on the racialized principle of "resemblance." They sought to foster an understanding of the history of harm perpetrated by the adherence to such destructive political criteria for membership. Keenly aware of the dangers associated with sacrificial logics, each writer engaged the problem of sacrifice as an essential presupposition of emancipatory political engagement. All sought to reconfigure its rhetoric and effects to facilitate African American freedom. Grasping that the relation between slavery and the American pursuit of happiness was bound up with whites' willingness to forgive their own glaring moral trespasses, Walker theorized the possibility and the need for blacks to choose to sacrifice to overthrow a morally bankrupt political regime. Gripped by his own vision of the heroic grandeur of the founders' sacrifices, Douglass tried to convince whites and blacks that the founders' revolutionary sacrifices had been made on behalf of slaves and women as well as free white men. Impressed by the cult of the founders among New England cultural elites, Du Bois theorized the quest for racial justice as the precious, but endangered, sacrifice of Northern heroes. Baldwin told stories that highlighted the sacrifice of the prospects for real beauty in everyday life to sustain myths about false and misleading past sacrifices. Yet he also called on Americans to sacrifice their current condition to create a world in which sacrifice would no longer be necessary.

Walker died shortly after publishing *An Appeal to the Colored Citizens of the World*, so there is no record of his thoughts about the adequacy of his vision. Douglass lived long enough to betray growing worries about the adequacy of his vision, however. Du Bois and Baldwin were clearer in their self-assessments. Opening his autobiographical *Dusk of Dawn*, Du Bois confessed to the impotence of scholarship as prophetic exhortation. To be precise, he confessed to the failure of the prophetic intervention he had undertaken in his magisterial *The Souls of Black Folk* and in *Darkwater: Voices from within the Veil*, his more apocalyptic and less celebrated text of 1920. Describing his scholarly and political activities during this period, he confided, "Crucified on the vast wheel of time, I flew round and round with the Zeitgeist, waving my pen and lifting faint voices to explain, expound and exhort; to see, foresee and prophesy, to the few who could or would listen."[11] Acute as ever at the ripe old age of seventy, Du Bois perceived the folly of these presumptions.

Baldwin came to a very similar judgment. He confessed to the continued allure he felt to exhort fellow citizens, despite having concluded that time had
proven such exhortation futile. In the twilight of his life, in 1985, he admitted
to the persistence of this allure: "If I were still in the pulpit which some people
(and they may be right) claim I never left, I would counsel my countrymen
to the self-confrontation of prayer, the cleansing breaking of the heart which
precedes atonement." Chastened (and perhaps wizened) however by deep disappointment and profound frustration, he confessed, "This is, of course, impossible. Multitudes are capable of many things, but atonement is not one of
them."[12] Both writers' confessions say something very important, but not necessarily decisive, about the adequacy of prophetic political critique as a mode
of late modern political reflection and engagement. Both writers admit individual failure, and each confession suggests that the roots of the current crisis
of prophetic political critique might be located within the tradition itself.

Prophetic Faith, Political Desire, and the Problem of American Expectations

Should we take Du Bois's and Baldwin's repudiation of prophetic political
critique at face value? Martin Buber, philosopher and scholar of the Jewish
Bible, has argued that the expectation of failure was an essential part of the
classical prophet's faith in the community's capacity to be brought to the
moment of decision.[13] If he is right, we might take the despair of their later
assessments as part and parcel of the plight of the prophet. Or we might situate this assessment of failure in relation to the exaggerated expectations
of success associated with the uniquely American notion of a covenanted
errand. On this reading, Baldwin's and Du Bois's despair might betray each
author's unwitting internalization of the promise of New World modernity
to make ultimate fulfillment and complete self-realization genuine possibilities for American selves and for the polity as a whole.[14] As marginalized
and dislocated but thoroughly modern and thoroughly American writers,
each author began with the languages and aspirations that he found ready
at hand. Each used his talents to interrogate these elements as thoroughly as
he could. The deep and perhaps constitutively human desire for wholeness,
sufficiency, and insight—a desire articulated by American culture as the reasonable expectation of modern American selves—might be inordinate, but
it is lodged so deeply and widely that it remains resistant to all but the most
attentive and merciless experiments in self-overcoming.

While it is quite possible that Du Bois and Baldwin succumbed to inordinate American expectations, this hypothesis is neither confirmable nor

incontestable. Both authors wrote of their deep appreciation of the ways in which American political evil was bound up with the tragic character of human existence.[15] For this reason, we cannot jump to any conclusions about the deepest longings of the hearts of these men. Yet even an uncertain and unconfirmable hypothesis opens space for contemporary leaps of faith. As long as conditions warrant prophetic intervention and these interventions are capable of addressing internal contradictions, leaps of faith concerning the prospects for reviving prophetic political critique may not be unreasonable. If this kind of leap is still possible in our time, then prophetic political critique may be in decline and under siege, but it may not yet be dead.

Darkness at the Heart of Sacrifice: The Courage of Black Women

As we saw in Chapter 4, Baldwin sought to excavate the slave's "covenant with life" as a refusal of sacrifice and a model for postsacrificial politics. He was not the first African American novelist to attempt to recover slaves' pre-political civic excellences from the critique, dissembling, and condescension of Walker, Douglass, and Du Bois, respectively. Ralph Ellison's great 1952 novel, *Invisible Man*, begins with an excavation of precisely this kind in its presentation of the invisible man's clever old ex-slave grandfather as the Delphic oracle who sets the invisible man on his way. As praiseworthy as the effort of both writers to recover the ground of African American cultural and political life might be, each author is tellingly brief in his exposition of the inner experiences of slaves and the contexts that set the stage for the exemplary slave's actions. Although James Baldwin opened the door for a consideration of myriad forms of emotional and physical vulnerability and a broader range of gendered and sexualized experiences, his work does not take up the specific experience of slaves.

Toni Morrison corrects these omissions in her extraordinary 1987 novel, *Beloved*. *Beloved* depicts a world made by slaves under conditions of American mastery, a world where integrity leads to hubristic resolution, courage leads to crime, and love leads to abomination. The central theme of the novel is Sethe's quest for the good life, a quest as genuine as one is likely to find in American literature. It is the quest of an enslaved black woman to protect her children and live free with her husband. Although Sethe is a remarkable woman for many reasons, the one that is most relevant to the discourse of the City on the Hill is that she bears the sign of the elect. Unlike her peers, Sethe was chosen by her captured African mother and chosen precisely so that she would survive and know her origins.[16] Sethe's mother was raped aboard the ship that transported her from Africa to the New World and coerced into nonconsensual sexual relations as a slave in America. She proceeded to dispose of all of her children except Sethe, her only child born of a freely chosen union. Thus chosen for life by her mother, Sethe is told of her special election: "She threw them all away but you. The one from the crew she threw away on the island. The others from more whites she also threw away. Without names, she threw them. You she gave the name of the black man. She put her arms around him. The others she did not put her arms around. Never. Never."[17]

Sethe is exemplary for another reason. As one of the novel's many female and male slaves who are raped or reeling from the rape of a loved one, she portrays a common vulnerability of slavery as well as a profound truth about the slave's encounter with American political evil.[18] "That anybody white could take your whole self for anything that came to mind. Not just work, kill, or maim you, but dirty you. Dirty you so bad you couldn't like yourself anymore. Dirty you so bad you forgot who you were and couldn't think it up."[19] As a woman who has survived all of these physical, sexual, and psychological abuses, Sethe represents a standing challenge to African American prophetic political critique that tacitly or expressly reinforced the gender codes undergirding both black politics and the U.S. political system. *Beloved* demands that an adequate account of the experience of American enslavement must not only include the experiences of enslaved women but also undertake an analysis of the implications of these lived experiences for U.S. politics. With the exception of Baldwin, whose politics of love as provocation presupposed an exploration of, and engagement with, vulnerability and intimacy, the thinkers I have examined sidestep the full implications of a sustained examination of sexual violation. By feminizing treachery, Walker fails even to engage with these experiences. Douglass makes a spectacle of the brutalized black female body and then conceals black women's testimony. In the process, he shores up his own public performance of masculinity and privatizes black women's trauma. Du Bois recovers these traumas for theoretical elaboration and political mobilization, but he sublimates them for the purposes of genuine scholarship.

In *Beloved*, Morrison builds on a long tradition of African American women's engagement with prophetic political critique. Women such as Maria Stewart, Ida B. Wells-Barnett, and Anna Julia Cooper insisted on their status as political thinkers when their male counterparts and the public more generally did not always take them seriously as such. Tellingly, they did not typically claim membership in the tradition of prophetic political critique, and they often refuted or disregarded its central arguments and practices. Each of these writers, in different ways, contests the prophetic political visions articulated by the thinkers described in this study and anticipates elements of Morrison's engagement with this tradition. Stewart invokes and claims the legacy of Walker, yet subtly revises his masculinist project of promoting martial virtue. Taking up the post-emancipation political evil of lynching, Wells-Barnett sees through the pretensions of American theologico-politics and contests African American appropriations of this discourse. Theorizing liberal democratic justice in light of the patriarchal exclusion of black women's theoretical, practical, and political labor, Cooper launches a powerful critique of black prophetic politics. Explicating Stewart's revisionism, Wells-Barnett's political realism, and Cooper's repudiation helps to sharpen and focus Morrison's engagement with this tradition.

Like Walker, who sought to "awaken the spirit of inquiry" within the souls of his "slumbering brethren," Stewart attempted to awaken blacks to the interrelation among liberation, moral improvement, and spiritual purification in the 1831 speech "Religion and the Pure Principles of Morality." In her attempt to "cultivate among ourselves the pure principles of piety, morality and virtue,"[20] Stewart, following Walker's example, also saw "the gross ignorance that prevails among us" as the crucial problem facing U.S. blacks.[21] More than simply a call to blacks to return to the agenda mapped out by the recently departed Walker, Stewart's exhortation sought to expand the prophetic role to include black women. Walker had preached to the "brethren" that "true happiness" under conditions of "natural enmity" lay in preparing to "glory in death." Stewart argued that her conversion to the Christian faith was a transformative calling that imbued her, and other women, with "that spirit of independence that, were I called upon, I would willingly sacrifice my life for the cause of God and my brethren."[22] Pledging "to devote the remainder of my days to piety and virtue," Stewart proceeded to negate Walker's figure of the treacherous slave woman, the gendered trope he deployed to link ignorance to attenuated masculinity. "Many will suffer for pleading the cause of oppressed Africa, and I shall glory in being one of her martyrs."[23] For the women and men in the audience who may not have caught her references to the text of the *Appeal*, Stewart made her engagement with Walker more explicit: "And if there is no other way for me to escape, [God] is able to take me to himself as he did the most noble, fearless, and undaunted David Walker."[24]

The first American woman to address a "promiscuous" combined audience of men and women, Stewart aimed at black women political appeals usually reserved for men: "Oh, ye daughters of Africa, awake! Awake! No longer sleep nor slumber, but distinguish yourselves."[25] Redressing the

Appeal's masculinist construction of political agency, Stewart called black women to practice civic virtue and to cultivate the "spirit of independence."[26] "Show forth to the world that ye are endowed with noble and exalted faculties."[27] Redressing the implicit exclusion of black women from Walker's martial public, Stewart illuminated the political potential in the everyday activities of ordinary black women. As mothers, Stewart argued, in accord with the ideology of republican motherhood, black women occupied an office charged with molding the character of future generations of black citizens. "Oh, ye mothers, what responsibility rests on you! You have souls committed to your charge, and God will require a strict account from you."[28] As wives, black women held an office uniquely empowered to revive the sagging and beleaguered political desires of black men. Under the guidance of politicized wives (and potential wives), black men's "souls would become fired with holy zeal for freedom cause." More provocatively, Stewart insisted that black women needed to cultivate among themselves a political solidarity originating in the common vulnerabilities of black women and guided by their aspirations for collective black flourishing. As members of a solidaritous community of this kind, black women, Stewart dared to suggest, could inspire each other to embark on the quest for glory Walker had prescribed for the "brethren" and to create the conditions for their own greatness: "Why cannot we do something to distinguish ourselves, and contribute some of our hard earnings that would reflect honor upon our memories, and cause our children to arise and call us great?"[29]

Even though Stewart sought to enlarge this tradition of political theorizing by redressing the gender biases of Walker, she also undercut the aims of prophetic political critique in ways that devastated its effectiveness as an analysis of American political evil. To be sure, Stewart at times deployed biblical prophecy to inveigh against American crimes and warned that divine retribution awaited an unrepentant American polity as Walker had done.[30] However, Stewart's jeremiad departed from Walker's in her fundamental revision of Walker's crucial notion of natural enmity, his account of the objective yet socially constructed relation of violent opposition between blacks and whites. Where Walker's *Appeal* mercilessly interrogated the U.S. polity's leading figures and relentlessly exposed the polity's moral deficits, Stewart argued that blacks could learn something from the example white citizens provided: "I have been taking a survey of the American people in my own mind, and I see them thriving in arts and sciences, and in polite literature. Their highest aim is to excel in political, moral, and religious improvement. They early consecrate their children to God, and their youth indeed are blushing in artless innocence. They wipe the tears from the orphan's eyes, and they cause the widow's heart to sing for joy."[31]

When Stewart called blacks to dedicate themselves to piety, morality, and religion, her conception of these practices and spiritual commitments aligned closely with the values of "Christian Americans," the group Walker had cast as nearly unredeemable enemies of "colored citizens of the world."[32] Stewart advises blacks to divine American political virtues and to "possess a spirit of virtuous emulation within our breasts."[33] Furthermore, Stewart seems to appropriate the political imaginary of America's covenantal origins at face value. "Did the pilgrims, when they first landed on these shores, quietly compose themselves and say 'The Britons have all the money and all the power, and we must continue their servants forever?' Did they sluggishly sigh and say, 'our lot is hard, the Indians own the soil, and we cannot cultivate it?' No, they first made powerful efforts to raise themselves, and then God raised up those illustrious patriots, Washington and Lafayette, to assist and defend them!"[34] Holding up these examples, Stewart repudiated the martial virtues in favor of emulation, moderation, and faith, and evacuated prophetic political critique of its political urgency and force: "Then, my brethren, sheath your swords, and calm your angry passions. Stand still and know that the lord he is God. Vengeance is his, and he will repay."[35]

Writing in 1892, roughly sixty years after Stewart and three years before the passing of Douglass, Cooper and Wells-Barnett advanced powerful political analyses of the African American predicament, including trenchant critiques of the tradition of prophetic political critique. Both writers built on Stewart's illumination of the particular vulnerabilities black women faced at the intersection of white supremacy and patriarchy and her discussion of how the black male theoretical enterprise tended to eviscerate black women's political agency from its conceptions of liberation and collective flourishing. Wells-Barnett took up the first of these concerns in *Southern Horrors* and *A Red Record*, her two unflinching analyses of American lynching. Cooper took up the second in *A Voice from the South*, her pioneering feminist theory of American politics.

Wells-Barnett concluded *Southern Horrors* with a lesson she claimed every "Afro-American should ponder well": "A Winchester rifle should have a place of honor in every black home, and it should be used for that protection which the law refuses to give."[36] Beneath this lesson, there were two additional ones that were interrelated and conceptually prior. The first was that conscience, whether posited as a collective phenomenon inhering within a political imaginary or as a faculty of the individual psyche, was at best a secondary factor in politics. Political and social change within the American polity, Wells-Barnett argued, was produced by the force created through deft organization and prudent exercise of social power. "By the right exercise of his power as the industrial factor of the South, the Afro-American can demand and secure his rights."[37] This lesson was connected to a second. Although terrorized, dominated, and exploited, blacks already possessed social power that they had heretofore exercised imprudently. With Washington and Du Bois, Wells-Barnett perceived that the rehabilitation of the South had become a national priority, one predicated on "northern capital" and "Afro-American labor." However, where Du Bois and Washington sought to mobilize the national power of Northern capital on behalf of black uplift—Du Bois, by appealing to patrician investments in the political imaginary of the City on the Hill, and Washington, by skillfully exploiting white fatigue with the "Negro problem"—Wells-Barnett urged blacks to re-imagine themselves as a politically integral source of self-generated power that could itself be made worthy of national and local consideration: "To Northern Capital and Afro-American labor the South owes its rehabilitation. If labor is withdrawn capital will not remain."[38]

Wells-Barnett's teachings were insights gleaned from her unflinching and unprecedented engagement with the problem of American lynching, a problem so pressing at the time of her writing that its relative neglect by major black male political figures, such as Douglass and Du Bois, ought to give students of prophetic political critique pause. As Wells-Barnett demonstrated in her analyses of the problem, the one hundred and fifty officially documented annual lynchings of blacks in the early 1890s constituted a political atrocity, an atrocity that warranted systematic study and radical intervention.[39] Douglass praised Wells-Barnett's studies of lynching, but his praise betrayed his silence and disengagement from the issue. Du Bois and Washington publicly condemned lynching, yet Du Bois, even in his role as progressive social scientist, never afforded it the central and systematic analysis it warranted, and Washington supported antilynching activities in relative secret.

As Wells-Barnett explained, lynching was a system of political intimidation, a deliberate practice of racial terror countenanced by all levels of government and designed to coerce blacks into submission to the newly emerging Jim Crow racial order. Sustained by the specious justification that lynching was punishment for the rape of white women by black men and fueled in part by white men's anxiety about consensual sex between black men and white women—which concealed white men's historic and ongoing violations of black women—lynching revealed the arbitrariness of American law, the hollowness of American justice, and the vapidity of American susceptibility to moral appeal. Like Walker, Wells-Barnett urged blacks to cultivate powers and implements of collective defense. Unlike Walker and his male heirs, Wells-Barnett refused to invoke the political imaginary of the City on the Hill. Grappling head-on with the dark tangle of violence and sexuality at the heart of American racial domination, Wells-Barnett espoused a political realism and urged blacks to think politically without the supports provided by the American political imaginary.

Wells-Barnett's contemporary, Anna Julia Cooper, witnessed how black male elites systematically denied black women educational opportunities, excluded them from positions of leadership, and refused to acknowledge their talents. A former slave in North Carolina, Cooper experienced firsthand the dismissal of black women's intellectual work when her black male colleagues at St. Augustine's Normal School and Collegiate Institute (a school for newly freed slaves) underestimated her as a student and, later, when Frederick Douglass failed to acknowledge her after the publication of her book, *A Voice from the South*.[40] Excluded, as all women were, from the National Negro Academy, an organization formed by Alexander Crummel, Francis Grimke, and Du Bois to promote racial uplift through intellectual leadership, Cooper witnessed the simultaneous production of patriarchal power and political authority within elite black political organizations. As a perceptive political theorist in her own right, Cooper not only grasped Weber's insight that prophetic political critique embodied a distinctive form of political authority and political desire but also perceived that, when knotted to the quest of black male political elites for patriarchal power, prophetic political critique had become a regime of power and knowledge that legitimated their narrow political ambitions. Among other important interventions, Cooper's *A Voice from the South* advances a subtle yet devastating critique of prophetic political critique as a mode of black politics.

To begin with, Cooper rejected the covenantal, or providentialist, conceptions of history that have underscored the political imaginary of the City on the Hill. Characterizing the West in general and the United States in particular, Cooper charged, "In the few hundred years we have had to strut across our allotted territory and bask in the afternoon sun, we imagine we have exhausted the possibilities of humanity." Her candid historical assessment describes a martial imaginary lacking in refinement and virtue. "Our God is power; strength, our standard of excellence, inherited from barbarian ancestors through a long line of male progenitors, the Law Salic permitting no feminine modifications."[41] Dispensing with this history, then, Cooper placed the U.S. "theatre of action" in a broader and more contingent historical movement in which nations rose and fell. In stages of emergence, development, and gradual improvement, societies might discern and liberate forces of social progress. In periods of stasis and decay, societies typically held firm to anachronistic or regressive cultural and political practices. According to Cooper, a society's ability to tolerate differences between its members and its capacity to devise institutional means to mediate conflicts and channel them in socially productive ways were among the most important factors that determined whether the society progressed or regressed. Because race and gender formed the principal lines of social differentiation and conflict in the United States, they could act as catalysts propelling the U.S. polity forward or backward in its historical development. As Cooper explained, "Equilibrium, not repression among conflicting forces is the condition of natural harmony, of permanent progress, and of universal freedom."[42]

According to Cooper, the United States was contingently positioned as an heir to the imperfect but impressive progress initiated by Enlightenment Europe. And, as a nation composed of deep differences of race, gender, region, and ethnicity that were not always honored by the polity, the United States possessed a unique opportunity to mobilize unprecedented historical progress if it could marshal the will and ingenuity to equilibrate its deep social differences: "The fact is this nation was foreordained to conflict from its incipiency. Its elements were predestined from their birth to an irrepressible clash followed by the stable equilibrium of opposition."[43] Although the term "foreordain" suggests that Cooper hoped to rehabilitate a providentialist account of American political development, Cooper refuses this move. Rather, she argues that conflict can degenerate into violence as easily as it can be channeled into socially constructive equilibrium. More to the point, Cooper insists that inasmuch as difference, rather than homogeneity, has always characterized the social composition of the actual inhabitants of the United States, conflict has always prevailed, although usually in latent form. Cooper thus repudiates an exceptionalist account of the American mission. Circumventing this pervasive trope, Cooper challenges readers to envision national purposes against a backdrop of historical contingency.

While Cooper lamented white America's antipathy to black citizenship and its failure to understand black problems, she was especially concerned with what she took to be the unrepresentative and impoverished political and cultural leadership provided by black men. "The part [black men] have had to play in American history during the last twenty five or thirty years has tended rather to exaggerate the importance of mere political advantage as well as to set a fictitious valuation on those able to secure such advantage."[44] Black men had monopolized race leadership, yet they had spectacularly failed to engage with the complex intersections of race and gender. Describing the predicament black women faced, in part because of the failure of black men's political leadership, Cooper states, "The colored woman of to-day occupies, one may say, a unique position in this country. . . . She is confronted by both a woman question and a race problem, and is as yet an unknown or unacknowledged factor in both." To make matters worse, Cooper explained, many black men's political ambitions inured them from considering the consequences of their "less liberal sentiments" and "conservative attitudes" on the lives of black women. "It may be," Cooper opined with undeniable poignancy, "that they do not yet see these questions in their right perspective, being absorbed in the immediate needs of their own political complications."

In Cooper's view, the ways in which black men constructed and practiced prophetic political critique served "to cloud or color their vision somewhat, and as well to relieve the smart and deaden the pain for them. Their voice is in consequence not always temperate and calm, and at the same time radically corrective and sanatory."[45] If true, this was a devastating charge. The prophetic political critic's purpose was to expose to the polity how black vulnerability to unjustifiable pain and unmerited suffering constituted a national investment in idolatry and represented a declension from the nation's covenantal origins and purposes. If black men remained anesthetized to the full measure of black pain, then they rendered themselves theoretically and practically inadequate to the rationale and moral grounds of the tradition and called into question the value of the kind of vision the tradition claimed to possess. As Cooper stated, leaving little doubt about her assessment of the quality of the tradition's vision, "It does not require a prophet's eye to divine [history's] trend and image its possibilities from forces we see at work around us; nor is it hard to guess what must be the status of women's work under the new regime."[46] If the nation were to progress, it would need to attend to problems of race. However, to attend to problems of race, the nation did not need prophets; it needed women and men of both races who could discern and manage potentially productive conflicts.[47] The nation would need to turn black men "who can let their interest and gallantry extend outside the circle of their aesthetic appreciation." Such men, Cooper explained, would not need to be prophets, but simply "a father, a brother, a friend to every weak struggling unshielded girl."[48] More importantly, the nation would need to help create conditions for the counsel of black women "who are so sure of their own social footing that they need not fear leaning to lend a hand to a fallen or falling sister."[49]

Taken together, the interventions of Stewart, Wells-Barnett, and Cooper force three interlaced questions to the fore: What occlusions of vision are produced when the African American political-theoretical imagination eviscerates black women's political agency from the historical record? What are the consequences of allowing engagement with political ideals and philosophical principles to obscure, or even supplant, engagement with real and ongoing political violence? How constructive, responsive, or reliable is a black politics that looks to black male ambition for its spiritual force? Morrison builds on this long tradition of black feminist political theorizing when she applies the deep knowledge that black women held regarding the relationship between the practice of American mastery and the problem of sacrifice, one of the abiding problems within the public philosophy of prophetic political critique.

When the model of desire that animates slaves' quest for the good life takes the experiences of enslaved women as its point of departure, then the deepest sources of slaves' integrity, courage, and love can encompass the experiences of mothers, sisters, daughters, partners, and wives, as well as fathers, husbands, sons, and brothers. As Morrison suggests in *Beloved*, heroic sacrifice under these conditions often flows from a mother's love rather than from a father's pride.[50] Sacrifice, then, takes a markedly different form. To protect her daughter Beloved from the humiliating violations that she herself had suffered as an enslaved woman, Sethe kills her, explaining, "If I didn't kill her she would have died and that is something I could not bear to happen to her."[51] In response to the incomprehension of her lover, oldest friend, and fellow former slave, Paul D., Sethe asks, "What he know about it? Who in the world is he willing to die for?" Referring to her method of securing a proper burial for her slain daughter, Sethe asks, "Would he give his privates to a stranger in return for a carving [in a headstone]?" As Sethe's testimony so powerfully reveals, a mother may sacrifice her children and herself, or more specifically, sacrifice herself by sacrificing her children and the future: "The best thing she was, was her children. Whites might dirty her all right, but not her best thing, her beautiful, magical, best thing—the part of her that was clean."[52] Given the horrifying consequences of the acute conundrum of infanticide as sacrifice, Morrison cautions us to be wary and skeptical of sacrifice talk. Indeed, Morrison seems to suggest that the political rhetoric of sacrifice may be a potent tool for the manufacture of passion, but, followed to its logical conclusion, such sacrifice would prove disastrous. Betraying the higher exigencies of African American survival, Morrison suggests that the rhetoric of sacrifice should be discarded as an essential precondition for real liberation. Given the centrality of sacrifice to the prophetic political tradition, Morrison's searing critique offers thoughtful grounds for abandoning the tradition: "This is not," she wrote, "a story to pass on."[53]

The Joshua Generation and the Professionalization of Black Politics in the Obama Era

On the cold morning of January 20, 2009, the most skeptical among us were shaken. It began when Aretha Franklin, royalty of American music, sang "My Country 'Tis of Thee," a song that rang out with ancestral cries and guttural moans. The roots of her rendition reached beyond and across the Massachusetts Bay colony of 1630 to the older settlement at Jamestown in 1619, reached back to what Baldwin described as the covenanting poetic practices of slaves trying to live on the whipping fields of American slavery. Then, a youthful and virtuosic black politician took the Presidential Oath of Office in the great republic, which, for most of its history, had been as committed to white supremacy as it was to Christian community and political liberty. On this day, a day like no other in the nation's history, formula was fact, moment claimed ritual, and skeptical cynicism had nothing to do but concede to solemnity as Winthrop's old words, "the eyes of the world are upon us," were spoken truly and infused with new vitality.

These old words were spoken frequently, perhaps more frequently and audibly than at any time in the nation's history. Print, radio, and television journalists, internet bloggers, and pundits—Left, Right, and Center—were in unusual accord. In electing a black man to its highest office, the U.S. polity had achieved an unprecedented feat of epochal significance, and the entire world was watching. Through the marvels of modern communication technologies, the inaugural spectacle enjoyed a global reach that was incomparable to any other spectacle of American political history and unimaginable by leading actors and spokesmen of earlier eras. The watching world was treated to a spit-polished and masterfully choreographed spectacle whose expert production and direction would have reddened the cheeks of Max Horkheimer and Theodore Adorno, co-authors of one of the earliest and most unsparing critiques of mass manipulation by the entertainment and media industries.[54] Those who watched twenty-four-hour cable news broadcasts outside the United States or webcasts provided by the three major American television networks were treated to American political theatre at its most sublime. Whether the intended public was a very small group of political elites, as it was during much of the republic's history, or whether it comprised the entire electorate and the world of electronically connected individuals, presidential inaugurations are dramatic performances that are tightly scripted for public consumption. Enhanced by ever-increasing expertise in representational techniques, fostered by market competition, and concentrated within the oligopolistic contest among a handful of media outlets, the racial drama playing itself out lent weight and interest to the political spectacle of the inauguration.

As the doors of the last whites-only space within the federal government swung open for Barack Obama, presidential blackness stood tall before a jubilant polity. American might and American promise seemed to join hands, and political power seemed to flow from freedom dreams, dreams that, until recently, had seemed heedless, excessive, and for some, even inflammatory. Behind these dreams were white votes from surprising places—Iowa, Louisiana, and North Carolina in the primary elections, and Ohio, Indiana, and Virginia during the general election. In postelection polling, some voters revealed that they supported Obama despite continuing reservations about black people. These hesitant and reluctant voters were a small part of a much broader coalition of white support, animated by a real conviction that the time had finally come: History had finally produced the black man promised by America's conception of itself as a covenanted liberal democratic polity that had, at last, turned the corner on its troubled racial past. Alongside these white voters stood robust support from Latino voters (six of ten), a level of support that was a surprise for many professional political observers and, for others, either a hopeful sign of a new era in coalition politics between African Americans and Latino voters or a terrible harbinger of the emergence of an unholy and un-American alliance.

In addition to this astonishing support from Latino and white voters, Obama received the nearly unanimous support of African Americans, a small number of whom had signed on as early as the 2004 Democratic National Convention, when the charismatic, and virtually unknown, candidate for the U.S. Senate gave the keynote address. That speech will probably be best remembered for its felicitous riff on the false divisions created by the rubric of "red states" versus "blue states." For a significant number of African Americans, however, what was most memorable was the peroration of the speech, in which the senator from Illinois distinguished "the politics of cynicism" from "the politics of hope" with a remarkable series of referents. "It's the hopes of slaves sitting around a fire singing freedom songs, the hope of immigrants setting out for distant shores, the hope of a young naval lieutenant bravely patrolling the Mekong Delta, the hope of a millworker's son who dares to defy the odds, the hope of a skinny kid with a funny name, who believes America has a place for him too."[55]

This was by no means the first time that the African American memory of slavery was injected into presidential politics. The Reverend Jesse Jackson had done precisely this at the 1998 Democratic National Convention. The first to deploy prophetic political critique within the high-stakes contest of American presidential politics and to subject it to this sphere's practical logics and spiritual imperatives, Jackson inserted the praxis into the eye of a storm when disillusioned black liberalism and assertive black nationalism swirled with angry white populism to discredit Democratic Party liberalism. Jackson boldly intoned, "We sit here together, a rainbow coalition, the sons and daughters of slave masters and the sons and daughters of slaves, sitting together around a common table to decide the direction of our party and our country."[56] As one of the most brilliant prophetic political exhortations in recent memory—albeit one delivered amid deep and widespread reservations about prophetic critique, such as those expressed by Baldwin in his later years—Jackson's speech conjured a robust and inspiring ideal of multiracial social democracy. Yet his vision of a rainbow coalition not only presupposed a unity comprising combatants in the long and continuing war for America's soul; in an attempt to conjure an alternative and oppositional set of sacrificial heroes, it also invoked the memory of murdered civil rights workers. Jackson preached (in the best and old prophetic sense of the word) common ground; however, he admitted that common ground was really an American "crossroads."

Obama's keynote address, given nearly twenty years later at the 2004 Democratic National Convention, said something quite different. According to Obama, the fraught but avidly sought "common ground" that Jackson had characterized as the lone road to peace available to combatants in America's unfinished civil and cultural wars, was an honorable vision. Yet, he intimated, this honorable vision unwittingly fed a politics of cynicism: "We are one people, all of us pledging allegiance to the stars and stripes, all of us defending the United States of America. In the end, that's what this election is about. Do we participate in a politics of cynicism or do we participate in a politics of hope?" As Senator Obama pointed out, the civil and cultural wars had not simply produced an unproductive stalemate; they had tragically mischaracterized American aspiration. Properly seen, he suggested, the true angel of American political history was hope, hope that had already knitted slaves, immigrants, veterans, gays and lesbians, and working-class whites together into a nascent political solidarity.

Many African Americans saw great significance and power in this early intervention by Obama. It had been nearly twenty years since a mainstream black politician with real political opportunities had spoken aloud about the freedom dreams of slaves at a major mainstream political event. This silence had something to do with the increasing political disdain for black griev-ance, which had originated (somewhat disreputably) in 1968 with the presi-dential campaign of Governor George Wallace of Alabama and had become both endemic and respectable since the election of Ronald Reagan in 1980. This silence also had to do with the penetrating and double-edged wisdom about the complex and unwieldy legacy of slavery and white supremacy artic-ulated by African American artists and intellectuals, such as Morrison. And it had to do with the decline of the tradition of prophetic political critique, a decline announced by Baldwin, hastened by and connected to the rise of black nationalism, and exposed by friendly but devastating criticism of the tradition leveled by African American political intellectuals.[57]

Obama's deft invocation of "slave's hopes" was rhetorically brilliant, as demonstrated by the peculiar enthusiasm that his first national speech gen-erated among pundits, party members, and political opponents. It was also philosophically intriguing. Obama appeared to channel Baldwin, excavat-ing and rehabilitating slave desire as an expression of American democratic virtue, as a form of the distinctive excellence of a democratic citizen. Begin-ning with Alexis de Tocqueville's account of the dehumanization of slaves in America, and culminating in Friedrich Nietzsche's withering and didac-tic genealogy of Western morality as flowing from the toxic spiritualization of slaves' resentment at the freedom of the strong, American political theory had deferred to American common sense about the meaning and value of the legacy of American slavery. According to this view, American slavery pro-vided a single object lesson. It was a political evil and a moral danger, both because enslavement betrayed individual rights and because the exercise of mastery inculcated a taste for tyranny. However, this is as far as the common sense analysis of slavery goes. Aside from confirming its malefic character and affirming its incompatibility with liberal democratic institutions, there was little to be gleaned from slaves' knowledge and experience that might serve as an example of political excellence. To discerning listeners, however, Obama's peroration in 2004 felt like a powerful gust of wind that had blown in from deep in the dishonored past. According to Obama, the hope of slaves was democratic desire, unsullied by the boundless quest for inordinate prop-erty and wealth.

Among other black voters, support for Obama was born from a deci-sive commitment made the night of the Iowa Caucus. As presidential can-didate Obama delivered his stirring victory speech before a rapt audience of white Midwestern voters, some decided that the difference between a credible black long shot and a flat impossibility was a leap of faith, one many Iowans already seemed to have made. For a number of black voters who rallied to his candidacy in these early days, Obama's sermonic cadence and affable seriousness—a blend of John Kennedy's virile optimism and patrician polish and Malcolm X's street wit and analytical brilliance—was an irresistible call to return to American politics.

For a larger number of voters, no doubt, candidate Obama became both recognizable and a cause, after the drama of the South Carolina primary, the drama that provided the Democratic primary campaign its moment of tragic sublimity. Former President Bill Clinton, a genuinely beloved figure among the black electorate for reasons other than his reliable support for traditional black Democratic concerns, cast aspersions on the black candidate's electoral chances, after Obama had just beaten the former president's wife, Senator Hillary Rodham Clinton, who had been the odds-on favorite to win the Democratic nomination. Most observers interpreted Clinton's aspersions as a crassly calculated decision, by one who knew the stakes, to mobilize white reaction against Obama. He seemed to think he could count on both black voters' blind affection for him and his wife and the paucity of political alternatives available to African Americans with liberal political inclinations within the mainstream American polity. For black voters who supported Obama in the aftermath of the South Carolina primary, Obama became an intimate because he appeared to be a black person who had proven himself competent and extraordinary and was vulnerable for precisely this reason. Black voters began to realize that they must close ranks, a realization they arrived at not without pity and fear, because their spiritual brother, the former president, had betrayed them to an old and familiar evil.

With a Jamestown wind blowing and resonating in the voice of Aretha Franklin, President Obama addressed a jubilant polity in crisis. Economic disaster loomed large on the horizon, military debacles festered, and American alliances were badly frayed. President Obama had to choose his words carefully. The previous administration had deployed the theological politics of America to strengthen American resolve after the terrorist attacks of September 11, 2001, and to justify American crusades—the preemptive projection of American violence to secure "the homeland" and promote what the administration declared to be a divinely ordained establishment of liberal democracy in places where God seemed to have revealed alternative political, economic, and social preferences. At this precarious moment in U.S. history, President Obama demonstrated that he was as brilliant a student of theologico-politics as he was a virtuosic statesman. His remarks were brief and austere, intended mostly to reassure an anxious and insecure polity. Under the circumstances, a full-throated invocation of the legacies of Jamestown as a live lament and source of democratic renewal would have been bold. Far less risky was an invocation of the City on the Hill, the well-worn legacy of Massachusetts Bay.

After quietly invoking Frederick Douglass, Obama quoted St. Paul: "We remain a young nation, but in the words of scripture, the time has come to set aside childish things." After St. Paul, Obama channeled Thomas Jefferson: "The time has come to reaffirm our enduring spirit, to choose our better; to carry forward that precious gift, that noble idea, passed from generation to generation: the God-given promise that all are equal, all are free, and all deserve a chance to pursue their full measure of happiness." Where candidate Obama had reformulated the terms of African American memory of slavery by replacing black grievance with black hope and, by implication, American shame with democratic virtue, President Obama then took the bold step of yoking black grievance and black hope together and recasting it as the confident and knowing preparation of black folk: "For us, they packed up their few worldly possessions and traveled across oceans in search of a new life. For us they toiled in sweatshops and settled the West; endured the lash of the whip and plowed the earth. For us, they fought and died in places like Concord and Gettysburg, Normandy and Khe Sahn." All were working, suffering, and waiting, the president insisted, "so we might have a better life." Then President Obama deployed Winthrop: "Our Founding Fathers, faced with perils we can scarcely imagine, drafted a charter to assure the rule of law and the rights of man, a charter expanded by the blood of generations. Those ideals still light the world, and we will not give them up for expedience sake."

Admitting that many of the most pressing problems facing the polity were new, President Obama went on to declare that the American future was secure because his election confirmed the truth of the real principle of movement within American history, a historical movement that revealed itself, it seemed, only on the basis of an antecedent adoption of the legacy of Massachusetts Bay as one's "point of departure." Within the parameters set by Winthrop's City on the Hill, the principle of movement was the quest to establish a model polity that would provide moral and political instruction to the world. When guided by this remarkable young president to see through this optic, the polity came into focus as having simply deferred, not forfeited, its covenanted purposes, when it committed the great sins of slavery and white supremacy. The angel of American history was quietly at work in the preparatory sacrifices made by slaves, immigrants, and settlers, sacrifices that now revealed themselves as racial progress. In electing Obama, the preparation of the polity had been completed, *the promise of America had been fulfilled*: "Our challenges may be new. The instruments with which we meet them may be new. But those values on which our success depends—these things are old. These things are true. They have been the quiet force of progress throughout our history." Stated in a minor (not to say blues) key, President Obama reaffirmed the spirit of American mission, construed American political evil as providential preparation, and identified racial equality as American redemption. President Obama subtly deployed the symbol of the "City on the Hill" by reasserting the link between the covenanted fate of the American polity and the cause of human dignity throughout the world. Perhaps more importantly, he recalled Americans to the political sacred by presenting himself as the custodian of America's triumph over American evil.

Although there can be no question of the political brilliance of President Obama's invocation of the City on the Hill, his appeal to the verities of America's sacred errand had far more in common with President Reagan's appropriation of this discourse than with the tradition of prophetic political critique. Perhaps the susceptibility of this discourse to conservative cooptation is itself a compelling reason to renounce any lingering critical potential for appeals to the City on the Hill.

As part of the intervention undertaken in *The Souls of Black Folk*, Du Bois counseled that premature demise of a worthy political project is cause for mourning, reflection, and self-critical rededication. Exhorting readers to remember the demise of the Freedman's Bureau, Du Bois noted, "The passing of a great institution before its work is done, like the untimely passing of a single soul, but leaves a legacy of striving for other men." By "legacy of striving," Du Bois sought to invoke a memory of a glorious inheritance of exemplary antiracist political desire, a precious tradition of civic longing for justice that was imperiled by the superior forces of white supremacy and by time itself. He invoked and attempted to make space for an ideal mode of civic engagement, a civic mode of antiracist action whose aim was to concretize the desire for racial justice, a desire as precarious as the elusive spirit Du Bois attempted to summon.

Du Bois offered his counsel "about the passing of a great institution" as part of his prophetic political intervention, not as the epitaph to his abandonment of prophetic politics in the 1940s. Given the momentous resources of the prophetic tradition to illuminate and critique political evil, and the enormity of the inequities that persist in our nation, the fundamental question is whether we can recover something of the faith Du Bois ultimately lost.

Notes

INTRODUCTION

1. Perry Miller, *Errand into the Wilderness* (Cambridge, Mass.: Belknap Press of Harvard University Press, 1956); Andrew Delbanco, *The Puritan Ordeal* (Cambridge, Mass.: Harvard University Press, 1989); Sacvan Bercovitch, *The Rites of Assent: Transformations in the Symbolic Construction of America* (New York: Routledge, 1993); Ernest Lee Tuveson, *Redeemer Nation: The Idea of America's Millennial Role* (Chicago: University of Chicago Press, 1980).

2. Reinhold Niebuhr, *The Irony of American History* (New York: Scribner, 1962). Niebuhr located this blindness in the secular presuppositions of the American creed, not the culture's theological presumptions. Yet, as I argue, the secular optimism of American political culture is an effect rather than a cause of the theological constitution of American political solidarity. Also see his *The Children of Light and the Children of Darkness: A Vindication of Democracy and a Critique of Its Traditional Defense* (New York: Scribner, 1960) and *Moral Man and Immoral Society: A Study in Ethics and Politics* (Library of Theological Ethics) (Louisville, Ky.: Westminster John Knox Press, 2001).

3. The best intellectual histories of prophetic political critique are Cornel West, *Prophesy Deliverance! An Afro-American Revolutionary Christianity* (Philadelphia: Westminster Press, 1982). See also Cornel West, *The American Evasion of Philosophy: A Genealogy of Pragmatism* (Madison: University of Wisconsin Press, 1989); Eddie S. Glaude, *Exodus! Religion, Race, and Nation in Early Nineteenth-Century Black America* (Chicago: University of Chicago Press, 2000); and more recently, Joanna Brooks, *American Lazarus: Religion and the Rise of African-American and Native American Literatures* (Oxford: Oxford University Press, 2003).

4. On African American prophecy as "vernacular political theology," see George M. Shulman, *American Prophecy: Race and Redemption in American Political Culture* (Minneapolis: University of Minnesota Press, 2008). For a different conception of black prophecy as a mode of post-colonial black "political-intellectual" work, see Anthony Bogues, *Black Heretics, Black Prophets: Radical Political Intellectuals* (New York: Routledge, 2003). A selective list of this rich and growing literature includes Robert Gooding-Williams, *In the Shadow of Du Bois: Afro-Modern Political Thought in America* (Cambridge, Mass.: Harvard University Press, 2009); Richard Iton, *In Search of the Black Fantastic: Politics and Popular Culture in the Post–Civil Rights Era* (Oxford: Oxford University Press, 2008); Juliet Hooker, *Race and the Politics of Solidarity* (New York: Oxford University Press, 2009); Barnor Hesse, *Un/Settled Multiculturalisms: Diasporas, Entanglements, "Transruptions"* (London: Zed Books, St. Martin's, 2000); Joy James, *Shadowboxing: Representations of Black Feminist Politics* (New York: St. Martin's, 1999); Michael C. Dawson, *Black Visions: The Roots of Contemporary African-American Political Ideologies* (Chicago: University of Chicago Press, 2001); Katharine Lawrence Balfour, *The Evidence of Things Not Said: James Baldwin and the Promise of American Democracy* (Ithaca, N.Y.: Cornell University Press, 2001); Danielle S. Allen, *Talking to Strangers: Anxieties of Citizenship after Brown v. Board of Education* (Chicago: University of Chicago Press, 2004); Charles W. Mills, *The Racial Contract* (Ithaca, N.Y.: Cornell University Press, 1997); Tommie Shelby, *We Who Are Dark: The Philosophical Foundations of Black Solidarity* (Cambridge, Mass.: Belknap Press of Harvard University Press, 2005); Eddie S. Glaude, *In a Shade of Blue: Pragmatism and the Politics of Black America* (Chicago: University of Chicago Press, 2007).

5. Eddie Glaude cautions against this danger as a particularly troublesome issue within contemporary African American political life. Advocating pragmatic interpretive strategies that highlight the tension between the exigencies of contemporary problem solving and the silencing that often attends the invocation of venerated historical figures, Glaude recommends a "post soul politics" that is more attentive to the contemporary references that inform and sustain African American cultural-political practices. I think there is a much greater role for veneration within contemporary black politics than he does, as I hope to make clear. Eddie Glaude, *In a Shade of Blue*. On the challenge of late modern acceleration of time on political reflection, political experience, and political action, see Sheldon S. Wolin, *The Presence of the Past: Essays on the State and the Constitution* (Baltimore: Johns Hopkins University Press, 1989); and more recently, Sheldon S. Wolin, *Democracy Incorporated: Managed Democracy and the Specter of Inverted Totalitarianism* (Princeton, N.J.: Princeton University Press, 2008).

6. Nietzsche explicates this problem with characteristic rigor. See Friedrich Nietzsche, *On the Advantage and Disadvantage of History for Life*, trans. Peter Preuss (Indianapolis: Hackett Publishing, 1980).

7. Aristotle, *The Politics*, ed. Stephen Everson, Cambridge Texts in the History of Political Thought (Cambridge: Cambridge University Press, 1988). For a good discussion of Winthrop's political thought, see Edmund Sears Morgan, *Puritan Political Ideas, 1558–1794* (Indianapolis: Bobbs-Merrill, 1965); for Puritan thought more broadly, see Miller, *Errand into the Wilderness*, and Delbanco, *The Puritan Ordeal*.

8. Alexander Hamilton et al., *The Federalist Papers* (New York: New American Library, 1961), 1.

9. Ibid., 198 (my emphasis).

10. Reagan was referring to court rulings that the display of the Ten Commandments in public school classrooms violated the First Amendment requirement of the separation of church and state.

11. On King as a prophetic critic, see Shulman, *American Prophecy*. Also see Cornel West, "Prophetic Christian as Organic Intellectual: Martin Luther King, Jr.," in *The Cornel West Reader* (New York: Basic Civitas Books, 1999).

12. Winthrop characterizes the political dimension of the errand as follows: "For the worke we have in hand, it is by mutuall consent through a speciall overruleing providence, and a more then an ordinary approbation of the Churches of Christ to seeke out a place of Cohabitation and Consorteshipp under a due form of Government both civill and ecclesiasticall." "A Modell of Christian Charitee," in Edmund S. Morgan, *Puritan Political Ideas, 1558–1794* (Indianapolis, Ind.: Hackett, 1965), 90. Miller, *Errand into the Wilderness*, 12.

13. Morgan, *Puritan Political Ideas, 1558–1794*, 93.

14. Augustine and R. W. Dyson, *The City of God against the Pagans* (Cambridge: Cambridge University Press, 1998), 960.

15. For his discussion of pride, see ibid., 537 and 936; for vanity, see 212 and 614; for corruption, see his discussion of the ends of the earthly city (632).

16. Morgan, *Puritan Political Ideas, 1558–1794*, 78.

17. Augustine argues that natural justice exists but is not always apparent. Augustine and Dyson, *The City of God against the Pagans*, 967.

18. Winthrop argues that natural justice fails to provide principles for dealing with enemies and provides no guidance on questions regarding duties of sacrifice—giving, lending, and forgiving. Morgan, *Puritan Political Ideas, 1558–1794*, 79.

19. Ibid., 92.

20. Ibid., 90.

21. Ibid., 92.

22. This probably has much to do with the subversive memory created by rival poets such as Nathaniel Hawthorne and Arthur Miller. For political theorists, the culprit may be Alexis de Tocqueville, who both celebrated Puritan prohibitions and applauded the Puritans for "carrying the legislation of a rude and half-civilized people into the heart of a society whose spirit was enlightened and more mild." Alexis de Tocqueville, Harvey Claflin Mansfield, and Delba Winthrop, *Democracy in America* (Chicago: University of Chicago Press, 2000), 38.

23. Morgan, *Puritan Political Ideas, 1558–1794*, 79.

24. Ibid., 78.

25. Ibid., 91.

26. Revealingly, Winthrop quotes Isaiah 58:6: "Is not this the fast that I have chosen to loose the bonds of wickedness, to take off the heavy burdens to lett the oppressed goe free and to breake every Yoake . . ." Ibid., 78.

27. Ibid., 84.

28. Ibid.

29. Ibid., 87.

30. Winthrop explains that resemblance explains God's love for humans, especially the elect, as well as a mother's love for her child and Adam's love for Eve. Ibid., 87, 78.

31. Ibid., 88.

32. Ibid., 89.

33. Winthrop acknowledges the difficulty thus: "If any shall object that it is not possible that love shoud be bred or upheld without hope of requital, it is graunted but that is not our cause, for this love is always under reward it never gives, but it always receives with advantage." Ibid., 88.

34. Ibid., 92.

35. Arendt simply followed the grooves worn into the European imagination by John Locke's characterization of America as a state or nature. Hannah Arendt, *The Origins of Totalitarianism* (New York: Harcourt Brace Jovanovich, 1973), 186.

36. As argued later in *On Revolution*, the political rises in America with the War of Independence, shines brightest during the ratification debates of the founders, and tragically recedes shortly afterward because participants within these debates were unable to enlarge and institutionalize their experience of constitution making. Alexis de Tocqueville provided a more complex account of the genesis of New World politics, highlighting its European antecedents in England as well as in the self-governing townships in sixteenth-century New England.

37. "Might have" is the key phrase here because Arendt was also reckless in her description of colonial atrocities in Africa. See Arendt, *The Origins of Totalitarianism*. For a more sympathetic assessment of Arendt's discussion of these genocidal massacres, see George Kateb, *Hannah Arendt, Politics, Conscience, Evil* (Totowa, N.J.: Rowman and Allanheld, 1984).

38. Niccolo Machiavelli, *The Prince and the Discourses* (New York: Modern Library, 1950); Frantz Fanon, *The Wretched of the Earth* (New York: Grove Press, 1963); Tuveson, *Redeemer Nation*; Mills, *The Racial Contract*.

39. Richard Slotkin, *Regeneration through Violence: The Mythology of the American Frontier, 1600–1860* (Middletown, Conn.: Wesleyan University Press, 1973); Toni Morrison, *Playing in the Dark: Whiteness and the Literary Imagination* (Cambridge, Mass.: Harvard University Press, 1992); Jill Lepore, *The Name of War: King Philip's War and the Origins of American Identity* (New York: Knopf, 1998).

40. As Alexis de Tocqueville noted, Puritan politics was the "point of departure" in the development of American democracy, the source of authoritative norms that decisively informed the past and current political practices of the United States. In his view, the forms established by Puritan settlers to order their collective life facilitated comprehensive political education in self-government: education in the competences of exercising and deferring to communal power, and education of mores, the affective habits and intellectual dispositions that constituted and contained individual imagination within prescribed boundaries. According to Tocqueville, containment of the imagination works alongside the enunciation of right and political obligation, both in terms of political legislation and in terms of culturally prescribed patterns of private association. Silent delimitation of what is permissible, possible, and desirable by mores supplements the coercion of law and shapes the formation of self-interest. Hence, mores are a critical foundation within the order of a polity, an authoritative form of soulcraft. Puritan religion provided this key form of soulcraft. However, as he also notes, the true genius of Puritan religion reached well beyond the Massachusetts Bay Colony theocracy. It extended in time and space, providing a seedbed for the robust religious practices that continued to contain the imaginations of eighteenth-century American revolutionaries and nineteenth-century citizens of American democracy. Hence, he insisted that there was an important lesson for Europeans here, but one especially important to his countrymen and fellow legatees of the French Revolution. Rather than honoring within the foundations of the American polity the Enlightenment assault on religious authority, as was done in the French revolutionary constitution, not only had Americans preserved unenlightened religious belief and practice but the polity had also managed to protect, promote, and legitimate the genius or Puritan soulcraft by sheltering it in the private sphere. Hence, the true genius of Puritan religion comes to view only when it is understood that the soulcraft devised and performed by Winthrop is essential to sub-

sequent operations of American statecraft. Tocqueville, Mansfield, and Winthrop, *Democracy in America*.

41. Patrick J. Deneen, *Democratic Faith* (Princeton, N.J.: Princeton University Press, 2005); Robert Neelly Bellah and Steven M. Tipton, *The Robert Bellah Reader* (Durham, N.C.: Duke University Press, 2006).

42. Bercovitch, *The Rites of Assent*. Also see Sacvan Bercovitch, *The American Jeremiad* (Madison: University of Wisconsin Press, 1978).

43. The classic account or religious resonance in American politics is Tocqueville's account of it as a form of hope that expresses the permanent needs of a being fated to die in the "short space of 60 years." Tocqueville, Mansfield, and Winthrop, *Democracy in America*, 284. For a good recent discussion of the enduring source, continuing challenge, and progressive possibilities of resonant religious vocabularies and practices, see William E. Connolly, *Capitalism and Christianity, American Style* (Durham, N.C.: Duke University Press, 2008).

44. The classic account is provided in Benedict Anderson's theory of the nation: "Communities are to be distinguished, not by their falseness and genuineness, but by the style in which they are imagined; [these communities] are imagined as limited because even the largest of them has finite if elastic, boundaries, beyond which lie other nations; [these communities] are imagined as sovereign because the concept was born in an age in which Enlightenment and Revolution were destroying the legitimacy of the divinely ordained, hierarchical dynastic realm; and [they are] imagined as a community, because, regardless of the actual inequality and exploitation that may prevail in each, the nation is always conceived as a deep, horizontal comradeship." Benedict R. O'G. Anderson, *Imagined Communities: Reflections on the Origin and Spread of Nationalism* (London: Verso, 1991), 6–7.

45. Charles Taylor, *Modern Social Imaginaries* (Durham, N.C.: Duke University Press, 2004), 23.

46. Wolin, *Democracy Incorporated*, 18.

47. Paul W. Kahn, *Sacred Violence: Torture, Terror, and Sovereignty* (Ann Arbor: University of Michigan Press, 2008), 97.

48. Ibid., 100.

49. Although prophecy is a social form practiced in divergent ways in many different cultures, the social and cultural critiques canonized in the prophetic books of the Hebrew Bible are the source for prophetic thinking in the United States. As George Shulman argues in *American Prophecy*, Hebrew prophecy is "a genre of speech and form of action" that reveals itself in a "mode of address, a particular 'register of voice,' and [set] of primal stories and constitutive metaphors" (3). Seen as a social practice of Ancient Israel and the United States, prophecy is a political office that consists of exhortation, bearing witness, forewarning, and poetic consolation (5). Its rhetorical forms are the jeremiad, theodicy, and the promise of redemption (10). Also see Michael Walzer, *Interpretation and Social Criticism* (Cambridge, Mass.: Harvard University Press, 1987); Martin Buber, *On the Bible; Eighteen Studies* (New York: Schocken Books, 1968); Max Weber, *Ancient Judaism* (New York: Free Press/Collier-Macmillan, 1967); Norman Podhoretz, *The Prophets: Who They Were, What They Are* (New York: Free Press, 2002). The primal story that orients prophecy is the story of Israel's divine election. According to this story, Israel is a national community constituted by a covenant with God, a reciprocal promise involving God's commitment to establish, protect, and exalt Israel, and Israel's promise to recognize, honor, and implement God's ordinances and world historic intentions and priorities.

50. "Prophecy, Apocalyptic, and the Historical Hour in Studies," in Martin Buber, *On the Bible* (Syracuse, N.Y.: Syracuse University Press, 2000). Also see Abraham Joshua Heschel, *The Prophets* (New York: Perennial, 2001).

51. Heschel, *The Prophets*, 159. Also see Podhoretz, *The Prophets*.

52. Shulman, *American Prophecy*, 5. Also see West, *Prophesy Deliverance!*, 214–215.

53. "The prophets stood in the midst of their people and were interested in the fate of the political community." Weber, *Ancient Judaism*, 300. Martin Buber argues that ancient Jewish prophecy is essentially a critical discourse that seeks to facilitate a decision about the status of the covenant by placing these fundamental issues before the community. The emergence of prophecy as a critical practice, along with the emergence of a literature that records the orations and deeds of these critics, suggests a culture of argument and reflection, as Michael Walzer argued in *Interpretation and Social Criticism*. However, the emergence of a group of persons tasked to perform these critical activities strongly suggests, as George Shulman has recently noted, that prophecy is an office, an institutional practice structurally related to other governing institutions of the community.

54. In 1787, the year delegates convened in Philadelphia to draft The Constitution of the United States, the Reverend Richard Allen and Absalom Jones led an exodus of black Philadelphians from segregated white churches to build what would become the first independent black church. Allen and Jones publicly enacted the imperatives of black prophetic Christianity. Yet neither writer develops a systematic theory of black politics or American politics. Nonetheless, as the oldest intellectual tradition of black America, prophetic Christianity precedes the praxis of prophetic political critique. However, while it provides the conceptual forms that prophetic political critics appropriate and revise to theorize the political, as well as the social imaginary that connects African Americans into a collective subject, it will take intellectual commitments of a very different kind to engage in political theorizing.

55. Cornel West, *Prophesy Deliverance!* Prophetic Christianity consists of interpretations of the Christian Gospel that highlight Jesus's kinship to the travails and tribulations of a people chosen to suffer horribly, yet prevail ultimately, and they read the meaning of his life and ministry in light of The Gospel of Luke's portrayal of him as a prophet: "And there was delivered to him the book of the prophet Isaiah. And when he opened the book, he found the place where it is written. The spirit of the Lord is upon me because he hath anointed me to preach the gospel to the poor, he hath sent me to heal the brokenhearted, to preach deliverance to the captives, and recovering of sight to the blind, to set at liberty them that are oppressed" (Luke 4:14–18).

56. My conception of prophetic political critique differs from the model of "redemptive prophetic" criticism described by Anthony Bogues. In *Black Heretics, Black Prophets*, Bogues describes an intellectual practice that consists of "healing, divination, and prophesy," where "prophesy" is principally the activity of eschatological prediction and eschatological prediction corresponds with a "millenarian" politics (19). Prediction of social disintegration is present in all of the thinkers studied here; however, it is less essential than provoking a collective decision by engaging with the covenantal presuppositions embedded within American theologico-politics. As Martin Buber and George Shulman (more recently) note, prophecy and eschatology are in deep tension with one another. Buber, *On the Bible*, and George Shulman, *American Prophecy* (Minneapolis: University of Minnesota Press, 2008). Recognizing individual agency within a contingent historical frame, the prophet calls their community to decide. By contrast, the prediction of the eschatologist enjoins an audience to comply with a predetermined fate. Bogues, *Black Heretics, Black Prophets*.

57. All of the writers I examine here conceived the prevailing forms of white supremacy of their day as political evil, and they sought to attenuate, deflect, and transform it
through their literary and rhetorical interventions. However, what distinguishes their
interventions from less sophisticated treatments of political evil is the degree to which each
writer (in different ways) went well beyond simplistic condemnation of the moral repug-
nance of white supremacy in order to grasp more fundamental relations between the dehumanizing violation of blacks and reproduction of American political solidarity. In doing
so, this group of writers leaves behind some of the most sensitive, candid, and creative
American writing about political evil ever articulated from within the tradition of American political thought. To understand the sophistication of these interventions is to gain a
deeper appreciation of what is at stake in the passing of this tradition.

58. For a moral philosophical account of political evil, see Claudia Card, *The Atrocity
Paradigm: A Theory of Evil* (Oxford: Oxford University Press, 2002). Also see John Kekes,
The Roots of Evil (Ithaca, N.Y.: Cornell University Press, 2005), 1; and John Kekes, *Facing
Evil* (Princeton, N.J.: Princeton University Press, 1990). For an excellent history of moral
evil as a problem of political theory, see Susan Neiman, *Evil in Modern Thought: An Alter-
native History of Philosophy* (Princeton, N.J.: Princeton University Press, 2002).

59. Andrew Delbanco, *The Death of Satan: How Americans Have Lost the Sense of Evil*,
1st ed. (New York: Farrar, Straus and Giroux, 1995). Moral philosopher John Kekes makes
a similar claim about the disappearance of the sense of evil. For Kekes, however, the relevant subject is the entirety of Western modernity, not simply Americans, and the source
of the erosion of this sense is the Enlightenment. Kekes, *Facing Evil*, and, more recently,
Kekes, *The Roots of Evil*.

60. In my reading, prophetic political critique qualifies as a genre of political philosophy because its practitioners consciously engage central questions of political philosophy
as well as facilitate or invent transformative politics. My conception of the prophetic critic
stands in contrast to the conception of the "political intellectual" described by many scholars working within the field of Africana studies. As I interpret the distinction, "political
intellectual" refers to the theoretical work involved in all black politics, but especially the
work of critics and activists. I do not wish to take issue with this conception, but only to
highlight the difference between it and my own. A good example of this approach is provided in Anthony Bogues, *Black Heretics, Black Prophets* (New York: Routledge, 2003).

61. I am building on George Kateb's definition, but as will become clear later, I am
revising it significantly. My insistence on evils committed by private citizens who act under
state protection is a departure from his view, which focuses on states and political movements. George Kateb, *The Inner Ocean: Individualism and Democratic Culture* (Ithaca,
N.Y.: Cornell University Press, 1992), 201.

62. The abstraction that is the chief offender for Kateb is patriotism.

63. Judith N. Shklar, *Ordinary Vices* (Cambridge, Mass.: Belknap Press of Harvard
University Press, 1984).

64. Judith N. Shklar, Stanley Hoffmann, and Dennis F. Thompson, *Redeeming American Political Thought* (Chicago: University of Chicago Press, 1998).

65. This problem maps onto a larger problem of the late modern world, according to
Connolly. The "acceleration at speed" that "compresses the distance" between different
faiths makes the quest for religious unity within territorial states a recipe for "persecution."
William E. Connolly, *Pluralism* (Durham, N.C.: Duke University Press, 2005), 29. Also
see his *The Augustinian Imperative: A Reflection on the Politics of Morality* (Newbury Park,
Calif.: Sage, 1993).

66. Connolly, *Pluralism*, 27.

67. For divergent views on St. Augustine's conception of evil, see Charles T. Mathewes, *Evil and the Augustinian Tradition* (Cambridge: Cambridge University Press, 2001); Paul Weithman, "Augustine's Political Philosophy," in *The Cambridge Companion to Augustine*, ed. Eleonore Stump and Norman Kretzmann (Cambridge: Cambridge University Press, 2001).

68. Augustine and Dyson, *The City of God against the Pagans*.

69. The formulation—"evil as policy"—is Kateb's. Kateb, *The Inner Ocean*.

CHAPTER 1: BLACK LIBERTY IN THE CITY OF ENMITY

1. David Walker and Charles Maurice Wiltse, *David Walker's Appeal, in Four Articles, Together with a Preamble, to the Coloured Citizens of the World, but in Particular, and Very Expressly, to Those of the United States of America* (New York: Hill and Wang, 1965), 17 (hereafter, *Walker's Appeal*).

2. Ibid., 12.

3. W.E.B. Du Bois, "The Talented Tenth," *Writings* (New York: Library of America, 1986), 844.

4. Christopher Leslie Brown, *Moral Capital: Foundations of British Abolitionism* (Chapel Hill: University of North Carolina Press, 2006). Also see Ian Baucom, *Specters of the Atlantic: Finance Capital, Slavery, and the Philosophy of History* (Durham, N.C.: Duke University Press, 2005).

5. For a discussion of Walker's predecessors, see John Saillant, *Black Puritan, Black Republican: The Life and Thought of Lemuel Haynes, 1753–1833* (Oxford: Oxford University Press, 2003). And, Richard S. Newman, *Freedom's Prophet: Bishop Richard Allen, the AME Church, and the Black Founding Fathers* (New York: New York University Press, 2008).

6. For an alternative view, see Wilson Jeremiah Moses, *Black Messiahs and Uncle Toms: Social and Literary Manipulations of a Religious Myth* (University Park: Pennsylvania State University Press, 1993), 46.

7. For a discussion of solidarity, see Tommie Shelby, *We Who Are Dark: The Philosophical Foundations of Black Solidarity* (Cambridge, Mass.: Belknap Press of Harvard University Press, 2005).

8. Walker and Wiltse, *Walker's Appeal*, 21.

9. Moses, *Black Messiahs and Uncle Toms*, 38.

10. Eddie S. Glaude, *Exodus! Religion, Race, and Nation in Early Nineteenth-Century Black America* (Chicago: University of Chicago Press, 2000).

11. Since Du Bois's pioneering insight that black churches effectively functioned as "governments of men," the interpenetration of the political and the theological has been widely accepted among scholars of African American religion. For the classic recent account of this, see Albert J. Raboteau, *Slave Religion: The "Invisible Institution" in the Antebellum South* (New York: Oxford University Press, 1980). Also see Cornel West, *Prophesy Deliverance! An Afro-American Revolutionary Christianity* (Philadelphia: Westminster Press, 1982). And more recently, Eddie S. Glaude, *In a Shade of Blue: Pragmatism and the Politics of Black America* (Chicago: University of Chicago Press, 2007).

12. Sheldon S. Wolin, *Tocqueville between Two Worlds: The Making of a Political and Theoretical Life* (Princeton, N.J.: Princeton University Press, 2001), 35.

13. This panoramic vision was increasingly pervasive in American public culture of the period. See Angela L. Miller, *The Empire of the Eye: Landscape Representation and American Cultural Politics, 1825–1875* (Ithaca, N.Y.: Cornell University Press, 1993).

14. Sean Wilentz, "Introduction," in *Walker's Appeal*, xii.

15. Ibid., 1.

16. Ibid., 76.

17. Aristotle and Stephen Everson, *The Politics* (Cambridge: Cambridge University Press, 1988), 69.

18. Walker and Wiltse, *Walker's Appeal*, 2.

19. By "conceptually" prior, I mean that for Walker, one must understand a particular problem first if one is to understand a larger problem, even if this larger problem appears in time as a more pressing problem. By "programmatically" prior, I mean that for Walker, taking meaningful action in regard to a particular problem may require that one first address an issue that seems marginal to the problem one ultimately wishes to address.

20. Edmund Sears Morgan, *American Slavery, American Freedom: The Ordeal of Colonial Virginia* (New York: Norton, 1975).

21. For an excellent discussion of this, see Joanna Brooks, *American Lazarus: Religion and the Rise of African-American and Native American Literatures* (New York: Oxford University Press, 2003) and John Ernest, *Liberation Historiography: African American Writers and the Challenge of History, 1794–1861* (Chapel Hill: University of North Carolina Press, 2004).

22. Walker and Wiltse, *Walker's Appeal*, 2.

23. Abraham Lincoln, "Address before the Young Men's Lyceum of Springfield," *The Life and Writing of Abraham Lincoln* (New York: Modern Library, 1940), 232.

24. Walker and Wiltse, *Walker's Appeal*, 3.

25. Brown, *Moral Capital*. Baucom, *Specters of the Atlantic*.

26. Walker and Wiltse, *Walker's Appeal*, 3.

27. Because Walker only implies this idea, it is impossible to know whether he is advancing something like a neo-Kantian conception of evil as a positive essence in opposition to the Augustinian conception of evil as privation. However, he appears to be closer to the position that Milbank attributes to the neo-Kantian position. See John Milbank, *Being Reconciled: Ontology and Pardon* (London: Routledge, 2003).

28. Walker and Wiltse, *Walker's Appeal*, 3.

29. Ibid.. My emphasis.

30. Ibid., 4.

31. "Second Inaugural Address," *The Life and Writing of Abraham Lincoln* (New York: Modern Library, 1940), 842.

32. Walker and Wiltse, *Walker's Appeal*, 7.

33. Ibid., 19.

34. Ibid.

35. Ibid., 20.

36. Ibid., 21.

37. Ibid.

38. Ibid., 22.

39. Ibid., 24.

40. Ibid., 27.

41. Plato, G. R. F. Ferrari, and Tom Griffith, *The Republic* (Cambridge: Cambridge University Press, 2000), bk. II, 375a–376c.

42. Walker and Wiltse, *Walker's Appeal*, 43.

43. For an extended discussion of this paradox, see Glaude, *Exodus!*

44. Walker and Wiltse, *Walker's Appeal*, 35.

45. Sacvan Bercovitch, *The American Jeremiad* (Madison: University of Wisconsin Press, 1978). Glaude, *Exodus!* David Howard-Pitney, *The Afro-American Jeremiad: Appeals for Justice in America* (Philadelphia: Temple University Press, 1990).

46. Walker and Wiltse, *Walker's Appeal*, 35.

47. Some have argued that las Casas ultimately comes to regret this proposal. As Davis points out, however, las Casas challenges the legality of enslaving Indians, and perhaps also Africans, but he never questions the justice of slavery itself. See David Brion Davis, *Inhuman Bondage: The Rise and Fall of Slavery in the New World* (New York: Oxford University Press, 2006), 354, n49. Also, as Jill Lepore notes, the New England Puritans also positioned themselves as more perfectly Christian than the Spanish using las Casas as a key text. Jill Lepore, *The Name of War: King Philip's War and the Origins of American Identity* (New York: Knopf, 1998).

48. Walker and Wiltse, *Walker's Appeal*, 36.

49. Ibid., 37.

50. Ibid., 38.

51. Ibid., 40.

52. Ibid., 46.

53. Ibid., 47.

54. Ibid., 55.

55. Ibid., 58.

56. Ibid., 47.

57. Ibid.

58. Thomas Jefferson and Merrill D. Peterson, *The Portable Thomas Jefferson* (New York: Viking Press, 1975), 186.

59. Alexis de Tocqueville, Harvey Claflin Mansfield, and Delba Winthrop, *Democracy in America* (Chicago: University of Chicago Press, 2000), 328.

60. "I advance it therefore as a suspicion only, that the blacks whether originally a distinct race, or made distinct by time and circumstances, are inferior to the whites in the endowments of both body and mind." Jefferson and Peterson, *The Portable Thomas Jefferson*, 192.

61. Walker and Wiltse, *Walker's Appeal*, 10 (also see 27–29).

62. Ibid., 50.

63. Ibid., 20.

64. Ibid., 26 (also see 11).

65. He admits, "I have several times called white Americans our natural enemies—I shall here define my meaning of the phrase." Ibid., 60.

66. Ibid.

67. Ibid., especially 11–16.

68. West, *Prophesy Deliverance!* Anthony Appiah, *In My Father's House: Africa in the Philosophy of Culture* (New York: Oxford University Press, 1992).

69. Jefferson and Peterson, *The Portable Thomas Jefferson*, 192.

70. Walker and Wiltse, *Walker's Appeal*, 27.

71. Ibid., 28.

72. Isaiah Berlin, *Two Conceptions of Liberty* (New York: Farrar, Straus and Giroux, 2000).

73. Walker and Wiltse, *Walker's Appeal*, 28.

74. Ibid., 29.

75. Ibid., 61.

76. "They do not know indeed, that there is an unquenchable disposition in the breasts of blacks, which when fully awakened and put in motion, will be subdued only with the destruction of the animal existence." Ibid., 25.

77. Ibid., 28.

78. Ibid., 29.

79. Ibid.

80. Sallust and John Carew Rolfe, *Sallust* (London: W. Heinemann; G. P. Putnam's Sons, 1931), 133.

81. By "black-modern," I am borrowing from the notion of "Afro-modernity" that Robert Gooding-Williams describes in his recent work on Du Bois. As he explains, "Afro-modern" refers to a distinctive genre of political theory that is concerned to explain the "political and social organization of white supremacy, the nature and effects of racial ideology, and the possibilities of emancipation." Robert Gooding-Williams, *In the Shadow of Du Bois: Afro-Modern Political Thought in America* (Cambridge, Mass.: Harvard University Press, 2009), 3.

82. Walker and Wiltse, *Walker's Appeal*, 25.

83. Plato, Ferrari, and Griffith, *The Republic*.

84. Walker and Wiltse, *Walker's Appeal*, 24.

CHAPTER 2: "GLORIOUS REVOLUTION" IN THE CITY OF MASTERY

1. Alexander Hamilton, James Madison, John Jay, and Clinton Rossiter (Publius), *The Federalist Papers* (New York: New American Library, 1961), 33.

2. "The Dred Scott Decision," in Frederick Douglass and Philip S. Foner, *The Life and Writings of Frederick Douglass* (New York: International, 1950), 169.

3. "The Present Condition and Prospects of the Negro People," in Douglass and Foner, *The Life and Writings of Frederick Douglass*, 244.

4. See Orlando Patterson, *Slavery and Social Death: A Comparative Study* (Cambridge, Mass.: Harvard University Press, 1982), 13. David W. Blight, *Frederick Douglass' Civil War: Keeping Faith in Jubilee* (Baton Rouge: Louisiana State University Press, 1989). Herbert Storing, "Frederick Douglass," in *American Political Thought*, ed. Morton Frisch (New York: Charles Scribner's Sons, 1971), Wilson Jeremiah Moses, *Creative Conflict in African American Thought: Frederick Douglass, Alexander Crummell, Booker T. Washington, W.E.B. Du Bois, and Marcus Garvey* (Cambridge: Cambridge University Press, 2004), and Sharon R. Krause, *Liberalism with Honor* (Cambridge, Mass.: Harvard University Press, 2002), respectively.

5. "Men of Color to Arms," in Frederick Douglass and William L. Andrews, *The Oxford Frederick Douglass Reader* (New York: Oxford University Press, 1996). For Douglass's account of "the slave party," see "The Present Condition and Future Prospects of the Negro People" and "The Dred Scott Decision."

6. For a good discussion of Douglass's conception of the more circumscribed politics of the plantation, see Robert Gooding-Williams, *In the Shadow of Du Bois: Afro-Modern Political Thought in America* (Cambridge, Mass.: Harvard University Press, 2009).

7. Charles Tilly, *Regimes and Repertoires* (Chicago: University of Chicago Press, 2006).

8. Aristotle and Stephen Everson, *The Politics (Cambridge Texts in the History of Political Thought)* (Cambridge: Cambridge University Press, 1988), bk. 1, 1252.

9. Describing his first realization of the natural clash of interests between masters and slaves, he says, "What he most loved, that I most hated. That which to him was a great evil,

to be carefully shunned, was to me a great good, to be diligently sought." Frederick Douglass, William L. Andrews, William S. McFeely *Narrative of the Life of Frederick Douglass, an American Slave, Written by Himself*, Norton Critical Edition (New York: Norton, 1997), 30. Also, "such is the relation to master and slave. Nature had made us friends; slavery made us enemies." *My Bondage and My Freedom* (New York: Dover Publications, 1969), 61.

10. Douglass's view on this issue evolved after his decisive break with William Lloyd Garrison, the charismatic founder of the American Antislavery Society.

11. "The American Constitution and the Slave," in Douglass and Foner, *The Life and Writings of Frederick Douglass*.

12. In his famous account of the regenerative powers of his violent resistance to the slave-breaker Covey, Douglass chose the metaphor, the "glorious revolution." See Douglass, *Narrative of the Life of Frederick Douglass, an American Slave, Written by Himself.* Also see *Colored Men to Arms* in Douglass and Foner, *The Life and Writings of Frederick Douglass* and his novella, "The Heroic Slave," in Douglass and Andrews, *The Oxford Frederick Douglass Reader.*

13. By "expedience," I refer to the strategic necessity of using all of the resources available to the Union. By "morality," I refer to Douglass's arguments in favor of enlistment as a catalyst for black civic confidence and identification with the larger purposes of America.

14. See "Address to Colored People," an early speech of 1848 in Douglass and Foner, *The Life and Writings of Frederick Douglass.* Also, see *West Indian Emancipation* in *The Life and Writings of Frederick Douglass.*

15. "Address to the People of the United States," in Douglass and Foner, *The Life and Writings of Frederick Douglass.*

16. Douglass, *My Bondage and My Freedom*, 361.

17. "The Unholy Alliance of Negro Hate and Anti-Slavery," in Douglass and Foner, *The Life and Writings of Frederick Douglass*, 387.

18. Valerie Smith, *Self-Discovery and Authority in Afro-American Narrative* (Cambridge, Mass.: Harvard University Press, 1987).

19. William L. Andrews and Henry Louis Gates, *The Civitas Anthology of African American Slave Narratives* (Washington, D.C.: Civitas/Counterpoint, 1999), 3.

20. Houston A. Baker, *The Journey Back: Issues in Black Literature and Criticism* (Chicago: University of Chicago Press, 1980).

21. Saidiya V. Hartman, *Scenes of Subjection: Terror, Slavery, and Self-Making in Nineteenth-Century America (Race and American Culture)* (New York: Oxford University Press, 1997), 80–90.

22. Ibid.

23. "Discourse on the Origin and Foundation of Inequality Among Men," in Jean-Jacques Rousseau and Donald A. Cress, *Basic Political Writings* (Indianapolis: Hackett, 1987). Alexis de Tocqueville, Harvey Claflin Mansfield, and Delba Winthrop, *Democracy in America* (Chicago: University of Chicago Press, 2000).

24. "Claims of our Common Cause," in Douglass and Foner, *The Life and Writings of Frederick Douglass*, 266.

25. On Douglass's investment in natural law and the problematic assumptions that inform this investment, see Charles W. Mills, "Whose Fourth of July?" and Frederick Douglass and "Original Intent," in *Frederick Douglass a Critical Reader*, ed. Bill E. Lawson and Frank M. Kirkland (Malden, Mass.: Blackwell,1999).

26. Douglass, *My Bondage and My Freedom*, 80.

27. "The Dred Scott Decision," in Douglass and Foner, *The Life and Writings of Frederick Douglass*, 168.

28. Patterson, *Slavery and Social Death*, 13.

29. David Brion Davis, *Inhuman Bondage: The Rise and Fall of Slavery in the New World* (New York: Oxford University Press, 2006), 31–36.

30. "I Am Here to Spread Light on American Slavery," in Douglass, *Narrative of the Life of Frederick Douglass, an American Slave, Written by Himself,* 113.

31. Ibid.

32. Few canonical political philosophers who treated the question of slavery had the interest or the heart to tackle this problem head on. Only St. Augustine spoke openly about it, and even he was uncharacteristically brief. When explaining the insurmountable fragility of friendship, St. Augustine explains that aside from loss of faith, the enslavement of a friend is the worst misfortune that one can experience. He states, "For not only are we anxious lest they be afflicted by famine, war, pestilence, or captivity, fearing that in slavery they may suffer evils beyond what we can conceive, also, there is the more bitter fear that their friendship will be transformed into perfidy, malice, and wickedness." Augustine and R. W. Dyson, *The City of God against the Pagans, Cambridge Texts in the History of Political Thought* (Cambridge: Cambridge University Press, 1998), 929.

33. Douglass, *Narrative of the Life of Frederick Douglass, an American Slave, Written by Himself,* 42. Discussions of sexual vulnerability and injury in slave narratives are often indirect. Authors struggle to find discursive strategies that will neither offend the conscience of white readers nor titillate white supremacist fantasies about black sexuality. Authors also grappled with the problem of their own experiences of shame and trauma, causing them to be selective in their personal disclosures.

34. Ibid., 50.

35. Frederick Douglass, *Life and Times of Frederick Douglass*, Centenary Memorial Subscribers Edition ed. (New York: Pathways Press, 1941), 138. Covey "knew just what a man or boy could do, and he held both to strict account," 136.

36. Ibid., 139.

37. *Narrative of the Life of Frederick Douglass, an American Slave, Written by Himself,* 43.

38. Ibid.

39. Ibid.

40. The shifting emphasis in this second biography from the frequency of beatings to his internal resistance to Covey's command might well have been related to the conditions under which the second autobiography was written. Douglass had shaken off the formal constraints of the slave narrative as well as the constraining tutelage of William Lloyd Garrison, conveying greater authorial freedom, both in terms of describing his experiences and in terms of choosing the image of himself to be presented to his readers.

41. Douglass, *Life and Times of Frederick Douglass*, 136.

42. On the nature of this kind of calculation, see Hartman, *Scenes of Subjection.*

43. The clearest statement of this view is provided by Tocqueville, Mansfield, and Winthrop, *Democracy in America*, 333. Also see David Hume's essay, "Of the Populousness of Ancient Nations," in David Hume and Eugene F. Miller, *Essays, Moral, Political, and Literary* (Indianapolis: Liberty Classics, 1985). Also see Alexander Hamilton, "Report on the Subject of Manufactures," in *Writings* (New York: Library of America, 2001).

44. Elaine Scarry, *The Body in Pain: The Making and Unmaking of the World* (New York: Oxford University Press, 1987), 30.

45. The best discussion of the importance of ritual as a structural support for mastery is provided by Patterson in *Slavery and Social Death.* He emphasizes the central importance of ritual action as the structural formation that facilitates "natal alienation," the radical severance of the ties of birth to both forebears and progeny. I explicate an equally

important affinity between ritual and gender construction and destruction following the provocative work of Hortense Spillers. See "Mama's Baby, Papa's Maybe: An American Grammar Book," in Hortense J. Spillers, *Black, White, and in Color: Essays on American Literature and Culture* (Chicago: University of Chicago Press, 2003). On the constitutive work of ritual as a social response to the challenge of identify formation and maintenance against historical contingency, see Beth Eddy, *The Rites of Identity: The Religious Naturalism and Cultural Criticism of Kenneth Burke and Ralph Ellison* (Princeton, N.J.: Princeton University Press, 2003), 2. Also see Danielle S. Allen, *Talking to Strangers: Anxieties of Citizenship since Brown v. Board of Education* (Chicago: University of Chicago Press, 2004).

46. Hannah Arendt, Joanna Vecchiarelli Scott, and Judith Chelius Stark, *Love and Saint Augustine* (Chicago: University of Chicago Press, 1996), 83.

47. Douglass, *Narrative of the Life of Frederick Douglass, an American Slave, Written by Himself,* 33.

48. Some might object, of course, that attributing a nihilistic fantasy to Douglass is to saddle him with a thoroughly contemporary (late modern) sensibility and therefore to project a distinctively contemporary pathology onto his fundamentally different experience of historical time. Insofar as this worry cautions against interpreting Douglass in a manner that displaces his own accounting of the experience, it ought to be taken to heart. However, if one considers the things for which Douglass himself believes he should have been killed, the nihilistic possibility seems plausible.

49. Douglass, *Narrative of the Life of Frederick Douglass, an American Slave, Written by Himself.*

50. Douglass and Foner, *The Life and Writings of Frederick Douglass,* 170.

51. Eric J. Sundquist, *To Wake the Nations: Race in the Making of American Literature* (Cambridge, Mass.: Harvard University Press, 1993).

52. "The Future of the Colored Race," in Douglass and Foner, *The Life and Writings of Frederick Douglass,* 194.

53. Douglass, *Narrative of the Life of Frederick Douglass, an American Slave, Written by Himself,* 64.

54. By the end of the middle of the nineteenth century, most white Americans ascribed to biological theories of racial inferiority that Thomas Jefferson initiated when he called for more scientific investigation into Negro inferiority in Query 14 of his *Notes on the State of Virginia.* During the seventeenth and eighteenth centuries, the prevailing description of black inferiority was an environmental one. For a good discussion of the intellectual history of white supremacy, see George M. Frederickson, *The Black Image in the White Mind: The Debate on Afro-American Character and Destiny* (Hanover, N.H.: Wesleyan University Press, 1971).

55. Tocqueville, Mansfield, and Winthrop, *Democracy in America,* 360.

56. "Address to the Colored People of the United States," in Douglass and Foner, *The Life and Writings of Frederick Douglass,* 332.

57. *Claims of Our Common Cause,* in ibid., 266.

58. "West India Emancipation," in ibid., 433. Douglass wrote a good deal about the effects of enslavement, the extensiveness of the degradation, and the strategies required to overcome it. At times, his claims came very close to those of Rousseau and Tocqueville, who suggested that slaves lose everything in their chains, including the desire to be free. At other times, he seemed to have internalized white supremacist evaluative rubrics. Douglass frequently made claims against colonization, not only referring to the "wilds" and "pestilential shores" of Africa, for example, but also claiming that proximity to American whites would be more beneficial for former slaves than emigration: "We believe that contact with

the white race, even under the many unjust and painful restrictions to which we are subjected, does more toward our elevation and improvement, than mere circumstance of being separated from them could do." In my discussion of Douglass's assessment of the effects of slavery, I do not wish to underplay these passages, but I do not believe that they capture the complexity of his considered judgments on this issue.

59. Douglass, *Narrative of the Life of Frederick Douglass, an American Slave, Written by Himself,* 52. Also see *My Bondage and My Freedom,* 255.

60. "Address to the Colored People of the United States," in Douglass and Foner, *The Life and Writings of Frederick Douglass,* 332.

61. Douglass depicts slaves' dim awareness of the full extent of their dehumanization in his discussion of slaves' indulgence in alcohol during holidays. Similarly, he intimates the pervasiveness of the slaves' sorrow over their predicament in his discussion of slave music. Douglass, *Narrative of the Life of Frederick Douglass, an American Slave, Written by Himself,* 51, 19. Also see *My Bondage and My Freedom,* 45.

62. For all the brevity of Douglass's depiction of this moment (in each of his biographical works), we must not lose sight of the immense existential transformation that occurs in Sophia Auld. When she assents to the principle and program of enforced illiteracy, she does not simply comply (however happily or grudgingly) as if she were simply quitting something, but she commits herself to a principle and marshals her personal resources to see to it that he does not acquire literacy. Douglass, *Narrative of the Life of Frederick Douglass, an American Slave, Written by Himself,* 31.

63. Herbert J. Storing, "Slavery and the Moral Foundations of the American Republic," in *The Moral Foundations of the American Republic,* ed. Robert H. Horowitz (Charlottesville: University of Virginia Press, 1986).

64. Douglass, *My Bondage and My Freedom,* 152.

65. Ibid., 154.

66. Douglass, *Narrative of the Life of Frederick Douglass, an American Slave, Written by Himself,* 126.

67. Douglass is no less adamant about mastery's evisceration of family ties within the communities of slaves. See his discussion of his relations with his own mother in ibid. Also see *My Bondage and My Freedom.*

68. Douglass, *Narrative of the Life of Frederick Douglass, an American Slave, Written by Himself,* 12.

69. For a good discussion of this point, see Moses, *Creative Conflict in African American Thought,* 24.

70. Douglass, *Narrative of the Life of Frederick Douglass, an American Slave, Written by Himself,* 14.

71. *My Bondage and My Freedom,* 60.

72. Deborah G. White, *Ar'n't I a Woman? Female Slaves in the Plantation South,* rev. ed. (New York: Norton, 1999).

73. Douglass, *Narrative of the Life of Frederick Douglass, an American Slave, Written by Himself,* 13.

74. Douglass, *My Bondage and My Freedom,* 59.

75. Hartman, *Scenes of Subjection.*

76. Ibid., 79. Melton Alonza McLaurin, *Celia, a Slave* (Athens: University of Georgia Press, 1991).

77. Douglass, *My Bondage and My Freedom,* 60.

78. "An Address to the Colored People of the United States," in Douglass and Foner, *The Life and Writings of Frederick Douglass,* 332.

79. Scholars have discussed this dynamic, particularly in relation to Harriet Jacobs, *Incidents in the Life of a Slave Girl* (Cambridge, Mass.: Harvard University Press, 1987).

80. Douglass, *Narrative of the Life of Frederick Douglass, an American Slave, Written by Himself*, 15.

81. Hartman, *Scenes of Subjection*. Fred Moten, *In the Break: The Aesthetics of the Black Radical Tradition* (Minneapolis: University of Minnesota Press, 2003).

82. Douglass, *Narrative of the Life of Frederick Douglass, an American Slave, Written by Himself*, 14.

83. Douglass, *My Bondage and My Freedom*, 59.

84. *Douglass, Narrative of the Life of Frederick Douglass, an American Slave, Written by Himself*, 14.

85. Ibid.

86. Douglass, *My Bondage and My Freedom*, 59.

87. Whether rooted in environmentalist theories of white supremacy of the eighteenth century or the scientific racism that replaced it in the nineteenth century, the commitment to the ideal of the absolute otherness of slaves was central to the American justification of slavery and of the exclusion of blacks, enslaved and free, from the putatively universal rights and immunities guaranteed by the U.S. Constitution. Indeed, it was this doctrine that enabled some defenders of slavery to argue that slaves should be enslaved for their own good. See George M. Fredrickson, *The Black Image in the White Mind: The Debate on Afro-American Character and Destiny, 1817–1914* (Middletown, Conn.: Wesleyan University Press, 1987).

88. M. I. Finley, *Ancient Slavery and Modern Ideology* (New York: Penguin Books, 1983); Patterson, *Slavery and Social Death*.

89. Orlando Patterson, *Freedom* (New York: Basic Books, 1991).

90. "Claims of our Common Cause," in Douglass and Foner, *The Life and Writings of Frederick Douglass*, 254.

91. Douglass, *My Bondage and My Freedom*, 148.

92. Ibid.

93. Ibid.

94. Ibid., 150.

95. Ibid.

96. Ibid.

97. Ibid.

98. In *Dred Scott*, Taney claimed to express the official view of the founders, devastating Douglass's central claim against Walker that there was a crucial distinction to be made between the slave power and the regime of the founders and American civil religion. In response, Douglass objected that the court had made mischief of the Constitution and the founders' intentions. For a discussion of this issue, see Charles W. Mills, *Whose Fourth of July?* and Frederick Douglass, "Original Intent," in Bill E. Lawson and Frank M. Kirkland, *Frederick Douglass: A Critical Reader*, Blackwell Critical Readers (Malden, Mass.: Blackwell, 1999).

99. Storing argues that constitutional rights to property among white men were privileged in the original constitutional settlement. This constitutional commitment thus confirms the rights of mastery. Douglass disagrees for the reasons stated earlier. Storing, *Slavery and the Moral Foundations of the American Republic*.

100. "The American Apocalypse," in Douglass and Foner, *The Life and Writings of Frederick Douglass*, 443.

101. *What the Black Man Wants*, 1865, in Douglass and Foner, *The Life and Writings of Frederick Douglass*, 158.

102. Ida B. Wells-Barnett, *On Lynchings (Classics in Black Studies)* (Amherst, N.Y.: Humanity Books, 2002), 29.

CHAPTER 3: ARISTOCRATIC STRIVINGS IN THE GILDED CITY

1. W.E.B. Du Bois, *The Souls of Black Folk, Writings*, (New York: Library of America, 1986), 547.

2. Ibid., 475.

3. Ibid., 42.

4. By "monumental history," I refer to edifying histories of the past told to facilitate imitation by persons in the present. The political histories of Rome by Sallust, Livy, and to a degree, the poet Virgil, provide classical examples of the genre. See Friedrich Nietzsche, *On the Advantage and Disadvantage of History for Life*, trans. Peter Preuss (Indianapolis: Hackett, 1980). By "critique," I mean a critical theoretical analysis of the conditions that must hold for a certain constellation of statements or ideas to be true. See Seyla Benhabib, *Critique, Norm, and Utopia: A Study of the Foundations of Critical Theory* (New York: Columbia University Press, 1986).

5. By "picturesque," I refer to the politicized aesthetic typical of mid-nineteenth-century painting. Angela L. Miller, *The Empire of the Eye: Landscape Representation and American Cultural Politics, 1825–1875* (Ithaca, N.Y.: Cornell University Press, 1993). Du Bois uses this aesthetic to represent the racial topography of the "Negro Problem," and by doing so, to alter the racial perceptions of his readers in the service of a multiracial nation. I draw from Sheila Lloyd, "Du Bois and the Production of the Racial Picturesque," *Public Culture* 17, no. 2 (2005): 277–298.

6. See Cornel West's analysis of Du Bois's enlightenment optimism, Victorian moralism, and overconfident rationalism, in Henry Louis Gates and Cornel West, *The Future of the Race* (New York: Alfred A. Knopf, 1996).

7. See his essay, "The Damnation of Women," in *Darkwater* in W.E.B. Du Bois, *Writings* (New York: Library of America, 1986). For a discussion of Du Bois's masculinism, see Joy James, *Transcending the Talented Tenth: Black Leaders and American Intellectuals* (New York: Routledge, 1997) and Farah Jasmine Griffin,. "Black Feminists and Du Bois: Respectability, Protection, and Beyond," *Annals of the Academy of Political and Social Science*, no. 568, (March 2000): 28–40.

8. Drew Gilpin Faust, *This Republic of Suffering: Death and the American Civil War* (New York: Alfred A. Knopf, 2008).

9. Alan Trachtenberg and Eric Foner, *The Incorporation of America: Culture and Society in the Gilded Age* (New York: Hill and Wang, 1982).

10. C. Vann Woodward, *The Strange Career of Jim Crow* (New York: Oxford University Press, 1974).

11. David W. Blight, *Race and Reunion: The Civil War in American Memory* (Cambridge, Mass.: Belknap Press of Harvard University Press, 2001).

12. Du Bois, *Writings*, 480.

13. Regarding the view of the North, see ibid., 398. Regarding the entrenchment of blacks at the bottom of the new economic order, see ibid., 478.

14. Ibid., 416.

15. Ibid., 415.

16. Ibid.

17. Augustine and R. W. Dyson, *The City of God against the Pagans* (Cambridge: Cambridge University Press, 1998).

18. Du Bois, *Writings*, 416.

19. Du Bois's derision of the white working class seems more ironic than expository in this context, although his own views about Southern white working classes are not much different. What seems undeniable, however, is that Du Bois's deployment of this language is a rhetorical strategy designed to identify with readers who hold these kinds of views. Ibid., 417. Also see "Of the Training of Black Men" and "Of the Sons of Master and Man" available in *Writings*.

20. Du Bois, *Writings*, 419.

21. Ibid., 418.

22. Ibid., 370, 537, 95.

23. Ibid., 418.

24. Ibid., 417.

25. Du Bois resembled the classical writers in that his commitment to republican politics did not entail a democratic conception of civic participation that required that all citizens must rule. For Du Bois and the classical writers, civic participation was perfectly consistent with political inequality; it could countenance this inequality by placing certain restrictions on who could hold power and other (perhaps less stringent) restrictions on who could select officeholders. As such, participation could as easily mean voting as it could mean some less decisive form of deliberation.

26. In terms of Du Bois's own categories, "spiritual strivings" are the fundamental internal motivations of individual persons, reflective of comprehensive evaluative schemes and fundamental orientations about the character of the world. As such, they reflect prevailing conceptions of "Truth, Beauty, and Goodness," but these strivings are also perennially vulnerable to the priorities implicit within the quest for wealth.

27. See Plato, *The Republic*, ed. G.R.F. Ferrari, trans. Tom Griffith (Cambridge: Cambridge University Press, 2000), 373a–73d; Sallust, *The War with Catiline*, trans. J. C. Rolfe (Cambridge, Mass.: Harvard University Press, 1995), 13; and Marcus Tullius Cicero, *De Re Publica, De Legibus*, ed. and trans. Clinton Walker Keyes, 213. (Cambridge, Mass.: Harvard University Press, 1994).

28. Baron de Montesquieu, *The Spirit of the Laws*, trans. Thomas Nugent, (New York: Haffner Press, 1949), 316. For an excellent recent discussion of the commercial republic, see Thomas L. Pangle, *The Spirit of Modern Republicanism* (Chicago: University of Chicago Press, 1988), 98.

29. For an excellent discussion of the ways Du Bois positions himself as a theorist of and partisan to American slavery, see Robert Gooding Williams, *In the Shadow of Du Bois* (Cambridge, Mass.: Harvard University Press, 2009).

30. The contractual dimension of enslavement functions at the level of political culture. Exclusion of blacks from civic protections and prerogatives functions as the contractual basis whereby whites consent to the unequal freedoms and privileges they enjoy in relation to one another. See Charles W. Mills, *The Racial Contract* (Ithaca, N.Y.: Cornell University Press, 1997). See Stephen Michael Best, *The Fugitive's Properties: Law and the Poetics of Possession* (Chicago: University of Chicago Press, 2004) and Ian Baucom, *Specters of the Atlantic: Finance Capital, Slavery, and the Philosophy of History* (Durham, N.C.: Duke University Press, 2005) for a discussion of black slaves as property and instruments of commercial exchange. Also see Judith N. Shklar, *American Citizenship: The Quest for Inclusion*

(Cambridge, Mass.: Harvard University Press, 1991) and Edmund Sears Morgan, *American Slavery, American Freedom: The Ordeal of Colonial Virginia* (New York: Norton, 1975).

31. Montesquieu, *The Spirit of the Laws.*

32. Du Bois, *Writings,* 479.

33. Saidiya V. Hartman, *Scenes of Subjection: Terror, Slavery, and Self-Making in Nineteenth-Century America (Race and American Culture)* (New York: Oxford University Press, 1997).

34. According to Weber, market practices are connected to and buttressed by deep religious commitments, but they remain eminently serviceable to modern capitalism. Max Weber, *The Protestant Ethic and the Spirit of Capitalism,* trans. Peter Baehr and Gordon C. Wells (New York: Penguin Classics, 2002).

35. Adam Smith and Edwin Cannan, *The Wealth of Nations* (New York: Modern Library, 2000). David Hume and Eugene F. Miller, *Essays, Moral, Political, and Literary* (Indianapolis: Liberty Classics, 1985). Thomas Jefferson, Frank Shuffelton, *Notes on the State of Virginia,* Penguin Classics (New York: Penguin Books, 1999). Alexis de Tocqueville, Harvey Claflin Mansfield, and Delba Winthrop, *Democracy in America* (Chicago: University of Chicago Press, 2000).

36. This motivation is alleged to foster punctual and productive wage labor. The clearest expression of this view is found in footnote 23 of David Hume's essay, "Of the Populousness of Nations" in David Hume, *Essays Moral, Political, and Literary* (Indianapolis, Ind.: Liberty Fund, 1985). For an alternative account, see Karl Marx, "Economic and Philosophic Manuscripts of 1844," in *The Marx-Engels Reader,* 2nd ed. (New York: Norton, 1978), 74).

37. Du Bois, *Writings.* He also elaborates on this in "Of the Dawn of Freedom," ibid.

38. Ibid., 419.

39. Ibid., 418.

40. See "Of Booker T. Washington and Others" in ibid.

41. Ibid., 398.

42. Ibid., 403.

43. Cornel West in Gates and West, *The Future of the Race.*

44. Booker T. Washington, *Up from Slavery: An Autobiography* (New Brunswick, N.J.: Transaction, 1997), 182.

45. Washington conceived slavery as a terrible misfortune rather than a manmade political evil. The former occurs for inexplicable reasons, covering all who come into contact with it as victims. Political evil, by contrast, refers to human action and tries, at its best, to distinguish perpetrators from victims, to assess whether reparations are owed, and to ensure that such action is prevented in the future. See *Up from Slavery,* chap. 1.

46. On Civil War memory, see Blight, *Race and Reunion.*

47. Washington, *Up from Slavery,* 148.

48. Ibid.

49. The civil rights cases established the precedent that Congress had no authority to outlaw discrimination by private persons and organizations, and *Plessy* established the constitutionality of segregation.

50. Washington, *Up from Slavery.*

51. See ibid., 155.

52. Ibid., 146.

53. Because Washington conceived real and effective freedom as the ability to coerce one's opponents through a granting or withholding of economic resources, he insisted that the most astute political act that blacks could undertake was to contribute to his effort

to build the institutional and social basis for the acquisition and maintenance of wealth. Washington insisted that blacks should cease agitation for citizenship rights because, as he believed, voting is a prerogative that is rightfully exercised by men of sense (some speci-fied level of education) and with a real stake in the community (property ownership), and because much anti-black hostility was simply the expression of the South's understand-able resentment at the conquering North's imposition of black male voting rights without regard for their actual fitness for citizenship.

54. Washington, *Up from Slavery*, 147.

55. Ibid.

56. Washington warned that the black third of the population would ultimately con-tribute to the success of the South, or they "will constitute one-third of the ignorance and crime of the South," one-third to the business and industrial prosperity of the South, or "a veritable body of death, stagnating, depressing, and retarding every effort to advance the body politic." Whatever threat is implied by this observation, however, is thoroughly domesticated by Washington's assurances about the true character of most blacks and the moderate and prudent character of his leadership.

57. Washington, *Up from Slavery*, 147.

58. Ibid., 149.

59. Du Bois, *Writings*, 393.

60. Ibid.

61. Ibid., 396.

62. Ibid., 400.

63. Ibid., 423.

64. Ibid., 400.

65. Du Bois's anxieties about Washington's power to facilitate a devaluation of black intellectual life is reminiscent of the worries of Alexis de Tocqueville, another aristocrat who feared that despotical power often required the liquidation of the intelligentsia. This is the clearest formulation of Du Bois's liberal democratic commitments (i.e., his claim that "criticism of writers by readers, of government by those governed, of leaders by those led— this is the soul of democracy and the safeguard of modern society.") Du Bois also high-lights the proto-demagogic effects of the imposition of Washington's authority on black America. See ibid., 395.

66. Washington, *Up from Slavery*, 149.

67. Du Bois, *Writings*, 400.

68. Ibid.

69. This essay was published originally in a collection of essays that included a piece by Washington himself. Ibid., 860.

70. Ibid., 399.

71. Ibid., 395.

72. Ibid., 398.

73. Ibid., 504.

74. Du Bois distinguished between evils stemming from natural and human-created sources. Encounters with natural misfortune and hardship generated a desire to "oppose and conquer nature." Ibid., 395.

75. Ibid., 396.

76. Ibid., 842.

77. Ibid., 395. For an excellent discussion of Du Bois's conception of black politics as leadership and its corollary construction of black suffrage as selection of elites rather than

group empowerment, see Robert Gooding-Williams, *In the Shadow of Du Bois: Afro-Modern Political Thought in America* (Cambridge, Mass.: Harvard University Press, 2009), 57.

78. Du Bois, *Writings*, 847.

79. I am not arguing that there is no class dimension to this category. Quite clearly, Du Bois distinguishes this class from other blacks, especially those he regards as "the submerged class" of black America, and working-class whites, poor whites, and the white elite. My principal claim, however, is that Du Bois is attempting to distinguish between the political life and the nonpolitical life, a more important distinction than the class distinction in understanding Du Bois's political theory as opposed to his cultural politics and social thought (broadly conceived). Also, Du Bois's formulation cannot be reduced to the all-too-common reading of Du Bois as an apologist for those blacks whom E. Franklin Frazier described as the "Black Bourgeoisie."

80. I borrow "freedom dreams" from Robin D. G. Kelley, *Freedom Dreams: The Black Radical Imagination* (Boston: Beacon Press, 2002).

81. Du Bois, *Writings*, 846.

82. Ibid., 842.

83. Ibid., 402.

84. Ibid., 476. Here Du Bois uses the social scientific language of his day to discuss racial uplift and the language of manliness to represent civilization. On these issues, see Michele Mitchell, *Righteous Propagation: African Americans and the Politics of Racial Destiny after Reconstruction* (Chapel Hill: University of North Carolina Press, 2004) and Gail Bederman, *Manliness and Civilization: A Cultural History of Gender and Race in the United States, 1880–1917* (Chicago: University of Chicago Press, 1995).

85. Du Bois hopes that the principles underlying the very best of American universities will one day enjoy a sovereign place within American civilization and political culture. See "Of the Wings of Atalanta" in Du Bois, *Writings*, 422.

86. Ibid.

87. Ibid., 383.

88. For a fascinating discussion of the black caretaker's ability to distinguish between the innocence of children and the guilt of adults of the master class, see Toni Morrison, "Rediscovering Black History," *What Moves at the Margin* (Jackson, University of Mississippi Press, 2008), 50.

89. Du Bois, *Writings*, 383.

90. Hazel V. Carby, *Race Men* (Cambridge, Mass.: Harvard University Press, 1998). For an alternative interpretation, see James, *Transcending the Talented Tenth*.

91. See Hartman's discussion of Harriet Jacobs in Hartman, *Scenes of Subjection*. Also see Toni Morrison, *Playing in the Dark: Whiteness and the Literary Imagination* (Cambridge, Mass.: Harvard University Press, 1992).

92. Du Bois, *Writings*, 436.

93. Ibid.

94. In claiming that he would not ask who was responsible for the Negro problem, Du Bois refused to push a very legitimate question that he never shrank from. He turned instead to an alternative question that appealed to and sought to energize an ethics of honor and shame. Du Bois explains, "After emancipation, it was the plain duty of someone to assume this group leadership and training of the Negro laborer. I will not stop here to inquire whose duty it was, whether that of the white ex-master, who had profited by unpaid toil, or the Northern philanthropist whose persistence brought on the crisis, or the National Government whose edict freed the bondmen; but I insist it was the duty of some

one to see that these workingmen were not left alone and unguided, without capital, without land, without skill, without economic organization, without even the bald protection of law, order, decency—left in a great land, not to settle down to slow and careful internal development, but destined to be thrown almost immediately into reckless and sharp competition with the best modern workingmen under an economic system where every participant is fighting for himself, and too often utterly regardless of the rights and welfare of his neighbor." Ibid., 478.

95. Du Bois, *Writings*, 504.

96. By "sovereignty," I refer to decisive political power, a notion informed by Thomas Hobbes's account of the institutional embodiment of the entire force of the community; Thomas Hobbes and Richard Tuck, *Leviathan* (Cambridge: Cambridge University Press, 1996); Carl Schmitt's notion that sovereignty is, above all, the power to determine when the rule of law is to be suspended; Carl Schmitt, *The Concept of the Political* (Chicago: University of Chicago Press, 1996); and the more recent work of Giorgio Agamben, who links the late modern expansion of surveillance and police power to the late modern state's capacity to distinguish bare life from specific forms of life and register an exclusive claim to protect it; Giorgio Agamben, *Homo Sacer: Sovereign Power and Bare Life* (Stanford, Calif.: Stanford University Press, 1998).

97. Du Bois, *Writings*, 429.

98. As a Congregationalist institution, Harvard was in some ways a religious institution whose character was more directly expressive of Puritan religiosity than any other institutions except for churches. Du Bois is clearly aware of this but suggests that a more secular impulse emerged at a later point, as the real architectonic principle.

99. Du Bois, *Writings*, 420, 23.

100. Ibid., 432.

101. Most Southern whites already thought of Reconstruction in precisely these terms, and not only justified their current practices of retaliatory and preemptive terroristic violence against blacks but also insisted on home rule of the South by true Southerners as the necessary precondition for sectional reconciliation with the North.

102. Du Bois, *Writings*, 430.

103. In addition to promoting resentment, projects of redemption may foster violence if they articulate politics as the quest for an antecedently guaranteed deliverance. For an excellent discussion of the consequences of projects of redemption, see George M. Shulman, *American Prophecy: Race and Redemption in American Political Culture* (Minneapolis: University of Minnesota Press, 2008), 249.

104. Du Bois, *Writings*, 481.

105. Ibid., 430.

106. Du Bois points out that cultured people routinely ask the wrong question about comparative levels of civilization: "Why has civilization flourished in Europe, and flicked and flamed in Africa? So long as the world stands meekly dumb before such questions, shall this nation proclaim its ignorance and unhallowed prejudices by denying freedom of opportunity to those who brought the Sorrow Songs to the Seats of the Mighty?" Du Bois, *Writings*, 345.

107. See West's discussion of this point in Gates and West, *The Future of the Race*.

108. Philip Pettit, *Republicanism: A Theory of Freedom and Government* (Oxford: Clarendon Press, 1997).

109. If the greatest danger to republican politics is the specter of demagoguery, understood as the direct result of a natural and inalterable dispensation in which the soaring

and overweening ambition of elites comes into contact with the easily manipulable narrow self-regard of common citizens, then the first priority of the polity is to ensure that such persons never get the upper hand. In "The Talented Tenth," the essay that was revised as "Of the Training of Black Men" and published the same year as the *Souls*, Du Bois states this concern with unrivaled clarity: "Do you think that if the leaders of thought among Negroes are not trained and educated thinkers, that they will have no leaders? On the contrary a hundred half-trained demagogues will still hold the places they so largely occupy now, and hundreds of vociferous busy-bodies will multiply." Ibid., 855.

110. Alexander Hamilton et al., *The Federalist Papers* (New York: New American Library, 1961), 46–48.

111. Like Publius, Du Bois casts the self-interested behaviors of ambitious elites such as Washington as the perennial and intractable source of political disorder. Like Publius, Du Bois's writings understand the desire for institutional forms that are designed to prevent demagogues as a kind of political common sense that naturalizes suspicion about the political competences of ordinary persons.

112. Du Bois, *Writings*, 435.

113. Thomas Jefferson crafted the blueprint for this process in a letter to John Adams in October 1813. Explaining to Adams that he agreed with him that there "was a natural aristocracy among men," whose "ground was virtue and talents," Jefferson also confided, "The natural aristocracy I consider as the most precious gift of nature for the instruction, the trust, and government of society." He asked his former rival, "May we not even say that that form of government is the best which provides the most effectually for a pure selection of these natural aristoi into the offices of government?"

114. As Tocqueville explained, "The territorial aristocracy of past centuries was obliged by law or believed itself to be obliged by mores to come to the aid of its servants and to relieve their miseries. But the manufacturing aristocracy of our days after having impoverished and brutalized the men whom it uses, leaves them to be nourished by public charity in times of crisis. This results naturally from what precedes. Between worker and master relations are frequent, but there is no genuine association." Tocqueville, Mansfield, and Winthrop, *Democracy in America*, 532.

115. In "Federalist 10," Publius admits that the best way to achieve this is to disempower the mass of citizens by institutionalizing extraconstitutional obstacles to majority formation. What Publius dare not admit, however, is that one of the best of these obstacles is the inculcation of a fear of demagogues among the mass of citizens, a threat out of proportion to other threats citizens might face as a direct result of consenting to the necessity of their disempowerment. If the mass of citizens believe that the rise of corrupt elites is the chief danger to their polity, they will scrutinize themselves and others like themselves for any sign of vulnerability. Achieving this, one will have cultivated a desire for a particular kind of elite politics without having had to make the argument for aristocracy. Hence, while the concern with the rise of demagogues seems, on the surface, as an anti-elite politics, in fact, it is a very effective way to convey aristocratic values to persons who are not and will not become aristocrats themselves. In either case, the crucial point to notice is that Du Bois thinks of politics in terms of elite contestation. The good elites or the right kind of elites are those who genuinely have the well-being of all—non-elites as well as elites—in mind when they deploy the power of the community. The wrong kind, of course, are those who have something else in mind, whether they are self-centered, ill-willed, or simply foolish. Well-ordered political life, in this view, institutionalizes conditions for the development and rule of the right kind of elites. Similarly, in this view, a disordered political life, a

politics that systematizes injustice or facilitates great political evil, results most often from the empowerment and rule of the wrong kind of elites.

116. Du Bois, *Writings*, 422.

117. Ibid., 419.

118. After enumerating the authors and subjects that students are exposed to, Du Bois suggested that the function of these universities is to inculcate the knowledge that the purpose of life is "not to earn meat, but to know the end aim of that life which meat nourishes." Ibid.

119. Ibid., 432, 20, 385.

CHAPTER 4: (MAKING) LOVE IN THE DISHONORABLE CITY

1. James Baldwin, *Go Tell It on the Mountain* (New York: Dell, 1985), 204.

2. James Baldwin, "This Morning, This Evening, So Soon," *Going to Meet the Man* (New York: Vintage, 1995), 162.

3. James Baldwin, *Tell Me How Long the Train's Been Gone* (New York: Vantage, 1968), 478.

4. James Baldwin, *Just Above My Head* (New York: Dell, 1979), 574.

5. James Baldwin, *The Price of the Ticket: Collected Nonfiction, 1948–1985*, 1st ed. (New York: St. Martin's/Marek, 1985).

6. Of the dangers of reading Baldwin as a political theorist, see Lawrie Balfour, "Finding the Words: Baldwin, Race Consciousness, and Democratic Theory," *James Baldwin Now*, ed. Dwight A. McBride (New York: New York University Press, 1999), 83. Bearing in mind this caution, I try to read Baldwin as a theorist of politics, as I believe she does, because he attends to questions and problems that are theoretical in nature and that should be central to academic political theory.

7. Here Baldwin recalls his third novel, *Another Country*, a bestseller published just one year before *The Fire Next Time*, in which Baldwin explores, among other important themes, the meaning and status of American exceptionalism when private crisis and personal catastrophe are vital supports in the maintenance and reproduction of the country as a malformed and unstable public.

8. Here Baldwin continues the discourse of American exceptionalism by casting antiracist politics as the exemplary practice of American citizenship and linking this form of citizenship to America's possibilities for unprecedented and exemplary human flourishing.

9. Although deliberative democrats will find this unpleasant to acknowledge, America's racially exclusive forms of public deliberation disqualify them as practices of democracy.

10. However, since Baldwin understood that catastrophe would not be distributed according to merit any more than was American justice and that the greater responsibility of white Americans for the coming catastrophe did not establish the innocence of blacks, catastrophic disintegration would mean that already beleaguered victims of white supremacy would now have to confront post-disintegration chaos. Preventing catastrophe was therefore an act of love, and love required exposing American innocence and willed ignorance and alerting "the authors of devastation" that an exorbitant price would soon be due. In this regard, Baldwin resembled Walker.

11. James Baldwin "The Price of the Ticket," *The Price of the Ticket: Collected Nonfiction, 1948–1985*.

12. James Baldwin, "Many Thousands Gone," (1951), in ibid.

13. Baldwin, *Go Tell It on the Mountain*, 34.

14. Ibid., 35.

15. Although Baldwin advocated representing the complexity and depth of black communal life—especially as it was lived within these kinds of church communities—he did not simply valorize this community or recommend that its practices be emulated.

16. James Baldwin, "The Creative Process," *The Price of the Ticket*.

17. For a discussion of Baldwin's struggle to represent black gay men's desire, see Marlon B. Ross, "White Fantasies of Desire: Baldwin and the Racial Identities of Sexuality," in *James Baldwin Now*. Ross perhaps overstates his case inasmuch as he neglects Baldwin's depiction of John Grime's desire for Elisha. I would also read Baldwin's depiction of Florence and Deborah's relationship as an obliquely queer representation.

18. Baldwin, *Go Tell It on the Mountain*, 217.

19. Ibid., 207.

20. Ibid., 209.

21. Ibid., 206.

22. Ibid., 216.

23. Ibid., 220.

24. This, of course, was one means among others. The others included inculcation of the spirit of obedience to the laws, ostracization of those who had become too rich or powerful, refraining from harming elites in matters of honor and harming the people in matters of money, and if possible, the maintenance of a large middle class. Aristotle, *The Politics (Cambridge Texts in the History of Political Thought)*, ed. Stephen Everson, (Cambridge: Cambridge University Press, 1988), bk. 5, 30.

25. In addition to Baldwin, "Many Thousands Gone," see his "Stranger in the Village" (1953), 86–89; *The Fire Next Time* (1963), 371–374; *No Name in the Street* (1972), 473–478; and "The Price of the Ticket" (1985), xiv, xviii, all in Baldwin, *The Price of the Ticket*.

26. James Baldwin, "Everybody's Protest Novel," *The Price of the Ticket*, 28.

27. Ibid.

28. Hannah Arendt, *Eichmann in Jerusalem: A Report on the Banality of Evil*, rev. and enl. ed. (New York: Penguin Books, 1994), 106.

29. Baldwin, "Many Thousands Gone," 66. For a discussion of racialization, see Michael Omi and Howard Winant, *Racial Formation in the United States: From the 1960s to the 1990s* (New York: Routledge, 1994); Charles W. Mills, *The Racial Contract* (Ithaca, N.Y.: Cornell University Press, 1997); and Kimberlé Crenshaw, *Critical Race Theory: The Key Writings That Formed the Movement* (New York: New Press, 1995).

30. Baldwin, "Many Thousands Gone," 69.

31. David Adams Leeming, *James Baldwin: A Biography*, 1st ed. (New York: Knopf, 1994).

32. Baldwin, "Many Thousands Gone," 71.

33. Bigger kills *ex nihilo*, as philosophers would say. Thus, there is no rebirth of self-consciousness since there is no substantive self to begin with. His act is such an event within the normal rhythms of his preconscious nature that he is compelled to think of it for no other reason than to calculate consequences and generate a justification for his fateful non-deed. In depicting Bigger Thomas, Wright flattens out and then radicalizes the notion of regenerative violence that Frederick Douglass's *Narrative* depicted so vividly.

34. Baldwin, "Many Thousands Gone," 72.

35. *The Poetics*, in Aristotle and Jonathan Barnes, *The Complete Works of Aristotle: The Revised Oxford Translation* (Princeton, N.J.: Princeton University Press, 1984). On Aristotle's conception of tragedy, see Walter Arnold Kaufmann, *Tragedy and Philosophy*, 1st ed. (Garden City, N.Y.: Doubleday, 1968). Also see Martha Craven Nussbaum, *The Fragility*

of Goodness: Luck and Ethics in Greek Tragedy and Philosophy (Cambridge: Cambridge University Press, 1986).

36. Baldwin, "Many Thousands Gone," 73.

37. Ibid., 77.

38. Ibid., 75.

39. Giorgio Agamben, *State of Exception* (Chicago: University of Chicago Press, 2005) and Carl Schmitt, *Political Theology* (Chicago: University of Chicago Press 2006).

40. Hence, there are what academic moral philosophers call utilitarian, deontological, and teleological justifications for this politicized self's motivations, but the highest, Baldwin's writings on love suggest, is neither of these. For, having both turned and learned from the eminent prospect of catastrophic racial violence (utilitarian), and having come to adopt principles of justice that are intrinsically best suited to the unique demography history has made of the country (deontological), the new American polity will have developed the maturity and prudence to exercise moral and political leadership in a world struggling with the vicious legacy of white supremacy (teleological). Nonetheless, while there are multiple practical justifications for such a course, the highest one, in Baldwin's view, is the ideal of love. And, as would seem to be implied by a conception of politics as service, political action would be laborious and exacting, requiring persons to undertake the hard and protracted labor of "insisting on" and "creating the conscience" of others. This labor is arduous because it involves trying to educate other selves that the very real privileges of whiteness that most nonblacks enjoyed as citizens of the old polity were meager by comparison to freedoms they would enjoy in the new; and moreover, that these very privileges, secured through allegiance to the old polity, were worth next to nothing because the old polity was truly on an inexorable crash course toward catastrophic disintegration. Thus, Baldwin acknowledged that the activity of "creat[ing] the conscience of the others" could not be a task for the lighthearted. Absent assurances that the particular competences and special purposes that Baldwin tried to build into his figure of the "lover," his program of political action could too easily draw persons from the ranks of would-be totalitarians, persons who might misinterpret his call to "insist on" and "create the conscience of others" as a license to molest others under the guise of trying to make them free. This is an abbreviation of the red herring that totalitarians of various stripes have claimed to find support for in eighteenth-century political philosopher Jean Jacques Rousseau's discussion of the relation between private interests and the general will. Rousseau is more subtle and complex than many of the purposes for which his ideas have been put. In either case, later I engage worries that Baldwin may promote some crypto-Rousseauianism. Jean-Jacques Rousseau and Donald Cress, *On the Social Contract*, in *The Basic Political Writings* (Indianapolis, Ind.: Hackett, 1987), bk. 1, chap. 7.

41. A fascinating question I pose later is whether the "lover" of *The Fire Next Time* is a politicization of Baldwin's conception of the vocation of the progressive artist. There is an obvious but not necessarily decisive connection between a conception of political activism as "creating the conscience of others" and artistic creation. Baldwin's account of the vocation of the artist is stated in "The Creative Process," where he describes the artist's struggle as a "lover's war." Precisely because these actors are engaged in a war where even defensive violence might precipitate a deeper spiral of violence, Baldwin's actors need to be the kind of people who can transfigure multiple and varied forms of violence into forms conducive to persuasion. There is something much deeper going on in Baldwin than simple reinterpretation of the principles of nonviolent direct action popularized by Martin Luther King, Jr. Baldwin's deeper appreciation of the breadth and complexity of white supremacist violence suggests to me an agonized kinship with David Walker.

42. This disorientation is made particularly vivid by the incoherence of the central political argument of the essay, which begins by portraying the ideology of American exceptionalism as a self-defeating illusion that undermines American efforts in domestic and international spheres (Baldwin, "Nobody Knows My Name," *The Price of the Ticket*, 184). After he identifies American exceptionalism as an illusion that disables America from doing what it wants to do in the world, he references it as a remedy (ibid., 193). As a northerner and an expatriate sophisticate, Baldwin would require time to make sense of what he experienced and to articulate a coherent political vision that grasped the complex specificity of southern life.

43. Baldwin, *The Fire Next Time*, 336. Here, Baldwin explains to his nephew that many persons will mistreat him, despite knowing that their actions are morally and politically objectionable. The reason for this, he explains, is that action implies commitment, and commitment exposes the self to danger.

44. Ibid., 356. Also see his discussion of Christianity's influence on the loss of conscience (352), as well as his discussion of moral cowardice as the foundation for radical evil (356).

45. The classic formulation of this worry is Karl Popper's *The Open Society and Its Enemies* (New York: Routledge Press, 2002). Also see Isaiah Berlin's classic essay, "Two Concepts of Liberty," in *The Proper Study of Mankind* (New York: Farrar, Straus and Giroux, 1997). While more sympathetic to a project such as Baldwin's, Berlin lays out this worry quite nicely in his discussion of positive freedom.

46. One can read Baldwin as a theory of political elitism or radical democracy. The first view would insist on treating Baldwin's appeals to particular highly refined elite persons (especially those reading elite, left-leaning journals, such as *Partisan Review* and the *New Yorker*). On the other hand, the democratic reading of Baldwin here would insist that the kinds of skills and competences Baldwin calls for are not only more widely available than is commonly supposed but also easily taught and learned by way of political education. This reading can claim that this is exactly what the civil rights movement achieved. As King explained in "Letter from a Birmingham Jail," nonviolent direct action was a highly refined structure of activism that succeeded in part because people had had enough of white supremacy and in part because the structure institutionalized the wisdom of self-examination, courage, sacrifice, and deference to higher law. In this way, the special competences and higher purposes to which Baldwin refers can be made widely available.

47. Baldwin came to defend the defensive violence practiced by the Black Panthers. He acknowledged the necessity and value of black self-defense against the aggressive and coordinated violence that police forces deployed in black communities across America. Nonetheless, Baldwin stopped short of encouraging or recommending their strategy. For Baldwin, the Panthers were an antidote to demoralization. They were a constructive moment in the historical effort of blacks to create a nucleus capable of devising new laws, but they were not a law onto themselves. He never joined them or recommended that other blacks join (Baldwin, *No Name in the Street*, 537).

48. Baldwin is claiming that this distinction holds across all societies. These "responsible actors" as Baldwin refers to them, are offices or institutionalized functions within given societies. Baldwin is not making any substantive claims about these other specific roles in society. There are more social roles than he mentions, and each of them allows for different kinds of performance. What distinguishes "responsible actors" from the vantage point of art is that they play a supportive role in the maintenance of the institutional order of society. See Baldwin, "The Creative Process," 316.

49. James Baldwin, "The Discovery of What It Means to Be an American," in Baldwin, *The Price of the Ticket*.

50. Baldwin, "The Creative Process," 316.

51. Ibid., 317.

52. Baldwin, "Everybody's Protest Novel," 29.

53. Baldwin, "The Creative Process."

54. There are two grand exceptions to this rule. The first is Katharine Lawrence Balfour, *The Evidence of Things Not Said: James Baldwin and the Promise of American Democracy* (Ithaca, N.Y.: Cornell University Press, 2001). Balfour's is the first sustained analysis of Baldwin as a political theorist, and one from which I have learned a great deal. More recently, George Shulman's treatment of Baldwin as a prophetic cultural critic is also an excellent and groundbreaking study. George Shulman, ed., *American Prophecy, Race and Redemption in American Political Culture* (Minneapolis: University of Minnesota Press, 2008).

55. Truthfulness as factual correspondence was supposed to distinguish these two genres from the novel and earlier premodern forms of fiction, such as ancient epic, renaissance tragedy, and the like. Both are importantly dependent on figurative and imaginative techniques that were once thought to be the exclusive provenance of literary fiction. Memoir was thought to be more reflective than autobiography, but both were presumed to rest on an authorial truthfulness that could be cashed out against a historical record.

56. Michel-Rolph Trouillot, *Silencing the Past: Power and the Production of History* (Boston: Beacon Press, 1995).

57. I am indebted to David Kyuman Kim for pointing out this crucial resemblance to me.

58. Baldwin, *The Fire Next Time*, 335.

59. Baldwin explicitly references the theory when he explains to his nephew that "the black man has functioned in the white man's world as a fixed star and immovable pillar" and that many whites fail to act, even while seeing the pernicious consequences of white supremacy, because "in the mind of most white Americans," action means a loss of their identity (ibid., 336).

60. Ibid., 334.

61. Hannah Arendt, *The Human Condition* (Chicago: University of Chicago Press, 1958).

62. Arendt, *Eichmann in Jerusalem*, 269.

63. Hannah Arendt, *The Origins of Totalitarianism*, New ed. (New York: Harcourt Brace Jovanovich, 1973).

64. James Baldwin, "Notes of a Native Son" (1955), *The Price of the Ticket*, 145.

65. This omission informs Balfour, *The Evidence of Things Not Said*; Shulman, ed., *American Prophecy, Race and Redemption in American Political Culture*; Leeming, *James Baldwin*; and, more recently, Eddie S. Glaude, *In a Shade of Blue: Pragmatism and the Politics of Black America* (Chicago: University of Chicago Press, 2007).

66. Baldwin, *The Fire Next Time*, 334.

67. Ibid., 335.

68. Ibid., 334.

69. Ibid., 335.

70. Both the idea and the expression—"Baldwin allows us to overhear a private conversation"—is taken from Shulman, ed., *American Prophecy, Race and Redemption in American Political Culture*.

71. I am deeply suspicious of such expectations, especially when I am a source of them. Yet having admitted this (and hopefully cautioned against affording too much weight to Baldwin's compliance with demands imposed by a profession whose standards

have functioned historically to exclude the political ideas of marginalized and oppressed peoples from being taken seriously as theory), I believe that Baldwin provides a brilliant and moving account that not only meets contemporary professional standards of epistemic circumspection but also transcends them.

72. Baldwin, "Notes of a Native Son," 140.

73. Baldwin, *No Name in the Street*, 531.

74. Ibid.

75. Baldwin, *The Fire Next Time*, 351.

76. Ibid.

77. On Arendt's problematic construal of the "social," see Hanna Fenichel Pitkin, *The Attack of the Blob: Hannah Arendt's Concept of the Social* (Chicago: University of Chicago Press, 1998). On Arendt's investments in whiteness, see Anne Norton, "Heart of Darkness: Africa and African Americans in the Writings of Hannah Arendt," in *Feminist Interpretations of Hannah Arendt*, ed. Bonnie Honig (University Park: The Pennsylvania State University, 1995).

78. Baldwin's political interventions are aligned in spirit with the political interventions that feminists (especially feminists of color, such as Audre Lourde, Toni Morrison, and others) are beginning and will continue to mount. However, he is less attentive to gendered violence and especially the way that the intersection of race, class, gender, and sexual orientation function as the primary modality of racialization and the violence that racialization entails for him. Although he is more attentive to questions of sexual orientation, especially in his novels, *Giovanni's Room, Another Country, Tell Me How Long the Train's Been Gone*, and *Just Above My Head*, he is less pointed in his public political interventions on behalf of these questions. Nonetheless, as Essex Hemphill and others have argued, Baldwin's pioneering depictions of queer black masculinities not only open a space in which gay black men can see their lives and struggles depicted with sensitivity and dignity but also help lay the groundwork for more assertive interventions that will follow.

79. Thomas Hobbes and Richard Tuck, *Leviathan* (Cambridge: Cambridge University Press, 1996).

80. On the issue of power as a form of coercion, see his discussion of the criminal character of American political and police power (341); his ambivalent rejection of Elijah Muhammad's proposition that no people have ever been respected without power (364); his discussion of American desegregation as a concession to the necessities of Cold War politics (371); his discussion of America's support for Western Germany after World War II (354); and his discussion of the power he felt as he whipped his congregation up during his sermons (346) in Baldwin, *The Fire Next Time*.

81. Ibid., 376.

82. Ibid., 368.

83. Baldwin says that the "paternal authority" he encounters in Elijah Muhammad makes him imagine the relation he might have established with his own father had they been friends. He also says that the source of Elijah's peculiar authority is "a pain so old and deep and black that it becomes personal and particular only when he smiles." As will become clear, one of Baldwin's big challenges is to address that "peculiar authority," which serving power as an end, is no less authoritative for doing so. Ibid., 360.

84. As Baldwin would go to explain, whatever reformation was occurring within black America, whether within or outside the Nation of Islam, was the result of the increasingly apparent dissipation and impotence of American and Western power. Within this widening vacuum, the political theology of the Nation appeared increasingly plausible to increasing numbers of blacks, especially those who were most crushed by white supremacy.

As Western hegemony recedes, new vitalities bubble up within oppressed communities and provide transformative hopes. Ibid., 354.

85. By "mode of textuality," I am simply referring to a kind of public political autobiographical writing that seeks to change readers' opinions, memories, and passions by way of extra-argumentative effects.

86. Baldwin, *The Fire Next Time*, 337.

87. Ibid., 338.

88. Ibid., 339.

89. Ibid., 340.

90. Ibid.

91. Ibid., 348.

92. Ibid., 349. Baldwin's discussion of those moments outside of church, usually at parties, where "rage and sorrow sat in the dark and did not stir," is quite revealing. In these moments, he explains, they achieved a freedom that was close to love. However, as he makes clear, these were not church functions.

93. Ibid., 345.

94. Ibid., 348.

95. Ibid., 362.

96. Ibid., 366.

97. Ibid., 360.

98. Ibid.

99. Ibid., 351, 354, 363, 366, 371.

100. Ibid., 363.

101. Baldwin, *Go Tell It on the Mountain*.

102. Baldwin, *The Fire Next Time*, 368.

103. Ibid., 340.

104. Ibid., 362.

105. Ibid., 364.

106. Baldwin, *No Name in the Street*, 552.

CONCLUSION

1. For a good discussion of the messianic impulse, see Wilson Jeremiah Moses, *Black Messiahs and Uncle Toms: Social and Literary Manipulations of a Religious Myth* (University Park: Pennsylvania State University Press, 1993). Moses's interpretation of the prevalence of this impulse within African American thought is quite different from mine. Also see Martin Buber's discussion of the apocalyptic in "Prophecy, Apocalyptic, and the Historical Hour" in Martin Buber, *On the Bible: Eighteen Studies* (New York: Schocken Books, 1968).

2. Joy James, *Transcending the Talented Tenth: Black Leaders and American Intellectuals* (New York: Routledge, 1997), *States of Confinement: Policing, Detention, and Prisons* (New York: St. Martin's, 2000), Melvin L. Oliver and Thomas M. Shapiro, *Black Wealth/White Wealth: A New Perspective on Racial Inequality* (New York: Routledge, 1997), William J. Wilson, *When Work Disappears: The World of the New Urban Poor* (New York: Vintage Books, 1997).

3. I borrow the term "afterlife of slavery" from Hartman's rich memoir. Saidiya V. Hartman, *Lose Your Mother: A Journey Along the Atlantic Slave Route* (New York: Farrar, Straus and Giroux, 2007).

4. Eddie S. Glaude, *Exodus! Religion, Race, and Nation in Early Nineteenth-Century Black America* (Chicago: University of Chicago Press, 2000). President Obama's speech of

March 4, 2007, "Selma Voting Rights March Commemoration," can be found at www. barackobama.com/2007/03/04/selma_voting_rights_march_comm.php.

5. Max Weber, *Ancient Judaism* (New York: Collier-Macmillan, 1967), 300.

6. Ibid., 288.

7. Ibid., 301. Later, on page 320, Weber explains that vulnerability to imperial predation and monarchial excess furnished problems of political context for the emergence of prophetic intentions, but these problems did not determine this intention.

8. "The Profession and Vocation of Politics," in Max Weber, Peter Lassman, and Ronald Speirs, *Political Writings (Cambridge Texts in the History of Political Thought)* (Cambridge: Cambridge University Press, 1994), 311.

9. Ibid., 312.

10. Ibid., 311.

11. W.E.B. Du Bois, *Writings* (New York: Library of America, 1986), 555.

12. "The Price of the Ticket," in James Baldwin, *The Price of the Ticket: Collected Nonfiction, 1948–1985*, 1st ed. (New York: St. Martin's/Marek, 1985).

13. "Plato and Isaiah," in Buber, *On the Bible*.

14. Shulman powerfully articulates this worry in his discussion of the lure of "redemption" quests within prophecy itself. George M. Shulman, *American Prophecy: Race and Redemption in American Political Culture* (Minneapolis: University of Minnesota Press, 2008).

15. Du Bois's awareness of the tragic comes through most clearly in his discussion of the fated failure of reconstruction; Josie's destruction by means of her exemplary virtue; black John's crime, resulting in part from white America's misapprehension of those black youth most ready for higher education; and Du Bois's autobiographical descriptions of his son's death. *The Souls of Black Folk*, in Du Bois, *Writings*. Baldwin states unequivocally that life is tragic because one day everyone must die. *The Fire Next Time* in Baldwin, *The Price of the Ticket*.

16. Toni Morrison, *Beloved: A Novel* (New York: Knopf, 1987), 60–61, 203.

17. Ibid., 62.

18. Ibid., 108, 19, 84–85.

19. Ibid., 251.

20. Maria W. Stewart and Marilyn Richardson, *Maria W. Stewart, America's First Black Woman Political Writer: Essays and Speeches* (Bloomington: Indiana University Press, 1987), 30.

21. Ibid., 28.

22. Ibid., 29.

23. Ibid., 30.

24. Ibid.

25. Ibid.

26. Ibid., 38.

27. Ibid., 30.

28. Ibid., 35.

29. Ibid., 37.

30. Ibid., 39.

31. Ibid., 34.

32. In places, Stewart qualifies her lavish praise of the "American people" by calling attention to American racism (35).

33. Stewart and Richardson, *Maria W. Stewart, America's First Black Woman Political Writer*, 49.

34. Ibid.

35. Ibid., 40.

36. Ida B. Wells-Barnett, *On Lynchings (Classics in Black Studies)* (Amherst, N.Y.: Humanity Books, 2002), 52.

37. Ibid., 51.

38. Ibid., 50.

39. Ibid., 58.

40. Mary Helen Washington, "Anna Julia Cooper, a Voice from the South," in *Black Women's Intellectual Traditions*, ed. Kristin Waters and Carol B. Conaway (Burlington: University of Vermont Press, 2007), 258.

41. Anna Julia Cooper, *A Voice from the South* (Xenia, Ohio: Aldine, 1892), 53.

42. Ibid., 160.

43. Ibid., 164.

44. Ibid., 136.

45. Ibid., iii.

46. Ibid., 132.

47. Nonetheless, Cooper was "an optimist on the subject of my country." Ibid., 165.

48. Ibid., 32.

49. Ibid., 33.

50. Morrison, *Beloved*, 164, 200, 203, 204.

51. Ibid., 200.

52. Ibid., 251.

53. Ibid., 275.

54. Max Horkheimer, Theodor W. Adorno, and Gunzelin Schmid Noerr, *Dialectic of Enlightenment: Philosophical Fragments* (Stanford, Calif.: Stanford University Press, 2002).

55. Transcript: *Illinois Senate Candidate Barack Obama.* Tuesday, July 27, 2004. www.americanrhetoric.com/speeches/convention2004/barackobama2004dnc.htm.

56. Transcript: Reverend Jackson's *1988 Democratic National Convention Address.* www.americanrhetoric.com/speeches/jessejackson1988dnc.htm.

57. Cornel West, *Prophesy Deliverance! An Afro-American Revolutionary Christianity* (Philadelphia: Westminster Press, 1982). West's attempt to wed prophetic critique with Marxist structural analysis remains the boldest attempt to resuscitate the tradition. His more recent attempt to inform prophetic critique with tragicomedy's reverent awareness of folly represents the deepest sense of prophetic critique's spiritual limits. See Cornel West, *The Cornel West Reader* (New York: Basic Civitas Books, 1999) and Cornel West, *Democracy Matters* (New York: Penguin Press, 2004). For more recent and somewhat harsher assessments, see Eddie S. Glaude, *In a Shade of Blue: Pragmatism and the Politics of Black America* (Chicago: University of Chicago Press, 2007); James, *Transcending the Talented Tenth*; and Anthony Bogues, *Black Heretics, Black Prophets: Radical Political Intellectuals* (New York: Routledge, 2003).

Index

Abernathy, Ralph, 157

Adam and Eve, 22

Adams, Henry, 127

Adorno, Theodore, 189

affluence, 169

African American prophetic political critique: black women, 179–189; vs. Bogue's "redemptive prophetic" criticism, 202n56; of colonial America, 18–19; decline of, 169–170, 178–179, 192; faith and desire in, 175–176; Jackson's Democratic National Convention speech, 191; King, 8; origins of, 1; and political evil, 19; as political philosophy, 203n60; political theorists' neglect of, 2; and sacrifice, 177, 188–189; and slavery, 18–19; and violence, 54–56, 145, 165–167, 172, 220n10, 223n47; West, 228n57. *See also* Baldwin, James; Douglass, Frederick; Du Bois, W.E.B.; Walker, David

African Americans: Baldwin on paradox of, 140; blackness, 137–141; churches, 122–123, 125, 204n11; and City on the Hill concept, 133–135; colleges, 119–120, 126; dignity of, 106; Du Bois on leaders, 108–111; enmity with whites, 43, 51–54, 135–136, 206n65; intellectual underdevelopment of, 31–33, 38, 42–43, 50–54; messianism, 28–29; political institutions of, 61; and politics, 172–173; repatriation to Africa, 47–50; sexism of, 55–56, 186–187. *See also* women

African Methodist Episcopal Church, 48

Afro-modernity, 207n81

Agamben, Giorgio, 141

Allen, Richard, 48, 202n54

America, 14–15, 34–36

American Antislavery Society, 62

American Colonization Society, 47

American exceptionalism. *See* City on the Hill concept

American Indians, 14–15, 167

American Prophecy (Shulman), 201n49, 202n56

Ancient Judaism (Weber), 173–174

Anderson, Benedict, 201n44

Anthony, Captain, 82–83

Appeal to the Colored Citizens of the World, but in Particular, and Very Expressly, to Those of the United States of America (Walker), 26–56, 177; audience addressed by, 27–28; economics of slavery, 34–35, 45–46; ignorance of African Americans, 31–33, 38, 42–43, 50–54; as jeremiad, 29, 44–45; racial enmity, 43, 51–53, 206n65; and religion, 28–29, 33–36, 43–47; as structural mirror of U.S. Constitution, 29–30. *See also* Walker, David

Arendt, Hannah, 14, 73, 136–137, 139, 152, 159–161

Aristotle: on concept of "city," 5; on constitutions, 30; definition of tragedy, 139; on habitual action, 73; on invention of domestic terrors, 135; on slavery, 37, 59, 81

artist/lover figure, 142–148, 154, 222n41. *See also* Baldwin, James

Stephen H. Marshall is Associate Professor in the Department of American Studies and the Department of African and African Diaspora Studies at the University of Texas–Austin.